CORN BREAD NATION 1

CORNBREAD NATION
John T. Edge, General Editor

CORN BREAD NATiON 1

THE BEST OF SOUTHERN FOOD WRITING

Edited by John Egerton

Published in association with the Southern Foodways Alliance,

Center for the Study of Southern Culture, University of Mississippi,

by the University of North Carolina Press

Chapel Hill and London

Manufactured in the United States of America

Designed by Richard Hendel

Set in Minion types by Eric M. Brooks

The paper in this book meets the guidelines for permanence and
durability of the Committee on Production Guidelines for Book
Longevity of the Council on Library Resources.

This inaugural edition of *Cornbread Nation* was underwritten,
in part, by a gift from the Atticus Trust.

Library of Congress Cataloging-in-Publication Data

Cornbread nation 1: the best of Southern food writing /

edited by John Egerton.

p. cm.

ISBN 0-8078-5419-0 (paper)

1. Food writing. I. Title: Cornbread nation one. II. Edge, John T.

III. Southern Foodways Alliance.

TX644 .C67   2002

641.3'0975—dc21   2002006417

06 05 04 03 02   5 4 3 2 1

CONTENTS

CORN BREAD NATiON 1

INTRODUCTION

At some point in the course of the Southern Foodways Symposium in Oxford, Mississippi, a couple of years ago—it could have been while we were scarfing up some of Leah Chase's bodacious gumbo, or when we were out in the little hamlet of Taylor wolfing down a ton of fried catfish and hushpuppies at an old grocery store, or even as we listened attentively to Dick Pillsbury's treatise on barbecue belts and grits lines and other landmarks of culinary geography— somewhere along in there, a rich and mellow idea seemed to hatch full-grown and muscular in several minds at once. This immaculate and spontaneous conception bounced up on the table in the shank of an after-dinner talkfest. It proceeded, as I recall, more or less like this:

"You know, what we oughta do is put together a book full of all this good stuff." (That must have been Ronni Lundy; she has a way of dreaming things up and then letting others think they discovered them.)

"Yeah, that's just what I've been thinking," someone else said. "Food is so central to the South we all like—the Good South of conviviality and generosity and sweet communion. What we've got here is a little band of food lovers who'll make any excuse to get together and cook, eat, talk . . . "

" . . . and write about it. At least half of us are writers of one stripe or another."

"That's probably because we don't know how to cook."

"The chefs are wannabe writers, and the writers are wannabe chefs—and when the twain meet to eat, the stories come rolling out like Cajun popcorn."

"So let's quit talking about it and do it."

"Do what?"

"A book. A collection of great food stories from the South."

And that, you might say, was the birth of a notion, more or less. We named it *Cornbread Nation*, a title the Southern Foodways Alliance previously used on its newsletter (which, henceforth, will be given another name to avoid confusion). *Cornbread Nation* is not a term freighted with any profound or universal meaning; it's just a catchy little phrase that calls to mind, for some of us, a timeless South where corn has been the staff of life forever, and cornbread in myriad forms has held a central place in the cookery of the region since the original people hunkered down to bake and break bread together.

It may come as a bit of a shock to some readers of this volume—the first in what we hope will be a long series of such collections—to learn that we borrowed the title from a Yankee. It appeared originally above an essay by John Thorne in "Simple Cooking," Thorne's widely read and admired food newsletter published in a small town on the coast of Maine. (I knew I liked this guy the minute I read his scathing criticism of antifat advocates "who treat lard as the moral equivalent of crack.") Thorne professes to be amused, even pleased, that we seized his words (titles can't be copyrighted) and used them to name our book. For our part, we are deeply indebted to him for advancing the symbolic thought that cornbread—that shared food in general—might somehow help to bind up the wounds of this entire nation-state and let us finally embrace the ideals embedded in our founding documents.

A little band of California hippies, several of them with Southern roots, must have had something similar in mind when they chose the name for their 1973 collection of poetry, fiction, and more-or-less-true stories: *One Lord, One Faith, One Cornbread*. There was nary a phrase about cornbread in that book, but a soon-to-be-famous poet and essayist among them, Wendell Berry of Port Royal, Kentucky, came up with the title, and his fellow writers embraced it like so many prodigal sons and daughters of the Mother South might be expected to pounce on a straight-from-the-oven pone of corn hot enough to fog your glasses.

Like theirs, ours isn't a treatise on cornbread (though the subject does come up a time or two in these pages). We're simply operating on the premise that if there's anything your garden-variety Southerner likes to do more than harvesting, preparing, or consuming the region's superlative food and drink, it probably would be talking and writing about the very dishes and libations that have sustained us through this vale of tears for centuries. That's what gave rise to the Southern Foodways Alliance in the first place: a love of our historical sustenance and a desire to organize an effective defense against its gradual disappearance.

The SFA was created in July 1999 at a Birmingham, Alabama, meeting of fifty people who shared a common interest in the food and beverage virtues of their native South (a roster of these founders appears at the back of the book). Drawing valuable lessons from the noble originators of two previous, unsuccessful efforts to form and sustain such a group, the SFA first secured an institutional base: the Center for the Study of Southern Culture at the University of Mississippi in Oxford. The center is the leading academic nexus of cultural studies in the region, having amassed almost a quarter-century of fruitful experience in a wide variety of initiatives, from conferences on William Faulkner and Elvis Presley to collections of blues music and such valuable publications as the massive and still-growing *Encyclopedia of Southern Culture*.

The organizers of the SFA appealed to the leadership of the center to nurture the fledgling group until it could make it on its own. Thus, we are a self-governing nonprofit institute within that structure, and our stated purpose—"to celebrate, teach, preserve, and promote the diverse food cultures of the American South"—is so compatible with the overall aims of the center that its principals seem as happy to have us there as we are to have their assistance. The SFA hopes in time to become a movable feast of programs and services reaching into the farthest nooks and crannies of the South.

The two previous organizational attempts—the Society for the Revival and Preservation of Southern Food, inspired by Edna Lewis, and the American Southern Food Institute, spearheaded by Terry Ford and Jeanne Voltz—might well have succeeded with institutional support. As it turned out, they pointed the SFA in a different and more productive direction—and Edna Lewis, Terry Ford, and Jeanne Voltz were among the fifty founders of the Southern Foodways Alliance.

Returning to the *Cornbread Nation* title for a moment, it needs to be said that we got more than just that phrase from our friend John Thorne. His essay, which appeared in a 1994 issue of "Simple Cooking" (later collected in his book *Serious Pig*), was full of food for thought about corn and culture. And it is every bit as pertinent to the Southern and American condition today as it was when he wrote it. In Thorne's capable hands, corn becomes a powerful symbol, a metaphor for national renewal. He writes:

If we dig past the clichéd image of the giving Indian and the (temporarily) grateful settler, what we find just beneath is something more complicated: an occasion of mutual recognition and, at the same time, a collision of cultures. This, simplifying, we might call "grain versus corn." Old-World grains—oats, millet, wheat, rye—required a careful, patient agriculture that reworked the same fields through the centuries. Those who owned the fields and the mills that ground what was grown in them owned the culture. Grain supports a feudal society of lords and serfs, a post-feudal society of landlords and tenant farmers.

A corn culture is more fluid. Corn is more adaptable as both a foodstuff and a crop. Skilled Indian agriculturalists could grow three crops of corn a year, and they could grow it almost where they wanted: here one year and somewhere else the next. Unlike wheat and similar grains, corn does not require plowed fields; it can be planted around the stumps of trees in freshly cleared plots.

Consequently, Indian culture itself was more fluid, not as hierarchical and not nearly as concerned with ideas of possession. . . . If the earliest colonists had had to depend on Old-World grains to survive in the New World, they would all have perished. The land could not be transformed that quickly, certainly not by a people who were not, most of them, skilled farmers. Much has been made of the importance of corn in sustaining the original colonies, but little if anything about its immediate and subversive effect on the new-born American character. If there are no peasants in this country, it is because a peasant is wedded—as his family before him and after him—to a particular piece of land. In America, however, a man could take a bag of seed corn and an axe and head into the wilderness, there to be "as much a great lord as any other."

. . . Cornbread Nation was populist, democratic, republican—all printed in small letters. It was a kind of agrarian radicalism, neither left nor right, that proposed that this nation would work best if it were a country of independent citizens, a majority of whom, whatever else they might be—artisan or woodsman or merchant—were also small landholders whose self-sufficiency would mean that they were beholden to no one. As equals among equals, they freely helped their neighbors and accepted help from them, not out of obligation but because it made good sense.

Lest he leave us clinging to an agrarian idealism that has long since vanished from the American landscape—including the landscape of the South—Thorne brings us gently back to reality. "In a money economy," he writes, "it is cash—not food—that is constantly in short supply; consequently, it is hard for us to understand the sense of wealth that a good corn crop gave to a small landholder, or to appreciate the fine distinctions that made it the type of wealth it was. Because corn is unique in being both a vegetable and a grain, it offers a wider range of culinary possibility than any other single food." No matter where we live in America, Thorne concludes, "the distance between cornfield and cornbread is growing fast," and we are powerless to prevent this disconnection.

It is that same sense of urgency, of impending loss, that breathed life into the Southern Foodways Alliance—and that now drives such programmatic efforts as the annual symposium, field trips to various Southern locales, budding oral history projects, and collections of exemplary food writing such as the one you are holding in your hands.

Our *Cornbread Nation* draws inspiration from a wide variety of sources— from Southern cooks and chefs, scholars and documentarians, writers and photographers; from the far-flung membership of the SFA, now totaling more than 400; from Southern social history; and from the contemporary landscape of the region's foodways. In selecting these articles, essays, scholarly papers, poems, and short stories, we tried to hew to the "cornbread philosophy" so well articulated by John Thorne and spelled out in the SFA statement of purpose—celebrating, teaching, preserving, and promoting the diverse food cultures of the South.

Individually, the selections in these pages can stand alone; they need no shoring up from us. Collectively, they buttress our conviction that nothing else the South has to offer to the nation and the world—with the possible exception of its music—is more eternally satisfying, heartwarming, reconciling, and memorable than its food. Our dishes and beverages express our faith, our good humor, our binding ties, our eternal joys and sorrows, our readiness for whatever awaits us. Without them, it seems reasonable to wonder if we would ever make it through first loves, playing-field defeats, revivals, bar mitzvahs, weddings, births, divorces, homecomings, funerals—the thousand-and-one big and little victories and defeats of life. In the words and pictures assembled here, we acknowledge with gratitude the abiding centrality of food in the ongoing life of the South. At the very least, the foods of our formative years linger in the mind more tenaciously—and favorably—than almost anything else.

Cornbread Nation aspires to be an approachable and intelligent pathway to the study of Southern foodways, an entrée (no pun intended) to the social and cultural life of the region. The book's time frame is three-dimensional, drawing primarily from 2001, secondarily from the period since the SFA's founding in 1999, and finally, in a few instances, from older archives. An editorial committee that included Jessica B. Harris, Lolis Eric Elie, and Fred Sauceman—with ad hoc assistance from our president, Toni Tipton-Martin, and our director and only paid staffer, John T. Edge—made the final selections, not based on a subjective classification of "the best" but rather on some real-life considerations: a general sense of inclusiveness and balance and, per-haps most important, the kind of writing that elicited from us laughter, tears, wonder, and delight. In a word, feeling.

So pull up a chair and help yourself. We hope you find enough to satisfy your appetite.

John Egerton, for the editors
April 2002

PEOPLE

Leah Chase

LOLIS ERIC ELIE

If it had been possible in the 1950s to see Dooky Chase for what it really was, everyone would have known it was just a shotgun house. A rather typical one, really. Though longer than most residences, it was about the same size as a whole lot of similar buildings around New Orleans where commerce was conducted in the front half and living took place in the back.

But no one saw Dooky's like that in those days. How could they when they had first viewed this place through Little League eyes, when the first time they ate in Dooky's or any real restaurant was when Morris Jeff Sr. brought them there for the end-of-season awards banquet? The place only seated sixty people, sixty-five if they really squeezed. But for the Little League banquets there were more than a hundred freshly washed bodies in Sunday-best outfits, all mortally afraid to be on anything but their best behavior. In the minds of every one of those hundred little faces, Dooky Chase would be remembered as a special place, large and grand.

As this grand vision matured, it would be the backdrop for classroom daydreams all around the city as boys and girls imagined that butterflies-in-the-stomach feeling of a prom date so special that it ended at Dooky Chase. The girls always ordered first. It was a custom owing less to etiquette than to economics. How else was a guy to know what he could afford to feed himself unless he had already calculated the cost of what his date ordered? It didn't even matter so much that a lot of mothers were certain to call the restaurant snooping around, asking, "Leah, what time did they leave?" Dooky's was still the place everyone wanted to go more than any other.

"When I was in school, that was our Waldorf-Astoria. That was like eating at Club 21," recalls Norman Francis, now the president of Xavier University of New Orleans. "When a guy said, 'I got a really special girlfriend, and I want to impress her,' we all knew where she was going."

In those days, Ray Charles defined soul. Anybody who had any musical taste at all listened to Ray. And anybody who listened to Ray certainly heard the way he made a special effort to alter the lyrics of "Early in the Morning Blues" so there would be no doubt as to what his favorite restaurant was:

I went to Dooky Chase
To get me something to eat.
The waitress looked at me and said
"Ray, you sure look beat."
Now it's early in the morning
And I ain't got nothing but the blues.

And it wasn't just Ray. All the other big-time celebrities stopped in at Dooky's, and taken as a whole, they certainly couldn't have been wrong. In 1948, when Louis Armstrong enjoyed the privilege of serving as the king of the Zulu parade, his float broke down at the end of the route. It didn't matter. The float stopped just a block or two away from Dooky Chase, and that's where he was headed anyway.

"No matter what time Nat 'King' Cole came, he wanted those eggs. He wanted four-minute eggs," Leah Chase recalls. "Lena Horne loved her fried chicken. Sarah Vaughan loved her stuffed crabs. She would eat four of those crabs and ask me to make her six to take home. Thurgood Marshall always came for his gumbo."

Dooky Chase began in 1941 as a small sandwich shop, financed by the profits its namesake earned from selling lottery tickets door-to-door. Emily Chase, the first Mrs. Chase in the restaurant business, was a master cook, albeit with a limited menu. Chicken, oysters, fish, or shrimp, take your pick, as long as you wanted it fried. But the restaurant, like its patrons, was due for some growing up. Dooky Chase had been a bandleader, playing jazz and rhythm and blues in New Orleans and on the road. He fell in love with a girl five years his senior. That age gap was itself scandalous, but perhaps not so scandalous as what this new bride proposed to do to the restaurant her in-laws had built all the way up from the ground, all the way up from nothing.

Leah Lange Chase, who had come from St. Tammany Parish at age sixteen in order to attend high school in New Orleans, had worked in French Quarter restaurants in the days before she met her husband. Her vision of what a restaurant should be had been informed by the time she had spent as a waitress and cook at the Coffee Pot and the Colonial. Neither was a fancy restaurant, really. But compared to the eating options available in the black community, these segregation-era, white-only establishments were positively luxurious.

Leah and the other two "colored" girls persuaded the owner of the Colonial to let them make a luncheon special every day to sell alongside the staple menu item, hamburgers. They started with Creole wieners and spaghetti, a simple, family-style dish but one that sold well at 65 cents a plate. It wasn't long after her marriage that Leah Chase began putting Creole wieners on the menu at Dooky Chase. That dish led to other more ambitious offerings, though none as wildly successful as those spicy sausages.

"The people did not know what a shrimp cocktail was. They thought it was something to drink," Leah Chase recalls. "So I'm trying to get my mother-in-law to understand how we served the shrimp cocktails in the French Quarter. She would say, 'Why should I change, I'm making a lot of money.' And she was making money. My mother-in-law used to sit there and cash checks on Friday evenings. Sit there on that table right in that front door with a cigar box. Maybe $5,000 or $6,000 in that cigar box. I remember one dish I was really so fascinated with, lobster thermidor. So I said, 'Okay, I'm going to do lobster thermidor.' Well, that lobster thermidor came back at me faster than it got out of here. Black folks were not into those cream sauces then. It was before integration."

There were all kinds of things wrong with segregation, but for a black business, that violently racist system offered one tremendous advantage: Black patrons were a captive market. Even in those turbulent days when the civil rights movement changed all of that, Dooky Chase still profited from its reputation as one of the few places that allowed integrated parties to gather for meals or meetings. "Movement people were always welcomed there. They never shied away from integrated groups," recalls Rudy Lombard, who would later celebrate Mrs. Chase and other black chefs in his 1978 book, *Creole Feast.* "It was like a haven. People could go there and count on being welcomed."

Dooky's held another attraction in those days: It was open late. In the early years, it would be crowded at 4 A.M. Even through the 70s, musicians would come there after their gigs and Dooky Chase himself would often come out and regale them with stories of his days on the road when, in lieu of payment, club owners sometimes would put a gun to the head of the bandleader and promise not to shoot if the musicians played another set.

Food in the South has always built bridges across political and social chasms virtually impassable by any other medium. And just as the restaurant became a symbol of the potential inherent in an integrated New Orleans, Leah Chase became a bridge builder and a civic leader well respected by New Orleanians black and white. Her election in 1978 to the board of the New Orleans Museum of Art was not only a testament to this status, but it also gave her an

Leah Chase, dipping a bowl of her fabled gumbo. Courtesy of Bruce Newman.

important entrée into a segment of the local upper class that had been relatively untouched by the gains of the post–civil rights movement era.

While there was a certain quaint authenticity in that sixty-seat dining room known as the Gold Room, it was becoming increasingly obvious by the early 1980s that the old shotgun house had been surpassed by its reputation. And though folks might have been too polite to say it, the old neighborhood surrounding Dooky Chase wasn't what it had been in the 1950s.

"A decision was made to become a major restaurant and stay in the neighborhood," recalls Kalamu ya Salaam, a writer and civil rights era veteran. "This neighborhood was across the street from a housing project. That decision could not have been made lightly. For the amount of money they spent they probably could have moved somewhere else cheaper. It was a gutsy call."

Tourists, or at least the timid among them, are sometimes frightened by these inelegant surroundings. They seem to forget that, if history is to be any guide, the crowded sidewalks of the famed French Quarter are far more dangerous ground than the stretch of Orleans Avenue where Dooky Chase stands.

By connecting two more shotgun houses to the old Dooky Chase, Leah Chase achieved her dream of owning an expanded full-service restaurant. Just

LOLIS ERIC ELIE

as before, the restaurant still has a take-out section, now with its own kitchen, that serves some of the best (and the least expensive) po-boys and red beans available in a city justifiably famous for these dishes. (Those in the know order the shrimp or oyster sandwiches in pan-bread, regular white bread somehow made more toothsome by the thickness of the slices.) But it is not the renovation or the expanded rooms for which this new building is best known. It is known now as the home of one of the most impressive art collections of any restaurant in New Orleans. And Leah Chase will tell you the story of this collection, beaming with enthusiasm painting by painting as she moves from a scene of cotton being weighed to the street parade in the huge New Orleans montage by Bruce Brice, from the woodcuts of Elizabeth Catlett to the stained-glass windows of Winston Falgout.

Of course the focus in a restaurant must be the art on the plate, the walls being at best a secondary consideration. The menu at Dooky Chase has changed little in the last decade. Shrimp Clemenceau—potatoes, peas, mushrooms, and shrimp married in a garlic butter—still stars, as does the chicken breast stuffed with oyster dressing. While the gumbo gets all the attention, the crab soup is quietly excellent. And perhaps as a nod to the old days, the Dooky Chase fryer still puts out some of the best fried chicken around. It is these dishes, and Leah Chase's personal warmth, that have made her an emblem of this city and its food culture. "She cooks the food New Orleans loves to eat," says Ella Brennan, the other matriarch of New Orleans restaurants. "Most of the people I have been there with are very prominent people in the community. They love Leah and they love the food."

The restaurant business is a young woman's game. Long hours, hot fires, and demanding customers are not the stuff of a graceful old age. Yet at seventy-eight, Leah Chase is still in the restaurant every day, doing most of the cooking and all of the meeting and greeting. Her staff is divided between mature workers who have been employed at the restaurant for a decade or more and youngsters—grandchildren and college students. At times, it shows; the service doesn't always have the same snap it once did. But what is unaltered is Leah Chase in person—her character and her commitment to this food and this community. "That's why I work hard here," she says. "I want it to succeed because people still expect so much."

Marie Rudisill

DAMON LEE FOWLER

"Imagine a morning in late November. A coming-of-winter morning more than twenty years ago. Consider the kitchen of a spreading house in a country town." So begins *A Christmas Memory*, Truman Capote's evocative and touching memoir of his childhood in Monroeville, Alabama. At the center of his memory is his cousin Sook Faulk and her annual labor of love—making fruitcakes for the entire world as she and Capote knew it.

He describes his cousin in ruthless but loving detail: "A woman with shorn white hair is standing at the kitchen window. She is wearing tennis shoes and a shapeless gray sweater over a summery calico dress. She is small and sprightly, like a bantam hen, but, due to a long youthful illness, her shoulders are pitifully hunched. Her face is remarkable, not unlike Lincoln's—craggy like that, but delicate too, fine-boned, and her eyes are sherry-colored and timid.

"'Oh, my,' she exclaims, her breath smoking the windowpane, 'It's fruitcake weather!'" In the background, Capote's teenaged aunt "Tiny" shared those days when Sook ran the kitchen of Jenny Faulk's rambling house. Shared them—and in her own way, has kept them alive.

Now imagine, if you will, another November, some seventy years later. It is not cold—and if winter is coming, it is impossible to feel that it will ever touch Hudson, Florida. The kitchen is spacious and well equipped but ordinary—there is no picturesque woodstove, no fireplace, no rocking chairs and rag rugs. Modern cabinetry lines the walls, and a modern range and refrigerator command attention. A sliding glass door looks out over a sandy backyard made patchy by the dogs who have the run of it.

But no matter: It is still fruitcake weather.

At the center of this kitchen is another small woman who also resembles a sprightly bantam hen. Her face is remarkable, too—stamped with the unmistakable features of a Faulk and lined by years of living and laughing. It is an intelligent and lively face, still full of the girlish enthusiasm that endeared her to the nephew who grew up with her.

But there her resemblance to Sook ends. She wears tiny, elegant black flats and her still shapely legs are encased in black stockings. She is well dressed, and her white hair is carefully contained in a tight, neat bun. And there is nothing timid about Marie Faulk Rudisill—known appropriately as "Tiny" in her childhood. Her dark eyes miss nothing, and she is not afraid of saying what she thinks—in a voice that is as large as she is small. But she shares Sook's passion for two highly misunderstood things: her nephew Truman Capote and fruitcake.

Rudisill, Truman Capote, Sook, and fruitcake are inextricably linked together, so it is no surprise that Rudisill's latest book, *Fruitcake: Memories of Truman Capote and Sook*, is much more than a cookbook or memoir; it is her tribute to all three. In more than two dozen recipes and a handful of essays, her affection shines through.

"I loved Truman Capote better than anything in this world!" she will tell you quickly, and just as quickly, she will admit that her relationship with him was complicated and at times uneasy. But she doesn't dwell on the difficult times; she'd rather recall the twenty-five-year-long practical joke that Capote pulled on his editor—or the time that Capote's ashes went missing from Joanna Carson's living room.

She loves fruitcake almost as much, and as she pries open a red and green tin and plunges a knife into a luscious ring of fruit-and-pecan-studded glory, you can smell this passion as the aroma of brandy and spice fills the room.

Her face still has the anticipation that must have been there on those long-ago Christmas Eves when she, Capote, and the other children used to sneak into the kitchen and pry open the fruitcake tin, digging into the cake with a fork even though they knew full well that they would be punished for it. That first, heady bite of brandy-laced cake was worth it.

"Fruitcake really is the queen of cakes!" she insists as she passes a thick, crumbling slice. "There is just nothing better—nothing!" Tasting it, you have to agree. The crude jokes about fruitcake seem silly and unfounded as its moist richness blooms on the tongue, stirring both memories of Christmases past and anticipation of those to come.

Rudisill has little patience with the tired old jokes about fruitcake and even less with the people who would dwell on her famed nephew's faults rather than his genius. "These people just don't know any better," she says. "They're just like the ones who didn't understand Truman because they didn't know him. They don't know fruitcake. They've never really baked one at home. They get those bought things and so of course they are disappointed. They don't know what good fruitcake tastes like."

Rudisill took her battle against bad fruitcake jokes onto national television when she appeared on *The Tonight Show*, hosted by notorious fruitcake-hater Jay Leno. The show ended in a good-natured draw, with Leno conceding he'd had worse and Rudisill claiming her fruitcake was not only historical but delectable.

Rudisill doesn't want you to miss out on what lies behind the cake—what she describes as "that whole feeling of the labor of love that making a fruitcake is. Just going out and buying the cake won't do it. You have to make it at home. A fruitcake is a love object. It's the whole process, from picking out the nuts to sorting the fruit. And the work—the hard work—and then when you're done, after all that work, sometimes you can't get the thing out of the pan! You have to be full of love to go through it!"

Still, modern cooks will find Rudisill's recipes easy to follow and should appreciate that fruitcake making is not nearly as hard—or risky—as it was in Sook's day:

"We used to go to the swamp to get the pecans. They grew right there with the cypress and the mayhaws. The pecans fell into the water, so you would scoop them up and take them home and spread them out to dry. There were water moccasins out there—sunning themselves right near us—but we were never afraid."

Today, we can relax in the knowledge that Southern-grown pecans come to us already shelled and picked and that we will not have to remember what kind of hardwood makes the right heat for cake-baking in the woodstove.

For those who still think it's not worth the effort or who think they don't have the time or stamina for making their own fruitcake, Rudisill's book is an inspiration—though not as much of an inspiration as she is. At eighty-nine, after a lifetime of cooking, she still loves it. She has already made her fruit-cakes for this year. When I last talked to her, she was busily making Thanks-giving dinner. From scratch. For fourteen. And the menu was staggering.

She didn't mind. Cooking is more than a passion for her; it's her way of showing her love. "I want my children and my grandchildren to have those memories. I want them to remember the love that I put into it. I mean, we have so much. Why shouldn't we give back something?"

Eugene Walter

JOHN T. EDGE

The canonization of modern American food experts began with the death of James Beard. The campaign gained momentum and mettle with the passing of M. F. K. Fisher and the attendant publication of various correspondence and recollections. Richard Olney got the nod when he died. Ditto Craig Claiborne. Julia Child has earned a berth in the firmament while still waltzing among us.

Sage choices, all. And yet they augur a fairly rigid gastronomic fraternity. I say it's time to loosen things up a bit.

I say, *Let Eugene Walter in.*

His voice was all honey and mud, a mellifluous brogue born of the Alabama black belt where he was reared. In his youth, Eugene Walter's blue eyes flashed with a jack-o'-lantern glint. In later years, a shock of white hair framed his wide face, giving him a foppish charm. He bore a temper that was quick and sweet. Though he loved his native Southland, he wore a disdain for conventional mores on his shirt-sleeve, reserving a circle in his own personal hell for the "so-called moral majority," which he declared to be "neither moral nor majority."

A thumbnail sketch of the late author's accolades should include the O. Henry citation bestowed on his short story "I Love You Batty, Sisters," the Sewanee-Rockefeller Fellowship granted for his *Monkey Poems,* and the Lippincott Prize awarded for his first novel, *The Untidy Pilgrim.* At the time of the novel's publication in 1954, Walter, just thirty-two years of age, declared himself to be "bored slapdab to death by the Sad Cypress school of Southern writing." He was not alone. One critic deemed his bildungsroman confection to be "a glass of champagne after years of buttermilk."

But even with that grocery list, we're just getting started. We have not acknowledged his longtime involvement with the literary journals *Botteghe Oscure* and the *Transatlantic Review* or that he was published in the first issue of the *Paris Review* and served as an advisory editor for nearly ten years thereafter. We have not delved into his work as a lyricist. Among other songs, he wrote the words to "What Is a Youth?" for Franco Zeffirelli's film, *Romeo and Juliet.*

Walter was a character actor in more than a hundred films, from *The Pink Panther* to *Gidget Goes to Rome.* For a Western called *The Ballad of Belle Star,* he played the role of a safecracker called Stickyfingers. He was a translator for Federico Fellini and acted in a number of his films, including *8½* and *Juliet of the Spirits.* Late in life, he appeared in a *Saturday Night Live* sketch, playing the part of an American tourist in Rome who, when presented with the check for dinner, collapses from a heart attack and drops head-first into a bowl of spaghetti Bolognese.

And we have yet to even broach the subject of Walter's culinary work, which moved his fellow Southerner, author John Egerton, to exclaim, "He is the once and future king of cookery writers!"

Eugene Walter's debut as a food writer came at the tender age of twenty when a letter he penned in praise of the cooking at a New York restaurant was passed along by a friend to *Herald-Tribune* columnist Lucius Beebe, who in turn published it for all to read. Over the course of a long and at times fitful career, he wrote, among myriad other articles, a treatise on gumbo for *Gourmet,* a paean to cabbage for *Harper's Bazaar,* and a dissertation on the proper preparation of tartar sauce for *Food Arts.*

He was nearly fifty, however, before Time-Life published his first food book in 1971. Entitled *American Cooking, Southern Style,* it was perhaps the best in a Foods of the World series that featured the likes of M. F. K. Fisher on the cookery of provincial France and Waverly Root on the cuisines of Italy. In succeeding years, he published two baroque-titled jewels, 1982's *Delectable Dishes from Termite Hall* and, in 1991, *Hints and Pinches.* Though all three works are rife with recipes, they are not, intrinsically, cookbooks. And their number is not the best measure of his powers.

"Eugene was our male Colette," says Michael Batterberry, a founding editor of *Food Arts* magazine and a longtime friend of Walter's. "He wasn't a capital F food writer. He didn't divorce his food writing from his life, or for that matter from his other writing. His love of food, his deep and classical reserve of knowledge, figured in everything he did. His work was extraordinarily, unwaveringly true to the texture of the South, to the daily cycles of life down there."

Down there, for Walter, was the languid Alabama port city where he was born. He considered Mobile to be a place out of time, where he witnessed "the end of the 18th Century and the beginning of the 22nd." The city was more

Eugene Walter at home. Courtesy of Don Goodman.

than a backdrop for Walter's writings. It was a character, a palpable and constant presence. "Down in Mobile they're all crazy," he wrote in *The Untidy Pilgrim*, "because the Gulf Coast is the kingdom of monkeys, the land of clowns, ghosts and musicians, and Mobile is sweet lunacy's county seat."

Walter grew up in the home of his grandparents. His grandfather was a fruit and vegetable importer, his grandmother the keeper of a boisterous household. "Midmorning in that house at the corner of Bayou and Conti Streets was a kind of mad levee," he once observed, "a morning party like those held by King Louis XIV of France, where people were received and the day's events were discussed. My grandmother would install herself in a rocking chair on the front porch to glance at the morning *Mobile Register*, shell beans, and sip a lemonade or iced tea."

His love of language—an appreciation that would serve him well in years to come—was born of necessity: "I remember sitting on the porch with my grandmother and the lady from across the street—the great-granddaughter of one of Napoleon's generals. And when they'd begin to gossip, they'd all start speaking French, you see, and they'd look at me out of the corner of their eyes while some very juicy tales were unfolded. From that time on, I decided I'd know exactly what they were saying."

Walter left home at the age of seventeen after securing a job with the depression-era Civilian Conservation Corps. (His favorite task was painting road signs. His favorite sign: Caution, Soft Shoulders.) A wartime tour of duty in the Aleutian Islands off the coast of Alaska and three-year sojourns in both New York and Paris followed. When, in the spring of 1954, Walter moved to Rome, he chose an apartment on a hillside overlooking what had once been Cleopatra's kitchen. And as he had done while living in France, Walter threw open the doors and bade all, "Welcome to extraterritorial Alabama." Twenty-five years would pass before he returned home for good.

Though it was very much in fashion for American expatriates of the day, Walter was not inclined to renounce his native region. Indeed, lest the distance from his beloved Mobile prove to be trying, he took certain precautions: Under his bed, he stashed a good-luck shoebox of red clay, dug from a gully near his birthplace. On his terrace, he tended a patch of okra. And on a plot of land near the Coliseum, he planted a crop of collards.

"In Rome I live as I lived in Mobile," he wrote years later. "I take a nap after the midday meal; there is always time for gossip and for writing letters. I eat Southern dishes: fried chicken, grits and spoon bread. . . . I enjoy guests, I stay up the nights of the full moon."

Walter thrived in Rome, cultivating his eccentricities as carefully as his collards. He was an inventive cook, an unconventional host, a celebrated story-teller with a reputation for embroidery that might best be described as rococo. His watchword: "The dinner table is the sunburst from which ideas go orbit-ing." Gore Vidal and Judy Garland, Truman Capote and Leontyne Price, Dylan Thomas and Isak Dinesen: all the world was in Eugene Walter's thrall.

He was quick to tell friends that, during one dinner at his apartment on the Corso Vittorio Emanuele, he crafted a stained-glass window out of gumdrops for Fellini. Rumor has it that at yet another party he dished up a platter of black-eyed peas and ham hocks for two certifiable princesses as a parade of cats sashayed down the middle of a table set with centerpieces of Silly Putty. More often than not, the evening's denouement came early in the morning, as his guests huddled together to toast fork-pierced marshmallows over flicker-ing candle flames. "When he was in his prime," recalls Robert Hunter, a friend from Mobile, "people said that there were two audiences you had to arrange while in Rome: the Pope and Eugene."

Walter was a fixture of the Italian *Cinecittà*. "Darling, I'll do anything," he said, "if they send a car and serve a good lunch." But he earned his keep as a translator of scripts and a sort of benign *agent provocateur*. While working on the 1970 Fellini film *Satyricon*, he made the acquaintance of a reporter from the Time-Life stable, in town to interview the great director. She was suffi-ciently impressed with Walter to suggest that he be the writer for a planned volume on the foods of the American South. "Two others had tried before me," he liked to tell people. "One was a Yankee who came down with a ner-vous breakdown after trying to deal with Southern women cooks. The other developed a liver problem researching fatback and fried chicken."

While most Time-Life authors worked on a two-year cycle, Walter was to complete his research and writing in two months. "When they phoned me I said, 'Let me think about this,'" he told Katherine Clark, whose oral auto-biography of Walter, *Milking the Moon*, is forthcoming. "But with one foot I was pulling the suitcase from under the bed and packing."

What followed was a tear across the southeastern United States, from Maryland down to Florida and westward to Arkansas. At the wheel of a company-issued station wagon was Mario Dubsky, a young Czechoslovakian painter of only slight acquaintance. Walter didn't drive. "I've never worn blue jeans either," he told friends.

Through literary contacts, Walter arranged entrée to poet Conrad Aiken's home in Savannah, Georgia, where he supped on turnip greens served from a sterling silver tureen. In Charleston, South Carolina, he sipped from bone china bowls brimming with sherry-scented she-crab soup. In Gee's Bend, Alabama, he bent an ear to church-mother Mrs. Eugene Witherspoon, who informed him that "watery grits goes with sleazy ways." And in Mobile, Walter and Dubsky spent days on end buzzing about Termite Hall, a gracious mansion in genteel decline, home of the redoubtable Mrs. John Marston. Walter called her "Mother West Wind" and plied her for the secret of her *sauce mahonaise*, which came replete with a lineage that would give a DAR chapter president pause.

Rather than being a hindrance, Walter believed his absence from the South gave him needed perspective. A taste of ham in Virginia sparked this reverie: "I have drunk from the centaurs' mint-verged spring in Thessaly, eaten apples and goat cheese in Arcadia, goose-liver pâté in Strasbourg, oysters at Colchester, couscous in North Africa, and perhaps only in the light of those experiences could I now come back to my native land and properly partake of Smithfield ham."

The text for *American Cooking, Southern Style*, completed after Walter returned to Rome, was nothing short of revelatory. A reader of today might be inclined to view the work as an elegy to a way of life in eclipse, but Walter saw cause for celebration as well: "Even among the tugs and hesitancies of Southern history there is reason to rejoice that all Southerners of whatever pigmentation or persuasion have retained an appreciation of the table as something more than just the place where one eats. . . . The immediate impact of Southern cookery . . . is one of great pleasure, but by implication its message is much more profound."

Yes, it is a cookbook. But it's also a paean to people and place with enduring appeal. "Eugene was proud of that book," confides Nell Burks, his longtime patron and dear friend. "He told me that was his best work of fiction."

Almost ten more years would pass before Walter, spurred by escalating political upheaval in Rome, returned home to roost in January of 1979. "I had gone to the mushroom shop up the block," he told a friend at the time, "and a policeman who raised his billy club to konk a demonstrator knocked out my front tooth, and I thought, 'I wonder what it's like in Mobile. It must be so peaceful.'"

He journeyed via steamer with more than 500 crates in tow, filled to overflowing with untold folios and novels and a small gallery's worth of paintings. Ever profligate, Walter arrived in Mobile virtually penniless, relying on old friends to arrange for lodging, first in a hotel, later in a tidy turn-of-the-century bungalow.

After an absence of more than thirty years, few people knew quite what to make of the fifty-seven-year-old eccentric. Walter was a cipher, a songbird-voiced dandy with a labyrinthine intellect, able to hold forth with equal gusto on the failings of Zeno and the charms of Dolly Parton. But *la dolce vita* was over.

"I stay home much of the time," he told a reporter, "unless of course, someone's buying dinner, and then I'm a boy with bells on. Otherwise, I simply rise and do a little sonnet writing, then take a nap, then read a little, eat a little, and then when there's an emergency (and there always is), I fill my bathtub with Jim Beam and swim my way to safety."

While his life in Europe had been a sprawling opera buffa, at home in Mobile he fought to keep up appearances. If someone tried to pigeonhole him about his work, Walter was likely to reply, "I feel the true poet need not know double-entry bookkeeping or how to repair an automatic dishwasher, but should be able to write in a classical meter, in many modes from the bawdy to the religious, depending on which direction he faces; should be able to lay on a party for three hundred with good choice of wine and food; should be able to lay out a garden, organize theatrical presentations, improvise comic scenes, write letters—not notes—know the names of wildflowers, decorate tableaux roulants; should be able to welcome politicians on official occasions and amuse children in chaos."

Some would argue that, in his final years, Walter was unfocused. Indeed, his later publishing career was scattershot. Articles appeared in *Food Arts* one month and the local literary review, *Negative Capability*, the next. The great majority of his new work was published as a weekly column in a local alternative newspaper. Slim volumes of verse and compilations of previously published short stories were released by vanity presses backed by friends. Occasionally, a university press stepped in to re-release an early work.

Many other books were slated for imminent release, including a novel, *The Blockade Runners*, and an untitled history of Mobile, which Walter described as "thick enough to hold a door open in high wind." A plethora of food books were planned as well, including *The Dainty Glutton's Handbook, The Ginger Fiend's Cookbook, Root-a-Toot-Toot: Rutabagas and Turnips, The Eggplant: What It Is and Why We Like It,* and *Dixie Sips and Dixie Sups and Sometimes We're Quite Reasonable.*

Two culinary works did make it into print, though neither garnered a wide audience. *Hints and Pinches: A Concise Compendium of Herbs and Aromatics with Illustrative Recipes and Asides on Relishes, Chutneys, and Other Such Concerns*—blazoned with Walter's fanciful pen-and-ink drawings of mango-eating monkeys, dancing cats, and crown-bedecked bulbs of garlic—is a funhouse encyclopedia, at turns scholarly and irreverent, while *Delectable Dishes from*

Termite Hall: Rare and Unusual Recipes is a treasure trove of arcana like patent leather pie, a tuna fish casserole topped with peelings of eggplant, and Walter's favorite dish, black-eyed pea patties, bound with milk and egg and spiked with his spice of choice, mace.

The books were pure, unadulterated Walter—suffused with his proclivities and prejudices. In an afterword to *Delectable Dishes*, he urges diners to "never use the dead dust sold as ready-ground pepper. . . . Freshly ground pepper has volatile oils which last about an hour after grinding. . . . But dead dust is only dead dust. . . . If like me, you love that bit of pepper on your steak or your salad, either take your pepper mill with you, or smash an ashtray when the waiter says they don't have one."

Eugene Walter died on Sunday, March 29, 1998. He was seventy-six years old. At a wake held that Wednesday evening, friends and family convened to tell tales of his life and share a meal of his choosing: chicken salad sandwiches, port, and plenty of nuts. Messages of good-bye were scrawled on the simple, metal casket, giving it a graffitied look reminiscent of a subway car bound for Brooklyn. A stuffed monkey, strapped with a bandolier of Mardi Gras beads, rode on top.

On Thursday, after a mass at the Cathedral of Immaculate Conception, his body was interred at historic Church Street Cemetery beneath a canopy of magnolia and oak. Perhaps a line from one of his Monkey Poems might serve well as a panegyric: "We've eaten all the ripened heart of life / And made a luscious pickle of the rind."

Edna Lewis and Scott Peacock

· ·

CHRISTIANE LAUTERBACH

In the senior-oriented apartment complex in Atlanta where they live, hardly anyone knows the housemates who share a unit on the second floor. He leaves early for work, looking for all the world like a cross between Elvis and Luciano Pavarotti. She rarely goes out, but when she does, she leans on his arm—a tall, grizzled African American woman with the bearing of a queen.

Some call Scott Peacock and Edna Lewis "the odd couple of Southern cooking." They seem like such unlikely housemates, the proud eighty-five-year-old black woman from rural Virginia and the thirty-eight-year-old white boy from a speck of a town in Alabama. These culinary soul mates are currently at work on a book, *The Gift of Southern Cooking*—her fourth, his first—mingling their voices in a work conceived as a coming together of two great chefs.

The two met in Atlanta thirteen years ago at an event for the American Institute of Wine and Food. An awed Peacock, then the chef at the Georgia governor's mansion, introduced himself to his idol, a woman many have compared to Alice Waters and Julia Child, during the cocktail party in Buckhead. "She was sipping whiskey," he remembers. "I asked if I could write to her." He didn't and was promptly forgotten by Lewis, the leading figure in the renaissance of traditional Southern cooking. One year later, for the same Southern food festival, Peacock was asked to assist her. He, of course, recalls every detail of these two encounters. She, with mischief dancing in her eyes, says, "I don't remember at all."

"She asked me where I had gone to cooking school," recalls Peacock, now the chef at Watershed. "And when I told her I didn't, she said, 'Let's have a chat.'" Lewis, also a self-taught cook, learned by watching her mother prepare food for the family. Peacock devoured her books and absorbed her gospel of flavors, and the two started cooking regularly at the kind of events where they spoke for the South on such matters as rendering lard, churning fresh butter, and using heirloom vegetables.

Their story is that of a mentoring turned into a deep, life-changing friendship. In her seventies, Lewis decided to retire near the settlement where she grew up, in Unionville, Virginia. She grew vegetables and milked her own cow. "You were bored," Peacock reminds her, joking that he rescued her from the dirt roads when he invited her to come work for Harry A. Blazer at Harry's Farmer's Market in 1992. "I made liver pudding," she recalls, quick to point out that she didn't have any problems with the famously difficult entrepreneur, then developing a line of Southern products in the test kitchen of his short-lived Alpharetta location. Blazer put her in a nice apartment on Mansell Road.

Lewis, who doesn't drive, relocated closer to town, off Ponce de Leon Avenue, after the gig with Harry's ran its course. She walked to Kroger every day in her high heels. One day, she fell on the street. About the same time, Peacock's landlord was selling the duplex where he lived in Morningside, and in a move that stunned both their families, the two decided to set up house in an apartment complex where she fulfilled the age requirement.

I met Edna Lewis in Atlanta twelve years ago during the second Southern Food Festival of the American Institute of Wine and Food, and because she was spending the night around the corner from my house, I got to drive her in my old Chevrolet Caprice. Ramrod straight, looking out of the window as if on a state visit, she was a most intimidating presence and an awesome responsibility. "What if someone runs into us and she gets hurt?" I remember thinking, paralyzed by everything I knew about her as an icon and irreplaceable treasure. She hardly spoke to me, but she was courtly and gracious. Her smile was my reward.

Like Julia Child, she is too tall ever to be invisible, and both have written seminal cookbooks that have been in print for decades. Once heard, their voices are unforgettable (Julia's, an almost comic warble; Edna's, thin and girlish, balancing exquisite politeness and wicked humor). "Julia? Yes, I know Julia; she is a bit of a mess," Lewis told me lightheartedly during a recent conversation over a late lunch at Watershed. She also shared her memories of Tennessee Williams ("He came to my restaurant every night"), the Roosevelts ("I worked on his campaign"), and Alice Waters ("We raised money together for Meals on Wheels—she and I were the only women").

When Berkeley's Chez Panisse, the defining restaurant for fresh American cuisine, turned thirty, Waters gave a birthday bash the *New York Times* called "the ultimate foodie class reunion." As part of the proceedings, Waters decided to honor some of the women from the culinary world whom she most admires: Cecilia Chiang, Marion Cunningham, Lulu Peyraud, and Edna

Lewis, whom the *Times* lauded as the chef "whose books celebrated the ingredients of her Virginia girlhood long before Chez Panisse was conceived."

In Atlanta, people stare at Scott Peacock and come forward to greet him at his Decatur restaurant or tell him they have seen him on television. But no one seems to care about Edna Lewis. In New York, she is recognized on the street. Hard-boiled restaurateurs who know a thing or two about celebrity roll out the red carpet for her.

Two years ago, when we arrived at Josephine's, a late-night French bistro on 42nd Street in Manhattan, Peacock was tired after cooking at a party in a West Village brownstone, where his mentor was the guest of honor. Lewis had been regal, distant, and sweet all evening, hardly doing more than nodding to the company. "You'll see," I was told.

No sooner had Jean-Claude Baker, one of Josephine Baker's many children, caught sight of her tall silhouette wrapped in one of the beautifully draped African dresses she always wears than he cleared the path and settled us where we could watch the crowd and hear the opera singer warming up by the piano. It got to be one o'clock and we were all falling asleep. Then Lewis came alive. Memories triggered more memories of how a young girl from a tiny farming community in Virginia had made it into the New York world.

"Everybody came to Café Nicholson," she said, speaking of the famous Upper East Side restaurant (now called Nicholson) where she was the chef from 1948 to 1952. In a small booklet put together for her eightieth birthday celebration at Bulloch Hall in Roswell, she says: "We always had Truman Capote and Tennessee Williams, and William Faulkner came when he was in New York. You could look over the dining room and see Eleanor Roosevelt; her children always came."

When I asked Lewis recently to tell me about her married life (she has been a widow for more than two decades), her face lit up with the mischievousness that is part of her personality. "My husband was a communist," she said (he was, in fact, part of a delegation that met with President Roosevelt to ask him to grant amnesty to the Scottsboro boys). "I was, too."

Born in Freetown, Orange County, a small Virginia farming community founded by her grandfather and his friends shortly after their emancipation from slavery, Lewis was raised around the school established by her illiterate forebears. "We grew our own food," says the woman who has influenced countless chefs but who left the cooking to her mother and older sister. Partly to help support her family, she moved to New York as a slip of a girl.

One job led to another, and soon Lewis was moving in a circle of artistic young friends who did the windows for department stores and cooked from cookbooks a food vastly different from the one she had grown up with. "I wasn't a chef," she remembers of the evening when John Nicholson asked her to become a partner and chef at his new restaurant, Café Nicholson—a place so lush and romantic that it served as a setting in Woody Allen's *Bullets over Broadway*.

The menu was small, elegant, and a far cry from Lewis's Southern roots. There she rose to prominence, not exactly forgetting where she came from but burying the family traditions deep in her heart while she cooked more sophisticated fare for Garbo, Dietrich, Elizabeth Arden, Diana Vreeland, and a cadre of Southern expatriates.

Lewis was never to be very far from the restaurant world. Even when she worked as a teaching assistant at the African Hall of the Museum of Natural History or in the typesetting department of the *Daily Worker*, the newspaper of the American Communist Party, she was hanging out with James Beard, baking for Dean & DeLuca, or catering private parties.

In 1953, she moved to New Jersey to raise pheasants. "I got an incubator; I built them a little house; but they all died of the sleeping sickness," she said sadly, remembering the failed experiment. After three more stints as a chef (at the Fearrington House near Chapel Hill, North Carolina; Middleton Place outside of Charleston; and Gage & Tollner in Brooklyn) and becoming famous for her Southern-style cooking, Lewis retired to Virginia.

Were it not for Scott Peacock and their affectionate bond, she might never have moved to Atlanta. She doesn't say much good about the city where she clearly feels isolated and bereft of the glamour, bustle, and recognition that used to be her daily bread in New York.

One can't meet Lewis without noticing how independent she is. I accompanied her and Peacock on a little escapade to Habersham Gardens, meant as much to cheer her up (she adores gardening and can make any old twig take root and burst into leaves) as to buy plants. While Peacock and I were trading stories (he is pretty new at growing stuff and I am an old pro), Lewis was musing about. Not only was she not following us, but she could hardly be followed herself. A white jasmine would be calling her name (she plucks flowers and sometimes snips things with a pair of scissors wherever she is); a hidden treasure would need a special visit. "Look at her," Peacock said with a mixture of pride and devotion.

The complex where they live is your average clump of low-slung brick buildings with outdated features. Climbing the steps, I could hear classical music pouring through the walls. Inside, I found a very private and colorful world reminiscent of New York in the 1940s, but with room for Southern country memorabilia.

The two collect with a vengeance. "She is horrible," he says, although he admits to having brought in more than his share of bizarre treasures: iridescent peacock feathers, antique lamps, blue Canton china, blooming orchids, layers of books, old photographs, and framed collectibles (anything from an X-ray of Peacock's grandfather's elbow to wonderful collages made for Lewis by some of her New York artist friends, such as Ken Scott and Norman Ives, who ended up teaching at Yale).

The kitchen, where Lewis sits in an overstuffed wing chair covered with an Ethiopian throw, is a riot of blended possessions. With objects from Buddhas to rolling pins, metal trays, and more crockery than many an antique store, the place hardly has any counter space. Lewis cooks for herself (she showed me her favorite little pan with a long handle) but often eats what Peacock brings from Watershed. She is a coffee addict, and she loves to read the *New York Times*. "I read the paper; he reads magazines and watches TV," she says.

Peacock and Lewis share an interest in books (such as Jean Genet's *Our Lady of the Flowers*) and gardening. The dining room doubles as the library, and the patio groans under the weight of dozens of massed specimens, including bamboo and tall water plants in big black tubs. Much of the décor is Peacock's attempt to keep Lewis amused and stimulated as well as comfortable. And while he showed me her hot-pink bathroom decorated with a small vintage radio and lots of pictures, it is clear that they don't invade each other's space.

It would be a grave misconception to assume that Lewis is a mother or even a grandmother figure in Peacock's life. He is deferential and invariably polite in a traditional Southern manner (mostly, he addresses her as "Ms. Lewis"), but he sometimes calls his flatmate "Old Woman" and jokes that she blames him for everything. On the subject of her being black and him being white, he loves to bring up the fact that they are both a quarter Cherokee.

"People will say that I exploit her celebrity," Peacock says, wary of the way their living arrangement is perceived. But looking at them, she making a grocery list for him, a pencil held in long fingers with perfect tapered nails, he looking fondly at her and telling me tales of her at seventy-five lugging a country ham on a train, one sees only the intimacy and timelessness of friendship. And if there is celebrity mythologizing ("I am the curator of the look," Peacock joked to me), it all takes place within a framework of earned respect.

The two are spending much of their time on their upcoming cookbook.

"It has her mother's gingerbread and my mother's cornbread," Peacock says, pointing out that it will carry more than 200 new and updated recipes.

As much social documents as cookbooks, Lewis's previously published works—especially *The Taste of Country Cooking* (1976) and *In Pursuit of Flavor* (1988)—include many memories of a time when homegrown was a way of life and people put up and cured their own food. Make your own baking powder (you'll avoid the chemical taste); cook pumpkin with onion and bacon; put lemon in the sweet potatoes; use pure leaf lard to make your pie crusts, she tells us. Her books resonated with professionals and novice cooks alike. "As the voice of one of the first communities of freed African-Americans, Edna Lewis captures the elegance of the palate of Virginia with both aplomb and grace," John Martin Taylor, author of *Hoppin' John's Lowcountry Cooking* and an authority on cookbooks, once said.

Lewis is, of course, no stranger to sophisticated techniques. After all, she was cooking filet mignon with béarnaise sauce at Café Nicholson, and her favorite dessert was chocolate soufflé. Her baking recipes are particularly refined, and she includes such tips as how to listen for signs that a cake is done. "When it is still baking and not yet ready," she writes in *In Pursuit of Flavor*, "the liquids make bubbling noises. Just as the cake is done, the sounds became faint and weak, but they should disappear."

Lewis is a fervent supporter of the organic movement and has been known to make appearances at the Morningside Farmer's Market with Peacock, who does all the driving. Mostly, though, the two keep to themselves, favoring quiet work and reminiscence over entertaining in their crowded and very private world.

Lewis and Peacock are so intertwined that when I eat at Watershed, I can't tell who is responsible for such recipes as grits with shrimp paste, salmon croquettes, pecan tart, and the ultimate Southern fried chicken. That may be her greatest gift: having inspired another chef to follow in her footsteps.

To Edna Lewis

NIKKI GIOVANNI

Dear Dr. Wilson:

Thank you for inviting me to participate in the *Encyclopedia of Southern Culture*.

I am enclosing a copy of my poem celebrating the eightieth birthday of Edna Lewis. I struggled with writing a new poem or memoir only to come to the conclusion that I had already done my best.

I first met Edna Lewis at Middleton Plantation, where she restored the culinary art to its original. I had been cooking Miss Lewis's quail recipe for years and had, in fact, forgotten that it was hers. When I read in *Food and Wine* that she would be cooking at Middleton, I immediately booked myself in for the week so that I could run the menu. After a day and evening I had the pleasure of Ms. Lewis joining me at my table. I had come to Middleton alone so I had read and sort of meandered. She came over and much to my amazement knew that I write poetry. She talked about meeting Langston Hughes and her days in Harlem. Then she asked if I cooked. I do and I am proud to say so. What is your favorite dish? You should try my quail I said. I then explained how I sautéed it. How I split the back, put a half-stick of unsalted butter and a bit of thyme and garlic, then browned on one side at medium heat then turned. I noticed a strained look coming over her face but I dismissed it as I raved about my dish. I also cook good lamb I said, and we moved the conversation along. That look on her face stayed with me until I got back home. I was living with my mother then (mother has since moved to San Francisco, then on to Blacksburg) and asked her where did we get our quail recipe. In one of those magazines she said. Mother is a pack rat so I started digging old *Food and Wine*s out. And there it was. Edna Lewis's Quail. My letter started: Dear Ms. Lewis: You must think I am an idiot. I've been cooking your quail recipe so long that I think it's mine. Will you ever forgive me????? And she has. And I still make great quail. I just give credit where credit is due.

So I wanted you to see how my relationship with Ms. Lewis evolved. I am proud to call her friend. And I am especially pleased with this poem.

Sincerely,

Nikki Giovanni

. . . .

The Only True Lovers Are Chefs,
or Happy Birthday, Edna Lewis

BY NIKKI GIOVANNI

it is practically amazing /// a show of immense proportions . . . more awe in-spiring . . . more death defying . . . more dangerous than hanging from some very thin rope at the top of the very big tent . . . more difficult than putting the lions and tigers in the same cage . . . more better than anything at all /// that mothers cook meals each day for ungrateful children and spouses

if we were fair about it /// we would enclose all kitchens in glass . . . so that the passers-by would stop and wonder at the Ralston's bubbling in the Pyrex dou-ble boiler each morning and the beauty of the four plates stacked against the four glasses tucking the forks and knives with that wonderful gentle touch of a napkin just kissing the edge /// if we were really fair we would hold contests for the ordinary housewife who is not an ordinary anything but a working mother though we recognize immediately that there is no concept of a work-ing father though we all are told men have families too so that we might reward the best housewife with some sort of Silver Plate and the best house-mother with a Silver Child and the best working housewifemother with a Sil-ver Husband studded with rubies and sapphires and one ¼ carat diamond /// if we were fair about it

but this is about love and there can be no better loving than bread pudding oh sure I know some people who think bread pudding is just food but some peo-ple also think creamed corn comes in a can and they have never known the pure ecstasy of slicing down the thicker end of an ear of silver queen that was just picked at five or six this very same morning then having sliced it down so very neatly you take the back of the knife and pull it all back up releasing that wonderful milk to the bowl to which you add a pinch of garlic and some fresh ground pepper which you then turn into a gently lit skillet and you shimmer

it all like eggs then put a piece of aluminum foil over it and let it rest while you put your hands at the small of your back and go WHEW and ain't that love that soaks cold chicken wings in buttermilk and gets the heavy iron pot out and puts just the right pat of lard in it at a high temperature so that when you dust the wings with a little seasoned flour the lard sizzles and cracks while the wings turn all golden on the outside and juicy on the inside and yes I'd say that's love alright cause that other stuff anybody can do and if you do it long enough you can do it either well or adequately but cooking /// now that is something you learn from your heart then make your hands do what your grandmother's hands did and I still don't trust anyone who makes meatloaf with instruments cause the meat is to be turned with your hands and while this may not be a traditional love poem let me just say one small thing for castor oil and Vicks VapoRub and "How is my little baby feeling today?" after a hard day's work so yes this is a love poem of the highest order because the next best cook in the world, my grandmother being the best, just had a birthday and all the asparagus and wild greens and quail and tomatoes on the vines and little peas in spring and half-runners in early summer and all the wonderful musty things that come from the ground said EDNA LEWIS is having a birthday and all of us who love all of you who love food wish her a happy birthday because we who are really smart know that chefs make the best lovers . . . .
. . . . especially when they serve it with oysters on the half-shell.

The Legendary Coe Dupuis, Moonshiner

CRAIG LaBAN

This is the summer of Coe's last batch. At least that is what I hear from his friends in Cajun country who dread the day there will be no more of his magical moonshine. Each spring in southern Louisiana, ever since the old man began feeding this terrible rumor, they repeat it without ever expecting it to come true.

Will this be the last year his copper still feels the slow heat of the flames he tends so meticulously? Since Prohibition, its coffin-shaped kettle has sent the sweet vapors steaming up through the cooling coils and down into the charred oak barrels. An American whiskey for the ages, kissed with a teaspoon of wild cherry bounce. Could this really be his last?

Edwin "Coe" Dupuis, ninety-six, sits in the massive cedar rocking chair in his kitchen parlor, frail body cocked in contemplation, King Edward "cee-gar" chomped between his jaws. The smoke curls up and disappears into the white waves of hair that frame his regal face. He moves to speak, sometimes in Cajun French, sometimes in English, often in a foggy mélange of the two.

"Probably so," he says with a sly smile, but the question does not engage him. Hospitality does. "Have a drink."

On the table sits a large jug filled with whiskey. I pour a splash. "More," Coe tells me, "more," until I fill it to the brim.

I had always heard that moonshine could make you blind or crazy. It was the secretly distilled rotgut of mountain men and gangsters out to make a fortune cheap and rough. Ruckus juice. Pop skull. Preacher's lye. Dead man's dram.

But what Coe makes is another creation altogether. The pure amber liquid tickles my nostrils with inviting, sophisticated warmth. As it slips across my tongue, waves of caramel, charred oak, and fruit flare but do not burn. The soft tease of a hum lingers, glowing long after the drink is gone. Dickie Breaux, the restaurateur and former Louisiana state representative who brought me here, likens Coe's whiskey to fine Armagnac. Jim Bozeman, the retired cardio-vascular surgeon and bourbon connoisseur who installed Coe's pacemaker twenty years ago, says, "It's not as good as Jack Daniels; it's much better." And Debbie Fleming Caffery, a photographer who is one of Coe's many devoted friends, tells him as they sway together on the porch swing, "It makes my cheeks hot after I drink it. It's a total aphrodisiac. Coe?" She wants his atten-tion. "Can you hear me? Aph-ro-dis-i-ac!"

"Don't use such big words," he whispers coyly.

I've come all the way from Philadelphia to speak with Coe, who is no ordinary backwoods moonshiner. Coe Dupuis is a wizard of whiskey, a Stravinsky at the still, a maestro of the mash. He has done for outlaw liquor what Robert Johnson did for the Delta blues, instinctively elevating a folk tradition into golden, liquid art. He makes it as a hobby now rather than for profit, but he still infuses it with the flavor and legend of a place that is rapidly disappearing.

I flew into New Orleans and drove two hours west to Cajun country, crossed the Mississippi and Atchafalaya, passed over stump-filled cypress swamps and moss-covered bayous, and arrived at his little cabin with a list of questions two pages long. How is the moonshine made? What about the old bootlegging days? What about Megan Barra, his student?

At first, he indulges my interest. But an hour into my weekend visit, his gray eyes become misty with indifference. He leans away from me with sus-picious distaste and waves as if brushing off a fly. "Quit talkin' about this whiskey business! You're not going to make none anyhow."

I have misjudged the moment. Today's interview is done. But Coe doesn't simmer for long. And besides, there's a party to prepare for tonight.

It was at Dickie and Cynthia Breaux's Café des Amis four years ago that Megan Barra, a graphic designer, and her boyfriend, world-renowned slide guitarist Sonny Landreth, had their first taste of Coe's moonshine.

"It was so smooth, everything else since tastes like gasoline," Megan says. "I went up to him and said, 'I love your whiskey.' And he said, 'Don't drink too much!'"

"Something about this extraordinary drink taps you inside and helps you use your own personal powers," Sonny says. "One guy I know got inspired to contact his biological mother after he drank it. And my road manager, well, he didn't have any back pain for months and months."

For Megan, it was also the beginning of something special. She painted an image of Coe as a younger man on a whiskey jug and gave it to him. They be-came friends, sharing stories and recollections. She took him more painted jugs: Coe beside his still; his late wife, Angeline, eternally pretty in her black hair and blue dress; and Sam, the pony that used to walk into his house and eat ashtrays full of cigar butts. Her visits soon evolved into something more intriguing: She became the moonshiner's apprentice.

"He said he was going to quit maybe two years ago, and we were like, 'Gosh, we love this stuff; what are we going to do?' I wanted to watch him and learn how, just like I learned to make gumbo from my grandmother."

This isn't the first time Coe has attracted followers. But none, he says, bothered to listen for very long. "They always start cuttin' corners, they start to try tellin' me how to make it," he says with disgust. "But Megan might. She might make it. She looks very interested, and she doesn't mind spending the time."

"I'm taking a chance, I s'pose"—Coe catches my eye—"but I've always picked good-looking girls." He gives Megan a mischievous smile, knowing her intense shyness. She blushes.

I am surprised to learn that Coe Dupuis is not a drinker, save for a porch-swing nip or a little whiff when he is blending.

"He can't handle that firewater," says his nephew, Adley Dupuis. "He gets mean if he drinks too much."

It seems a strange contradiction, considering moonshine has been a constant in his life since 1928. Then twenty-four, he decided to supplement the modest income he made fishing the Atchafalaya River with a little home brew. He acquired his copper kettles and the finer points of distilling from some Kentuckians who were installing high-power lines in the region. To compete with other local bootleggers who sold their whiskey fresh out of the still, he aged his spirits from six months to two years in burnt oak casks and then sold it for nearly twice as much, $5 a gallon.

A good bootlegger needs a poker face, he says, raising a hand with a ring finger that was shortened by a fan belt: "Don't be afraid. Nuh-uh."

A great bootlegger knows quality sells: "Take your time, and don't sell cheap. . . . C'est dans les barils, c'est dans les ans." The secret is in the barrels. It's in the years.

The significance of Coe's whiskey goes far beyond the occasional sip. It is his claim to fame. It is his way of marking seasons. He sets his mash to ferment only when the bayou sun reaches the peak of its summer swelter. And it is what Debbie Caffery calls his "mystic magnet," the force that draws all walks of people to his front porch. After film director Francis Ford Coppola showed up a couple weeks before I arrived, Megan began planning a portrait of Coe and "Francis" on a jug.

Recent episodes of heart failure have given Coe's friends a scare, but he insists on living alone where he can watch *The Price Is Right* every day and listen to his tape of country singer Jimmie Rodgers. Coe still drives his truck to town, although not always in a straight line. He has a daughter, but she lives in Indiana; friends whisper that a son committed suicide some years ago. Nephews and friends keep him in their sights.

"When you're around him, you realize that it's all about how you look at life," Sonny says. "He sees us young people running around at a frantic pace, always trying to accomplish, trying to be successful. But he has a more simplistic view: 'Don't worry 'bout nothin.' Be your own man. And don't take anything for granted.' The moonshine is incredible, but it's really Coe. If there was no more, not even a drop of moonshine, I'd still come over to visit because I've never met anyone like him."

Megan and Adley take me inside the stuffy shack Coe calls his office. Wasps hover overhead, attracted by the cane sugar in the plastic trash cans in the corner. These are where the mash ferments, a slurry of water, sugar, cracked corn, and yeast that foams and gurgles from four to twelve days before it's ripe. Coe stirs it with a paddle, filling the room with the smell of yeast.

When it's ready to be distilled, the mash goes into the kettle. The joints are sealed with thick dough, and the three gas burners below are set just enough to boil but not enough to stir up any impurities. The pure vapors rise up through a copper cone and into a tube that spirals down through a seventy-five-foot coil into a barrel of cool condensing water. When the alcohol comes out—fifty gallons take twenty-four hours—it drips down a little thread, ready to be distilled a second time.

Coe can stay up for forty-eight hours on end, a perfectionist tweaking the flames, discarding the toxic first half-gallon, unperturbed by temperatures above 100 degrees. "All he wants is alcohol," Adley says. "And it's just as clear as water, man, just as clear as can be. That's white lightning."

The fresh liquor goes into ten-gallon charred oak barrels he only uses once. Then, after two years of wooden slumber, the rich caramel-colored whiskey emerges. Coe keeps a hydrometer for proofing alcohol in the box it came in seventy-two years ago. It happens to be the only thing he can read, but he rarely needs it anymore. His whiskey, Jim Bozeman says, is almost always exactly 80 proof.

How will the novice become so proficient? "I came every other day last fall just to watch that batch," Megan says. "I felt like I could do it. I'm still not sure that mine will taste like his. But I want it to. Because when he goes, there's no more. And I would hate for this recipe to die with him. Just to carry it on is important. Because it's a good thing. Simple as that. It's good."

Coe's whiskey is not for sale these days. You have to be a friend. Rather than money, he receives presents of artwork or sugar-dusted beignets or sometimes Crown Royal, the most expensive whiskey Coe could find in the liquor store and, therefore, he feels, a fair exchange. He doesn't drink it, of course, but sometimes he gives it as a wedding present.

When moonshine was Coe's livelihood, most customers lived between Lafayette and Baton Rouge. During Prohibition, local parish bosses—sheriff, judge, and clerk of court—were among his most ardent fans.

"If you can't get along with the law," he says, "that's tough."

Work on oil and dredge boats gave Coe useful contacts in the North. One of his best customers, Jim Bozeman tells me, was a seafood purveyor in Cincinnati whose regular train shipments of buffalo fish from Atchafalaya station concealed barrels of whiskey.

"J'ai fait quelques sous," Coe admits. He made a few pennies.

Coe's small cabin belies the accumulation of many pennies with its rusting metal roof and gloomy wood-paneled rooms stagnant with late spring heat. "Joliment chaud!" says Coe, reveling in the "beautiful warmth."

"He is not the destitute-looking person you see in this old house. He could have a very nice house but doesn't want it," Bozeman says. "He bought a truck a year ago that must have been the only one sold in the entire state the last ten years without air-conditioning or radio."

Nevertheless, speculators aren't uncommon at Coe's door. A Louisiana senator came by not long ago, Bozeman says, his eyes asparkle with designs of making lots of money.

"Coe told me, 'He was just a *couillon*, a big shot. Doesn't he understand you can't make any money on this because the taxes are so high?'"

The tense relationship between illegal distillers and the government dates back to George Washington's 54-cent-per-gallon whiskey tax of 1791, which led to a farmer rebellion in southwestern Pennsylvania. At one time, the tariff made up 60 percent of the domestic taxes the government collected.

The antagonism hit its apex during Prohibition, when small-time bootleggers like Coe Dupuis got their start, contributing both to the local trade and to the flow north of Southern booze and smuggled European liquor. Louisiana's swampy maze of a coastline and easy access to the Mississippi have always attracted smugglers, from the pirate Jean Laffite to the drug runners of today. Even during Prohibition, New Orleans was a party town. Legendary government agent Izzy Einstein set a record there for finding a drink—within thirty-five seconds of his arrival.

By the light of the moon. Courtesy of Vanishing Georgia Collection.

Even though amateurs may now brew beer and make wine, distilling spirits at home is still illegal, whether for sale or for personal consumption.

Temperance is no longer the issue, but taxes are. The federal tax on a gallon of 100-proof alcohol is now up to $13.50, and the government doesn't want to lose that revenue to home distillers. Health concerns are another matter. Poorly made moonshine—sometimes condensed in lead-contaminated radiators—can cause brain damage, blindness, or even death.

And yet the renegade art of moonshining persists. Every so often the federal Bureau of Alcohol, Tobacco and Firearms comes across huge illegal distilleries capable of distributing millions of dollars in untaxed hooch. During Operation Desert Storm, GIs made moonshine in far smaller quantities to relieve the stress of war in the dry Middle East.

And then there are the legendary craftsmen like Coe.

Norbert LeBlanc, an alligator hunter, is showing me the swamp near Coe's house. His people do a little moonshining, too, using a recipe that's been in the family for generations, but they ferment their mash with dried peaches instead of cherries.

"Anybody can buy whiskey in town, but when you make it, it gives you something a little extra. It's a novelty now, really. But it's something the Cajuns are going to lose if they don't keep it up, like how younger generations don't speak French anymore."

He uncovers a recycled Crown Royal bottle filled with deep red liquid. I can smell peach peels when I don't breathe too deeply. But then I do, and fire fills my nostrils. The taste is even more vivid than the smell, with buttery richness fizzling into a rough and heady burn. At 106 proof, only a few sips leave me punchy. "Coe's is pretty good," Norbert says. "Course, mine is better, naturally."

From Coe's front porch, you can see the fields of sugarcane across the street rising into the horizon like a vast green fringe. His cabin is set like a surprise in the shaded bend of a two-lane road, corralled by a woven bamboo fence painted red, green, and white. Twirling in the front yard is a funky menagerie of wagon-wheel mobiles, dangling ax picks, wrenches, a grinding stone, a ship's bell. Dickie Breaux says the irrepressible Cajun urge to render something beautiful out of nothing is responsible for Coe's lawn fantasies.

And his whiskey.

"Watch out for quicksand!" Norbert calls to me over his shoulder, but I've already slipped off a cypress log and sunk knee-deep into the sandy clay banks of the Atchafalaya River. We are just below Bayou des Ourses, near where the Dupuis clan lived in the 1920s.

We've motored for hours in Norbert's boat through the twisting bayous, entered the powerful river, and circled around an island. We have pulled over to do some exploring.

Coe Dupuis's original stills were not too far away. We pass the ruins of railroad pilings where Atchafalaya station used to be. As I sink into the soft suction, surrounded by deer tracks and dragonflies, it is easy to imagine nimble-footed swampers like Coe—100-pound sacks of sugar on their backs—disappearing into the thick veil of willows and cottonwoods as their government pursuers struggle in the mud.

In his most productive years, Coe says he made up to 800 gallons of moonshine a trip. Even in 1929 he made a nice profit. Somehow people found the money for his whiskey: "Oh, yeah, 800 gallons wouldn't last too long."

Coe was caught once, in 1928, when a customer's irate wife tipped off revenuers, who burned his kettles. When Coe went to court in Opelousas with twenty-seven other bootleggers, his attorney—the lieutenant governor of Louisiana—got him acquitted.

"The poor fellas," he says of the revenuers, "were people just like us. They had their job, I had mine."

Even so, Coe tells the epilogue with sweet satisfaction. A man approached him one day and asked for a match. The man's whiskey-loving brother was angry, he told Coe, because he'd been one of the revenuers who had burned Coe's camp.

"Yeah? Well, tell your brother to come back," Coe said. "'Cause y'all didn't burn it all. Tell your brother to come back 'cause I got plenty left." The government men had missed the fifty-gallon barrels buried under their feet.

Today is my last day with Coe, and for the first time, we will be alone together. No more protective nephews to translate his foggy dialect. No more parties or beautiful women to distract us. Just a pesky *couillon*, as he calls me (in jest, I think), and the reluctant subject.

Debbie encouraged me last night as she prepared to leave for New Mexico, a bottle of moonshine tucked into her suitcase, ready to test her latest boyfriend.

Coe can be a demanding friend, she said, especially as his health declines. He wants his friends around when he wants them around. "But it's still always fun to go over. A lot of old people are crotchety and nobody wants to be around them. But Coe is lovable. He is like some kind of mystical being that wears the same perfume my grandmother did. And it's the smell of good memories.

"Here, bring him this," she said, handing me an empty Crown Royal bottle. "This'll score you points."

When I get to his house, Coe looks at me funny, noting the fierce pink sunburn I'd acquired that morning.

"I went out to the Atchafalaya River today with Norbert."

"Sho nuff?"

"I wanted to see everything—where you grew up, the old train station, Bayou des Ourses. It was beautiful. I got stuck in the mud."

He laughs at my dirt-caked shoes. "That sand is somethin'. Need to know where you are going. I'm glad that you saw that. I haven't seen that for fifty years."

He is pleased when I give him Debbie's Crown Royal empty. Then I bring up the subject of Father Allen Breaux, whom I'd also seen that morning, and he becomes unusually sheepish.

Coe's relatives sent for Father Allen, who is Dickie's brother, when Coe was ill. They asked the priest to give Coe the anointing of the sick. He went, but he knew not to push too hard. Coe has been to church only four times in his life, and though he believes in God ("My buddy!"), he has little use for ritual.

"He's a nice guy," Coe says of Allen, whose own grandfather was a moonshiner. "But a priest is a priest, and when he came, I didn't know what to do."

What Allen found was a man at peace.

"In fact, I find myself attracted to what he's about," Father Allen says. "He's a real craftsman, and there's no greed in his operation. He has lived a really full life."

I tell Coe this and he smiles.

"I ain't got much, but you see what I got. Maybe I can do better than that, but that's enough for me. If I could only work a bit to keep my yard the way I like, I'd be glad.

"You ever see a crawfish pond?" He grabs the serpent cane and rises out of his chair. "C'mon, let's go."

I drive Coe down a dusty street, an arid strip of dirt and gravel that he himself carved alongside a narrow bayou. The water is low today, its banks dry and parched. But as we turn a corner, the landscape that unfolds takes my breath away with its lushness.

A vast grass-fringed pond opens under the blue sky for a half-mile in either direction. Its glassy surface is entirely covered with purple water lilies, and the air is full of graceful long-necked birds. It could be a sanctuary for great blue and white herons, snowy egrets, and ibis, loping down to perch over the flooded crawfish traps.

"This is mine," Coe says, waving his cane toward the acres he bought in 1937. For each acre, he paid $6, just about the cost of a gallon of moonshine. The price was right.

This is the place where Bozeman met Coe thirty years ago, sloshing methodically through the muddy pond in his rain slicker while younger men checked their traps in boats. Today two people wave from the pond, thick-necked and sweaty beneath their straw hats as they haul forty-pound sacks of crawfish onto a truck. They salute Monsieur Coe in French.

His whiskey, they tell me, is the best: "C'est du bon l'ouvrage. Ca se boit bien." It's fine work. Drinks nice.

We drive back toward his house but turn first onto a shaded drive nearby. It leads to a compound of two attractive houses, rustic-looking contemporaries with big glass windows. Modern sculptures of figures crinkle-wrapped in metal sheets dot the manicured lawn.

"This was my boy's house," he says. It is the only time he has mentioned his son. "I sold it."

My tour of Coe's empire is over, and we are back where we began, sitting in the beautiful heat of his dark kitchen, savoring a last cup of moonshine. It is just barely on the sweet side of a man's drink. Dark with wild cherry, charred with a bourbony oak that makes my gums tingle.

I will miss this taste.

"You can't be in too much of a hurry to make something like that," he tells me.

"What about Megan? Think she's going to do it?"

"Peut-être," he says with a thin grin, baring his blunted teeth. Maybe.

"Did you ever show her the real McCoy?"

"Oooh no. Not yet."

"Well, what are you waiting for, Coe? Isn't this your last batch?"

"Nuh-uh," he says with a smoky sigh. "I'm going to make some this summer, and next summer, and the next summer. I got gallons of it left."

I toast the news and drink another. Then I rise to thank him. From his cedar rocking chair, he grasps my hand and holds it. His misty gray eyes suddenly bore into me with rings of white sharpness.

"When you comin' back?"

"Soon, I hope. Soon. Good-bye, Coe."

He stops me, holding up his stubby-fingered hand.

"Good-bye is for dead people. The right word is au revoir. Au revoir, au revoir. I'll see you again."

Dori Sanders, Peach Farmer

AMY ROGERS

Spring had come early—too early, in fact. By February the peach trees were in bloom; by March the tiny fruit buds had appeared. Yes, it was beautiful to see, but farmer Dori Sanders was worried. If there was another cold snap, the young peaches could freeze and the crop would be lost. There would be no fruit to sell that summer at the family's farm stand in York County, South Carolina.

It happened. The peaches did not survive the early spring cold of 1997. What would Sanders do when the customers began arriving in June, looking for those wonderful peaches to put in pies, cobblers, and homemade ice cream?

That was the summer Dori Sanders sold rocks. Not just any old rocks, but 100 percent genuine FARM rocks, each with its own certificate of authenticity. She sold them to kids and she sold them to grown-ups. She carefully washed the peach-sized hunks of rosy quartz, polished them up to look pretty, set them out on the farm-stand tables, and when people stopped to ask what she was doing, she told them, "We don't have any peaches, but we do have farm rocks that you can take home with you today."

Sound far-fetched? Not for the woman who has turned her memories of life on the family farm into two successful novels and a cookbook. The youngest of ten children, Sanders grew up near Clover, South Carolina, where her father was principal of a two-room schoolhouse. Even though resources were often scarce in rural schools, Sanders is emphatic about the richness of her education, stating simply: "We had books."

As a child, she read Hawthorne and Homer, George Eliot and James Joyce (although she admits it wasn't until many years later that she learned Eliot was a woman and Joyce wasn't). When her Daddy came home at the end of the day, she'd run to him, eager to tell him what was on her mind. "He told me, 'Write it down,'" she says with a laugh. And so she did, beginning her letters to him, "Dear Mr. Sanders . . ."

"If you grow up on a farm," she says, "you learn by doing." Tall for her age, she taught herself to drive a tractor before she was ten. Soon the young girl grew into a woman. But instead of moving away and seeking a different kind of life, as many of her siblings did, she remained on the farm, where she still works today—with her brothers Jarvis and Orestus and her sister Virginia Malone—to bring forth from the earth not only peaches, but sweet potatoes, greens, melons, okra, tomatoes, crowder peas, and silver queen corn.

She rises early every day, before the sun, as farmers have for generations. "As soon as it's light enough to see, we start picking and gathering. We pick okra and pull corn," her strong hands demonstrate, "down and twist." When the sun moves higher in the sky and brightens up the day, it's time to pick the peaches, when you can see the perfect blush that signals the time is right.

"There is no electricity at the farm stand, so we must pick fresh every day," Sanders explains. For customers to drive from 20, 30, even 40 or more miles away, the produce and the place it comes from must be extra special. Maybe it's the easy banter among the Sanders family and their customers. Or maybe it's a desire to remember a way of life that's becoming rare. But whatever it is, people come. Many sit under the tin-roofed "porch" and find that hours go by while they chat and feel the rhythms of life all around them: the cars pulling in and out, the hugs and hellos from friends, the breezes that blow gently through the leaves as the peaches slowly ripen.

And it was watching from this place, "looking at the landscape of my youth," that inspired the storyteller in Sanders. One day, she saw a funeral procession pass by, and in one car rode a little black girl who waved at her.

Later that day, she saw a white woman drive past, sad in her own way, alone in her car. What if I put them together, Sanders asked herself, that woman and that little girl? The seed of Clover's story was planted, and it grew into a novel that was an international bestseller.

Critics praised *Clover* for its gentle humor, wisdom, and freshness. They compared Sanders to Willa Cather, to Zora Neale Hurston, even to Maya Angelou. But the pull of success couldn't tug hard enough on Sanders to take her away from the farm, even after she wrote another novel, *Her Own Place.*

Her publisher had noticed that food cropped up often in Sanders's stories and suggested she write a cookbook. *Dori Sanders' Country Cooking* was the result. "Food is a major topic of conversation," the author explains. "If it weren't for the weather, who died, and food, we wouldn't have any conversation!"

A farmer rarely rests, and Sanders is no exception, rambling around the farm in a 1974 Ford pickup truck she calls Yellow Boy and still driving her Massey Ferguson 235 tractor. "There is always something to do," she says.

When the summer growing season ends, it will be time for autumn greens, dark and leafy. There will be rows and rows of trees to prune and seeds to buy for next year. And Sanders is at work on another writing project, a non-fiction work for which she is calling upon her own personal memories and recollections.

If next winter is too mild or spring is too harsh, the family will cope with quiet confidence. "The weather can be very crippling in its way, but the farmer can also in his own way become a little more resourceful," Sanders says. There are fish in nearby streams, wild berries, muscadine grapes. And what if the delicate peach blossoms should freeze again next year? What if there are no peaches to sell?

The author who remained on her family's land despite her successes in the literary world has a philosophy. "If you have survived up to that point, you can surely survive what's ahead. We will survive because we are farmers."

From the Recipe File
of Luba Cohen

MARCIE COHEN FERRIS

Luba Tooter traveled from Odessa to America in September of 1912. Hers is a tale familiar to scores of other Jewish immigrants who made similar journeys from Europe between 1881 and 1924 in the wake of Russian and Polish pogroms. Less familiar but equally important are Luba's life in Arkansas and the letters and recipes she left behind, which reveal a compelling, significant network of women's friendships. These friendships surface in recipes, letters, and cookbooks, where they reveal how foodways shaped networks of community, family, and sisterhood.

With their parents, Harry and Mollie Tooter, Luba and her brothers, Milton, Maurice, Edward, Joseph, Albert, and George, traveled in a horse-drawn wagon for over two months. Claiming that they were going to a family wedding, the Tooters packed just enough baggage to appear that they were leaving for vacation rather than making a permanent exodus from Russia. After an arduous journey to Rotterdam that required an illegal crossing of the Austro-Hungarian border, the family boarded the *America* and squeezed into small steerage compartments for their ten-day journey to New York. At the age of ninety-two, Luba's youngest brother Joe still remembers a small cubicle on the ship where Jewish passengers gathered to observe Rosh Hashanah and Yom Kippur. Their cousin, Minnie Issacson, met the family after they were cleared through Ellis Island and took them to an apartment she had rented in Brooklyn. Luba was fifteen years old when her family arrived in New York. Eight years later, she married Samuel Joseph Cohen, a Russian Jew who had immigrated from Minsk in 1912. They soon moved from New York to Blytheville, Arkansas.

Luba died in 1985 at the age of eighty-eight. In her Arkansas home, she left a wooden recipe box and the rolling pin with which she had made noodle dough as her mother had done in Odessa. Stuffed into the box was a disorderly collection of recipes written on scraps of paper, notepads from her husband's construction company, stationery from the Statler Hotel in New York and the Peabody in Memphis, bits of wallpaper, backs of envelopes, and her personal cards with the inscription "From the recipe file of Luba Cohen" printed across the top, along with recipes clipped from the *Memphis Commercial Appeal.*

When Luba arrived in Arkansas in 1920 as a young bride, she brought both recipes of her native Russian foods and those of American dishes she discovered during her years in New York City. She soon blended these recipes with Southern recipes in Blytheville, where she quickly developed friendships with her predominantly non-Jewish neighbors. Their cards for "Mrs. Thornton Scott's cocoon cookies," "Julia's jam cake," and "May Dixon's cook-while-you-sleep cookies" filled her recipe box, along with cut-out newspaper recipes for peach jam, pecan tarts, Brer Rabbit Molasses cookies, crabapple jelly, grasshopper pie, and "Mother's Best Hush Puppies," removed from the back of a cornmeal package. Luba's recipes for food favorites from the 1950s such as "tutti fruitti rolls," "perfect tuna casserole," Chinese egg rolls, veal scallopini, and Jello molds suggest how she acculturated by incorporating popular American dishes and entertaining styles.

Luba also had recipe cards from her Jewish friends who lived in Blytheville and nearby small towns in northeastern Arkansas and the "boot heel" of Missouri, where their husbands were merchants, doctors, engineers, and manufacturers. By 1947, these families had raised the funds to build Temple Israel in Blytheville. Because her husband, Samuel, known as Jimmy, had little interest in the temple and Jewish life, Luba remained at the edge of the Jewish community. A constant exchange of recipes with her "temple friends" for dishes like "Fanny Weinstein's matzoh balls," "Lillian's strudel," "Lena's mandel-brodt," and "Minnie's honey cake" preserved her cultural identity in a place where there were no connections to distant family and Jewish memory.

Recipes from Huddy Horowitz and her mother Lena also appear in Luba's box. Huddy married Luba and Jimmy's son Jerry in 1946 and moved with him to Blytheville. Reared in an active, traditional Jewish community in New London, Connecticut, Huddy embraced the small Jewish community at Temple Israel in Blytheville, where deep friendships developed through temple activities and the preparation of food for holiday meals and special events. Huddy explained that "the temple was our connection to our close friendships, our place of worship and identity. It held us all together, and the support was enormous."

One well-used recipe in Luba's box was chicken chop suey or chow mein,

Huddy Cohen, the author's mother, preparing lemon fluff. Courtesy of Marcie Ferris.

the dish she prepared when entertaining her family. Why did she cook a dish so "un-Jewish," so foreign to her Russian roots? Chow mein was a dish she had discovered in New York. Living in Brooklyn from 1912 to 1920, she and many other Eastern European Jews first encountered Chinese restaurants, where they enjoyed this inexpensive food that did not mix milk and meat, as proscribed by kosher law. And pork, a forbidden food for Jews who kept kosher, was minced too small to recognize. Chinese cuisine featured garlic, celery, onion, overcooked vegetables, chicken dishes, eggs, sweet and sour dishes, and hot tea, tastes that an Eastern European palate appreciated. While the Chinese called their dumplings wontons, Jews looked into the same steaming bowls of chicken broth and saw kreplach.

On Luba's kitchen shelves was *Tried and True Recipes*, a guidebook to Southern cooking published in 1922 by the Alabama Division of the United Daughters of the Confederacy. There was also the small, spiral-bound *Art of Chinese Cooking*, published in 1956. Luba's recipes, cookbooks, and Russian rolling pin reveal her experiences as a Russian child, a New York immigrant, and finally a Southern housewife.

Luba Cohen's life suggests how Southern Jewish foodways reveal a cultural history. We are what we eat, and the foods people enjoy as well as those they avoid reveal their cultural identity. Charged with the preparation of their families' meals, Southern Jewish women shaped their cultural identity through food. Their history survives in nontraditional sources such as recipes, menus, letters, journals, and cookbooks.

A Confederacy of Sauces

JACK HITT

While I was back home last spring in Charleston, South Carolina, doing some work with my nephew, we decided to drive over to a barbecue joint one afternoon for some pulled pork and sauce. The place I like is called Melvin's, famous for both its good barbecue and its fine pedigree. Melvin is a Bessinger, a clan whose name in South Carolina has the same kind of power that barbecue legends like Gates or Bryant have out in Kansas City.

But my nephew warned me that lately there had been a feud. Barbecue had somehow gotten mixed up with issues of race and heritage. Ugly fighting words had been exchanged, leaving a residue of aggrieved feelings. The quarrel had finally touched the third rail of contemporary Carolina anger, the only topic more sensitive than sauce recipes, Strom Thurmond jokes, and Charleston genealogy combined: the meaning of the Civil War. And once again, the war had re-enacted its old bitterness, setting brother against brother—only not at Gettysburg this time but in a hickory pit redolent with crackling.

"Buying a barbecue sandwich is now a political act," my nephew explained to me. "You have to declare which side you're on." On a culinary level, barbecue is one of those democratic dishes that have an inexplicable power to start fights, like pizza. People defend their favorite pit as passionately as a homeland (ask any Gates fiend about Bryant's), and chefs guard their secret recipes (which tend to involve strangely commonplace ingredients like A.1 Steak Sauce or red wine vinegar or margarine) with a paranoia worthy of Coca-Cola or KFC. But in South Carolina, barbecue has also become an occasion to vent what should be declared the state's official emotion: aggrievement. See, ours is different from yours.

If you were to draw a line north from Charleston to Columbia and shade in most of the low country to the east, you would form the Devil's Triangle of barbecue. There, the sauce is based on mustard, not tomatoes, and vinegar, not brown sugar, is the dominant back-taste. I have a friend these days from Kansas City. I brought up the subject of mustard-based sauce at his dinner table the other day and was hooted down for daring to speak about such a hideous abomination when a bottle of Gates's finest was actually present at the table. Of course, I wasn't comparing anything, I was just—all I was saying was that mustard, that sauce. . . . I went home that night feeling, well, aggrieved.

The first shot in South Carolina's modern barbecue war occurred when the state legislature lowered the Confederate flag from the capitol dome in Columbia on July 1, 2000. The flag had been flying there since 1962, and in 1999 the NAACP had initiated a boycott of the state to force it down. The lowering of the flag, at high noon, was covered live on television with an O. J.–like camera shot of the flag being carried down the dark internal steps of the dome. The tone of the TV broadcast was lugubrious, funereal, and, of course, aggrieved.

That afternoon, Maurice Bessinger, who has nine restaurants in and around the capital, hoisted the Confederate flag over each one.

"I surrounded the city of Columbia with Confederate flags," Maurice explained when I went to visit him at his headquarters. "I didn't even tell my wife. I had it all planned." As a character, Maurice is not unknown around the state. (He once owned a plantation-size piece of land and named it Tara.) He looks like a cross between Colonel Sanders and the rich guy on the Community Chest cards in Monopoly: a bantam rooster of a man with snowy hair and mustache. In addition to his Maurice's Bar-B-Q restaurants, he sells his trademark yellow sauce, dubbed Carolina Gold, in stores, with his own image smiling down from every bottle. He built a big bottling plant in 1993 that supplied 3,000 grocery stores from Tampa to New York with his stuff. His hickory fires burned twenty-four hours a day and consumed so much wood that Maurice bought an entire plantation near Columbia merely to supply himself with the sixty cords he needed each week. By 1999, Maurice had created the largest commercial barbecue operation in the country.

Just inside the door of his main restaurant is a set of tables that form a kind of shrine to Maurice's ancestors and his beliefs. There are pictures of his parents and grandparents, as well as framed letters from his heroes, George Wallace and Pat Buchanan. (Maurice's main pit doubled as the state's Buchanan for President headquarters in 1996.) The tables hold pamphlets on a range of subjects, one titled "McCarthyism and Lincolnism" and another that traces the symbology of the Confederate flag back to "4,000-year-old hieroglyphics," when the flag was "used by Jehovah-God in prehistoric times to fight battles for liberty and freedom."

"The whole thing wouldn't have happened if it wasn't for John Monk,"

Maurice told me. Last August, Monk, a local newspaper columnist, quoted one of the pamphlets explaining the relationship between the Bible and slavery. "Many of those African slaves blessed the Lord for allowing them to be enslaved and sent to America," it said. (In my experience, I have found that blacks can get grouchy when Southern whites talk knowingly on the issue of slave gratitude.)

Alarmed by Monk's column and fresh from their victory on the flag issue at the capitol, black leaders felt aggrieved by Maurice's flag-raising, and they held a news conference to express their views. At the time, Maurice was close to inking a deal to take his sauce national, expanding beyond his East Coast base. But in September 2000, faced with growing public pressure, Sam's Club pulled his sauce from its shelves. The next day, Wal-Mart, too, banned Carolina Gold and was followed by Food Lion, Harris Teeter, Bi-Lo, Kroger, and Publix. But the venerable Southern chain Piggly Wiggly (a.k.a. "the Pig") held out. A spokesman announced that the Pig would defend its customers' right to choose.

Enter a North Charleston minister, James Johnson, who met with the director of the Pig as the official representative of the Southern Christian Leadership Conference in the South Carolina low country.

"I told him we had the buses from the churches and that we'd have them parked next to each of his stores to bus every customer to Harris Teeter if we had to," he recalled. The Pig caved quickly.

"I lost about 98 percent of my bottled-sauce business," Maurice said. He wouldn't divulge precisely how much his overall sales (both restaurant and retail store) had fallen. But he estimates that he has lost $20 million from the boycott. Today, his bottling plant, which cost him millions to build, is largely idle.

Not long after the boycott began, a yellow sauce quite similar to Maurice's began to fill up the empty shelves of the Piggly Wigglys around Charleston. In the wake of Maurice's fall, a market niche had appeared, and right away an entrepreneur had seized the advantage.

"He opened the door because of his flag views, see, and we took the chance—why shouldn't we?" said the new kid on the block: Melvin Bessinger, Maurice's older brother. Still sporting some blond hair and piercing blue eyes at age seventy-eight, Melvin, the owner of Melvin's Southern BBQ and Ribs in Charleston, considers himself an old-line egalitarian: "I don't say anything about black people, as long as they're educated and do right. I don't hold myself up as better than nobody."

Melvin's son David, who works with Melvin, said that right after they got into the Pig, they secured Maurice's old shelf space at the Bi-Lo. Maurice was enraged. He went public with a nasty sound bite that he recited several times for me as well: "I taught Melvin everything he knows about barbecue sauce — but I didn't teach him everything I know."

Then an unlikely avenging angel appeared to smite Maurice's enemies: enter Johnson, once again. The minister says he got a call from a local television station that fed him a tip about all Bessinger sauce being the same. So Johnson called for yet another boycott.

"What happened was that black people saw our sauce in the Piggly Wiggly downtown on Meeting Street," Melvin told me. "They thought Maurice was putting his sauce in our bottles and calling it Melvin's." This confusion forced Melvin to speak publicly. He issued a press release through his attorney, officially denying his brother. "Melvin and his brother do not share political or social views," it said. "Despite their being brothers, they do not speak to each other. Melvin's views on the Confederate flag, slavery, and race relations are not those of his brother."

Stories appeared on the wire services about the dispute, saying that the only conversation that had passed between the two brothers in years was an aggrieved grunt of "Hi" at their sister's funeral last October. In Charleston, Melvin's son David said they had taken "Bessinger" off their bottle entirely. "I'm ashamed to use my last name," he told the *Charleston Post-Courier*.

Soon thereafter, Johnson held a news conference at Melvin's. He said he had been shown convincing evidence that Melvin's bottling operation was different from Maurice's, and he publicly endorsed Melvin's sauce.

When I later asked him, out of the glare of the TV lights, for his true feelings about the sauces, Johnson confessed: "I've never tasted Maurice's, to be honest. The truth is, I don't even eat barbecue. I try to avoid pork and the red meats."

Johnson explained that he had always avoided Maurice's restaurants. He knew about Maurice long before the flag controversy, he said. Maurice had been an outspoken Wallace supporter during the civil rights movement. Maurice maintained segregated dining facilities and separate entrances for blacks and whites until a 1968 Supreme Court decision (*Newman v. Piggie Park Enterprises*) forced him to change his policy.

On a hot and humid day in Columbia, I walked to the front steps of South Carolina's capitol. Maurice had invited me to attend a rally to condemn the lowering of the Confederate flag, with a big Bessinger barbecue afterward. Turnout was pretty high, I'd guess 500 people, mostly wearing dour expressions. The mission was to express aggrievement, especially for the politicians who had voted to take down the flag—a.k.a. the "turncoats." Flags flew everywhere—tiny ones for the kiddies, large swaying flags cocked in flag holsters for the real zealots. I was mildly afraid, as if someone might suddenly point at me and start ululating.

The politicians speaking that day, including the state's lieutenant governor and attorney general, knew their crowd well. There was no pig-biting demagoguery, only laurels for the nobility of dying for states' rights and the repeated assertion that the flag and the war never involved slavery, just high-minded constitutional theory. All of this got wrapped up in honey-tongued rhetoric and tied with a bow called "heritage"—reminding me once again how little contemporary Confederate history has to do with the past.

What neo-Confederates really want, paradoxical as it may seem, is not to be thought of as racists. The people in the crowd were tired and agitated over having to answer for Lester Maddox and Bull Connor forty years later. In an age of identity politics, when every group can boast of some noble and brave past, neo-Confederates want one too. To effect this, they look at the multiple and confusing causes and interests that erupted into the Civil War and remove from that historical tapestry the threads of slavery, racism, and hatred. What's left is honor in battle, the cause of states' rights, and heritage. That is the truth they want the Confederate flag to stand for today.

All of which partly accounted for one of the minor celebrities meandering through the crowd—Stanley Lott. He was the very picture of wartime suffering. Clothed in rags, he carried a huge Confederate flag while a necklace of large porcelain battle flags jangled against his chest. But what really distinguished Lott at the rally was that he's black. Wearing a grim face, he was hunched over, it seemed, from the weight of all the heavy metaphor he bore. A white woman beside me, dressed in antebellum widow's weeds and matching bonnet, stepped up to him hesitantly.

"Yes, ma'am," Lott said in greeting. "Nice day for a rally. Nice day." The woman tugged at her elbow-length lace glove until her pale hand was free. She stretched it across the radius of her hoop skirt. "I just want to shake your hand," she said. Her voice cracked, and she began to cry. "For knowing the truth."

"Yes, ma'am," Lott said, comforting her hand and confirming her truth. "Yes, ma'am."

Maybe 200 people turned out at the postrally barbecue at Maurice's bottling plant. He had set up a giant shed to seat 500, so the gathering looked like a failure. The machines were walled off by pallets of Maurice's boxes, each stamped with the word "Kosher." Maurice, a lay preacher, began the long afternoon of speeches.

"This is our only hope," Maurice explained, pointing to the giant Confederate flag behind him. "As the government gets more and more tyrannical, they will hand over more power to a world government. And then the Antichrist will just come in and say, 'Thank you very much.'"

Maurice is comfortable weaving religion with barbecue: there is a weekly Bible study session at each of his pits. Later on, in the privacy of his office, he let slip a secret of his sauce. "The recipe," he said, "is in the Bible."

"Does it start with Jesus' parable of the mustard seed?" I joked. Maurice's eyes flared, as if I had correctly guessed that his middle name was Rumpelstiltskin, and he refused to discuss it further.

"You can just say that my Carolina Gold is a heavenly sauce," he said. "I believe that after the Rapture there will be a big barbecue, and I hope the Lord will let me cook."

Bessinger sauce has always had mythic qualities, even in its origins. Like Jack of Beanstalk fame, the Bessingers' father, Joe James, took a desperate risk during the depression in order to feed his eleven children: he sold the family's only working assets, a cow named Betsy and a mule, and used the proceeds to open a restaurant. His gamble paid off. Joe's Grill, halfway between Charleston and Columbia on the old highway, was soon jammed with visitors. What people seemed to really go for was Joe's tangy mustard sauce.

During World War II, eleven-year-old Maurice worked in the restaurant while Melvin, seven years older, fought the Germans. Melvin landed at Normandy, was captured in battle, escaped from a POW camp, and was hidden from the Nazis in a Munich attic by a German woman. When Melvin returned to South Carolina with a Purple Heart and a Bronze Star, his father proudly brought his war-hero son into the restaurant—the same restaurant where Maurice had been working every day. Maurice was not happy.

"Daddy said he had put in the will that I would get the restaurant," Maurice said. "But after he died in 1949, the will couldn't be found. Momma gave the restaurant to Melvin. She always preferred him because his looks sort of favor her people, you know. Melvin was always Momma's pet." Maurice ran off and joined the army, eventually serving in Korea.

"Maurice never has liked me," Melvin said. "I don't know why. I think he's jealous. I think in his heart he loves me, though, because I love him."

Melvin might want to read Maurice's new book, titled *Defending My Heritage*. In it, Maurice describes Melvin as a vicious and sadistic older brother who stole food from him during the depression. One violent beating by

Melvin left an eight-year-old Maurice with "bloody stripes up and down my back." The book is bound to attract attention outside the family as well. In it, Maurice defends segregation because "blacks prefer the company of blacks while whites prefer the company of whites" and describes his earliest Jewish customers as "quite stingy and difficult to serve."

Given the volatile family dynamic, it's not surprising that in the decades after the war, the Bessinger brothers opened and closed barbecue pits all over the low country of South Carolina. Upon returning from Korea, Maurice and another brother, Joe Jr., opened Piggie Park in Charleston. The place no longer exists except in legend. You ordered from your car on scratchy metal intercoms, and young girls came out to snap a tray onto your open car window. I remember that the onion rings were as big around as cup saucers, coated with a smooth, thick batter and deep-fried. I also remember that all the whites parked under a central tin roof and the blacks parked against the wall.

On this trip, I decided to taste all the Bessinger sauces fresh from their respective fires, all in a single day. I ate at Maurice's in Columbia and then drove to Charleston. There, Melvin's two pits occupy James Island and Mount Pleasant. Another brother, Thomas, has a place on the Savannah highway. Yet another, Robert, has two pits in North Charleston. None of the brothers compete side by side with the others. They have spread out and covered the low country. I grew up being told that yellow sauce was my cultural heritage. But it's clear that without the siblings' anxieties and their nomadic habits, Joe Sr.'s recipe would have died out after Joe's Grill closed. South Carolina would have remained just another outpost in the national camp of red barbecue sauce.

In the meantime, the brothers' interpretations of Dad's original sauce have created subtle but noticeable distinctions. Maurice's is definitely sweetened (probably for mass-market consumption) and tastes yummy at first. Melvin's has a strong, good burned flavor, but my guess is that some of that derives from liquid smoke. Robert's is serviceable. And then there's Thomas's. Thomas avoided me strenuously when I tried to discuss the family brouhaha, getting his secretary to lie and say he wasn't in as I called him from my car phone and stared at him through the window. Still, in my opinion, his was the best, terrifically balancing the tangs of mustard and vinegar with a wood fire's charry flavor.

"They have an ego problem," Robert said when I caught up with him. "Melvin wants to be the chief, and Maurice wants to be the major chief." Robert admits that he doesn't have quite the ambition of his brothers. He doesn't bottle his sauce or even trick out his store with barbecuey decor like old scythes or yokes. There's a picture of Arnold Palmer near the cash register.

Robert checks the books every morning and plays golf every afternoon. He makes a living and can't understand how it all came to this.

"If we make politics out of barbecue, then what's next?" he said. "Political hamburgers? Political french fries?"

Probably. Maurice said that even though the grocery store chains have banned his sauce, some stores sell it out of the manager's office in brown paper bags and others stock it out in the open. Johnson confirms that he occasionally gets reports of Maurice's sauce being slipped back onto the shelf, and he has to revive his threats to get it taken off. According to Maurice, heritage groups like the Sons of Confederate Veterans have started coming into his shops, and they have made up for the loss in black business. Of course, blacks now avoid Maurice's altogether. The old segregation of the Piggie Park days has reconstituted itself for a new age.

In the heyday of the civil rights movement, many Southerners resented the federal government for singling out the Southern states for special remedies on the argument that segregation imposed by law was different from de facto separation of the races. The reaction back home, naturally, was to feel picked on and then aggrieved. Now, Southerners can be proud that their racial divide is strictly voluntary, just as it is everywhere else.

JACK HITT

Interview with Kim Wong,
Clarksdale, Mississippi

CARRIE BROWN

I was born in China and came to the United States when I was about twelve or thirteen years old. I lived with my sister in Connecticut and went to school there for a year. My dad had a store in Pride's Point, Mississippi, and he needed me to help him out. So I moved to Mississippi in 1950 and finished school down here. In Connecticut, the school was bigger and there were places to go—the YMCA, the beach, birthday parties, and a skating rink. In Mississippi, I had to forget about all of that because it was a small town. But you compare Mississippi to where I came from in China, and Mississippi is good! In China, we don't have anything. Where I was born, there was no running water, no electricity. In Mississippi, at the grocery store, I eat anything that I want, and it doesn't cost me anything.

There was no integration in the schools then. It was all segregated. But my dad went to the school board and said that I was going to an integrated school in Connecticut. So, they say, you try him in the white school. I was the first Chinese boy that ever went to the white school. There were no blacks; there were no Asians. I was the first one, and it was decent going to the white school. I tried to do everything. I wanted the people to see that I'm not the stereotype that they think I am, and I never had any problem at all. Out of thirteen people in my class, I was the only one to get elected to go to Boys State, so I proved myself. I was determined to be someone that they didn't think I was.

When my father retired in 1955, I took over his grocery store, and in 1973 I opened a Chinese restaurant in Clarksdale. I was running a restaurant, running a grocery store, and teaching martial arts at the same time. It was during that time that I discovered a product in the kitchen. My wife usually rendered a Boston butt in the pot and put the pure lard in the homemade biscuits. People from all around here, they come here in the morning to eat biscuits and sausage and drink coffee. Now we would throw away the by-products of the

59

Pork rind king Kim Wong. Courtesy of Elizabeth DeRamus.

lard, which I would find out later were called "cracklings." Some cooks made crackling bread with these tasty bits of pork.

One day in the grocery store I saw a couple of kids fighting over a bag of pork skins. A person came in and said, "You know, those pork skins are good, but it's not as good as my grandma's cracklin' bread." I asked about crackling, and then I realized—my wife was throwing that away every day. So I cooked it, seasoned it, put it in a bag on the counter, and gave it to the kids when they came in. Some of the kids would say, "The only time we have cracklin' bread is in the winter time when my grandmother and grandfather slaughter a pig in the backyard. But that's what this is and it's good."

CARRIE BROWN

Before long the kids would not buy the pork skins; they would buy the Zip-loc bags of cracklings I had on the counter. I couldn't produce enough. A salesman started buying packets and selling them to his friends. He said I had a market and suggested I call the FDA department in Jackson. So I called the FDA. A couple of weeks later, one of the inspectors came in to see me, and I told him the story. He said, "Oh yeah, you can do it." So I am the one who invented packaged pork cracklings, and people can now have them year 'round.

I feel only the United States can give me this opportunity. If I were in China, I would have never had this kind of opportunity. I feel like I am privileged. This is a great country, and I'm proud of it. That's why I served my country in Korea, and I do everything I can to serve my community. I like the culture of Mississippi, I like the people of Mississippi, and I like the quietness and the friendly neighbors. In Mississippi when I go outside, everybody says, "Hey, Kim! How ya' doin'?" All my friends are here, so I feel very, very much at home in Mississippi.

Craig Claiborne Remembered

JAMES VILLAS

"Jim, it's Craig," croaked the voice on the phone early one morning. "I'm in jail."

"My God, what for?" I reacted with alarm.

"Whatta you think? Drunk driving again. Can you come get me?"

It didn't matter to the cops of East Hampton that they'd locked up the celebrated cookbook author and food columnist of the *New York Times*. But since he was Craig Claiborne, the otherwise routine news would make headlines everywhere, as it had before.

Others were quick to pass judgment, but naively or not, I interpreted Craig's behavior simply as another indication of his lifelong appetite for risk. Here, after all, was the journalist who had ventured into Vietnam at the height of the war just to sample the cuisine; the adventurer who had ingested potentially poisonous fugu in Japan; the gourmand who enraged the Vatican by spending $4,000 on a single meal in Paris; the critic who dared to cross swords with the irascible restaurateur Henri Soule of Le Pavillon fame by siding with the chef, Pierre Franey, when he resigned after a bitter dispute. Here, too, was the editor brave enough to quit his prestigious job at the *New York Times*.

There has never been any question in my mind that it was Craig Claiborne, not James Beard or Julia Child, who first introduced Americans to the glories of great cooking and fine dining. If this conviction strikes today's professional foodies as heretical, so be it. Despite Beard's saintly legacy and Julia's phenomenal celebrity, the truth is that it was Claiborne who pioneered this country's gastronomic sophistication back in the 1950s, when he invaded the Women's News pages of the *New York Times* and, not long after, published his monumental first cookbook. As the newspaper's food editor, he put all ethnic food on the agenda when most people only wanted to read about French cuisine—and in the process, he discovered Paul Prudhomme, Madhur Jaffrey, Diana Kennedy, Marcella Hazan, Virginia Lee, and other groundbreaking chefs and cookbook authors. He introduced Americans to everything from French *coulibiac* of salmon to Greek *garides* to Chinese sea slugs. A complex and private gentleman, Craig never sought approval from his peers; he preferred to be left alone in his work and his personal life. Some perceived him to be a snob, but by maintaining a guarded sense of mission virtually unknown to others in the field, he almost single-handedly established, articulated, and popularized a new system of gastronomic standards in food writing, restaurant criticism, and recipe testing that remains as valid today as it was forty years ago.

We first met around 1970 at a press reception aboard the ss *France* in New York harbor, not long after Craig had pronounced the first-class Chambord dining saloon the greatest restaurant in the world. We tried to chat, but he was besieged by photographers, journalists, and fans.

"Good God Almighty," Craig finally whispered to me in exasperation; "I can't take any more of this. What say we clear out of here and go where we can talk?"

Minutes later, we were perched at a quiet table in the Oak Bar of the Plaza Hotel, sipping ice-cold Beefeater martinis and discussing not only the *France* but the South—the way all displaced Rebels tend to do when they're alone together. Still a relatively unknown greenhorn in New York City's vibrant food world, I was unquestionably dazzled to be in the company of its renowned and most respected exponent. In a forthright but courteous manner, he inquired about what I was working on and even invited me to visit him sometime in East Hampton. He told me about lecturing and cooking with his collaborator, Pierre Franey, aboard the ship.

What astounded me most, however, was how little Craig alluded to his passion for food and fine dining. Here was the country's foremost authority on gastronomy, and he didn't care to talk shop or flaunt his culinary knowledge. For him, to sit for hours and dwell on the components of a certain dish or to go on inordinately about such-and-such restaurant or to extol at great length the talents of some superstar chef was as annoying and boring as using a cell phone in a restaurant. Erudition, enthusiasm, and conviction were to be communicated primarily in an author's writing, not in a social milieu more conducive to conversation about recent travels and books read, music, politics, and sex.

Later, after he had convinced me that I should buy my own house in East Hampton, I suppose that I came to know Craig as well as any friend was allowed to. We cooked and entertained together, traveled and judged numerous contests together, got drunk and unruly together, and were always there to help and console each other when misfortune struck. I had a standing invitation to his formal, high-profile New Year's Eve dinners, graced by the likes of Jean Stafford, Joseph Heller, Lauren Bacall, Arthur Miller, and some of the world's most famous chefs. And on other festive occasions, he and a brigade of helpers would produce at his home a staggering buffet of Chinese, Scandinavian, or Mexican dishes, or he would coax someone like Maida Heatter to make a dozen different cakes for a communal tasting.

Over the years, I spent many a morning in Craig's kitchen while he and Pierre Franey worked on recipes (to country music or Verdi blaring in the background) that would appear in the *New York Times* and in their books. And while I'm the first to credit Craig with being one of the most brilliant, exacting, and dedicated journalists I've ever known, it's also true that this legend who taught America so much about cooking was himself not a very accomplished cook and would never have attained such heights of success had Pierre (and other professional chefs) not been at the stove. To point out a few of Craig's salient limitations may seem disrespectful—the only justification being that his flawed example taught me that an eminent food journalist must be a master chef no more than a connoisseur of Bach needs to be expected to perform the composer's preludes and fugues with immaculate precision.

Equally important to me was the totally unpretentious way that Craig approached food and restaurants in general. Contrary to his public image as the authoritative bon vivant nourishing himself exclusively on the world's most exotic foods, his tastes actually couldn't have been more elemental. He indeed relished an elegant caviar roulade as much as a Mongolian hot pot or an intricate striped bass baked in phyllo pastry, but if you wanted to see his blue eyes light up, mention Southern fried chicken or lowly French blood sausages or pumpkin cream pie. Once, when my mother invited him to dinner after a TV appearance in Charlotte and asked what he'd really love for her to prepare, without a second's hesitation, he specified spaghetti and meatballs. Another time, I asked him casually what he would say if forced to name a style of food he preferred over all others. "Well," he said after a moment of reflection, "actually, you know, I don't take the cuisine business all that seriously, since for me food is strictly a matter of pleasure. So I'd have to say . . . yes, I'd definitely say . . . any dish made with ground meat."

One thing I learned from Craig came initially as a great surprise: While still issuing his weighty New York restaurant reviews in the *Times*, he stated one night at a lousy Italian place that he was, frankly, bored with restaurant criticism and "wouldn't give a damn if most of the restaurants in Manhattan were shoved into the East River." The job had become frustrating, futile, and even demeaning, and one reason he was drinking so much was simply to endure

yet another evening of dining out. At the time, I attributed Craig's bilious out-
burst to either momentary disappointment or too many glasses of Barolo,
but, sure enough, not long after, he resigned this duty at the paper. "A restaurant is either good or bad, period," Craig would repeat in private over the
years, "and for a critic to venture anything more than a brutally objective ver-
dict and the essential details of an operation is both ludicrous and an egotisti-
cal indulgence."

Typical of his enormous generosity, Craig had willed the majority of his famous East Hampton estate and vast library to the Culinary Institute of America, a gesture that inspired me to take a nostalgic drive over to the house last
month for the first time in ages, just to look around. The grounds were pretty
unkempt and overgrown (Craig had been sick for years before he died), but as
I peered through the glass doors and windows, only a 1996 *New York Times*
wall calendar in the kitchen gave an indication that Craig was not at home,
writing or cooking or preparing to entertain guests. Time had stood still, and
in my imagination, I saw him in his half-glasses at the IBM typewriter on the
kitchen island as Pierre sautéed a handful of vegetables at the gas range. In
comes Paul Bocuse to bone and stuff squabs with foie gras and truffles, then
Diana Kennedy to teach Craig and me the right way to make tortillas, followed
by Paul Prudhomme lugging a chest full of fresh crawfish.

As the vision intensifies, I see Betty Friedan helping Craig set the long, pine
refectory dining table, while farther back in the spacious, terra-cotta-tiled living room overlooking the water, Sirio Macioni refills Betty Comden's and
Charles Addams's glasses with champagne. As Craig mixes himself another
vodka and soda and moves into a small room next to the glass-fronted, re-
frigerated white wine cabinet to change the classical tape, Marcella Hazan,
Jacques Pépin, and Craig's loyal cookbook editor, Joan Whitman, review the
elaborate Scandinavian buffet that stretches across almost the entire length of
one wall. Once again, the old crowd is together, the party is in full swing, and
Craig is happy.

TIMES

Dinner Rites

RICK BRAGG

The meal we all live for, the one we gather for in my momma's house after the
first frost and gentle fall have faded the splendid green from the foothills of the
Appalachians, is really born months before in the damp, thick hot of an Alabama summer. People here still call that time of late summer the dog days, a
time when the sun glares white, like an old man's blind eye, on the pine bar-
rens and frame houses, until the afternoon thunderstorms come down like a
fist and then blow themselves out, quick, leaving the ground to steam. Thanksgiving is just a cool dream, then, for most of us, except for the man in the garden, a hoe in his hand, planning ahead.

It all begins, that wonderful November meal, with that tall, thin man, his
silver hair hidden by a straw hat, moving slowly between rows of sweet corn
and tomatoes and beans, being careful with his feet because any fool knows
that the copperheads like to rest there, among the stalks, waiting for a field
mouse. The man, my Uncle John, is not afraid of snakes, but they can flat spoil
an otherwise uneventful day. Besides, as I have heard men say here, in summer
it's just too damn hot to get bit.

Corn is a science, maybe even an art. Pick it too soon and you waste it because there will not be enough on the cob to shave off even with the sharpest,
oldest butcher knife, and people who grew up poor cannot live with themselves if they waste food. Pick it too late and all it's fit for is hogs. But pick it
just right, Lord God Almighty, and it is a reason to live. My Aunt Jo loves to
capture just when it turns creamy, starchy, and put it up in freezer bags for the
winter.

Uncle John Couch and my Aunt Jo, who helped raise me along with my
Uncle Ed Fair and my Aunt Juanita and my Aunt Edna, know the garden the
way their mommas and daddies knew it, by feel, by smell, by something almost like magic. To call this a simple life shows a city person's ignorance.
There is nothing simple about working a shift at Goodyear and then toiling
bent over until the heat and the sweat bees run you into your house. But it is

a rich life, rich because the food that will line the countertops in my momma's kitchen on Thanksgiving Day comes from the red dirt just outside the door, which beats the bald hell out of anything else. The tomatoes, the beans, the peppers will all be canned in kitchens where the air is spiced with salt and vinegar and set in a cool, dry place until November. Everyone knows it will be the turkey, swimming in pale yellow butter, that will steal the show, but without those steaming pots of vegetables crowding around it, the main attraction would be, well, nekkid.

Like I said, my Uncle John knows gardens. He also knows turkeys. Uncle John, on the fourth Thursday in November, is a valuable man.

The women usually rule the kitchen in the houses that perch on the hills and inside the valleys that make up the counties of Calhoun, Cleburne, Clay, Cherokee, St. Clair, and Talladega here in the northeastern part of Alabama, not far from the Georgia line. But on one day each year, many of them grudgingly allow their men to enter that sacred, mysterious domain to help with the turkey, just the turkey. I do not really know why this is, why these pipe fitters, steelworkers, rubber workers, cotton-mill workers, and shade-tree mechanics are brought into the kitchen on this one particular day. I have asked and been told simply, "Well, they just are. Go sit down."

Men do cook here, but outside. They are allowed to flip the hamburgers, turn the ribs, and spin the pig but are usually not trusted with anything, as we say, "'lectric." "Your Aunt Jo says I can mess up a kitchen boiling water," says Uncle John, in explanation. Aunt Jo is a small woman, but it is best not to mess with her.

I asked Aunt Jo, before I asked Uncle John for the recipe, if there was any secret to the turkey, anything he might not share with me out of cussedness. There was one thing she said. "Your pan has to be at least thirty years old. We won ours at Coleman's Service Station. Every time you bought gas, you put your name in. And we won." The pan, once a shiny stainless steel, has been burned gold by four decades of Thanksgivings and Christmases. "Twice a year. That's all we use it. That's why it's lasted." Funny to think that the pan will outlive me, will be passed down and down. It's nice thinking that.

It is a covered pan with a small opening in the lid to let steam out, and that is one tiny secret to the turkey's tenderness. The important thing, Aunt Jo said, is not to care what it looks like when it comes out of the oven. "The legs always fall off," she said, because it is so tender.

In our house, presentation doesn't count for a whole lot. It's the cooking that matters, and Uncle John has done exactly the same thing for forty years.

Listen to him: "The first thing I do is slide a whole pound of butter inside the turkey, which is laying back-down. Then I coat the whole thing all over with poultry seasoning. That's black pepper, garlic powder, onion salt, some paprika, and a little bit of sage."

I am beginning to taste it now. The bird is a beautiful gold, specked with sage and black pepper, and when he raises the lid, the steam billows out and permeates the kitchen, the dining room, everything. And you hope, hard, that the premeal prayer will be a short one.

The dressing is my Aunt Jo's job, and she does not cook it so much as she creates it. Listen to her: "Start the night before with a big pan of cornbread cooked in an iron skillet. The day of Thanksgiving, mix in some chicken juice—broth, but I call it chicken juice. Dice up an onion, a big onion, and mix in the sage and some salt, because we're salt eaters. Edna said last year I used too much sage, but I didn't hear nobody else complaining."

She bakes it in the oven in a shallow pan until the top is crispy, gold-brown, and the inside is pale yellow, creamy. "Some people go to the store and buy dried bread cubes and call that stuffing," she says, and I get the feeling she would rather eat a bug.

My momma handles it from there. She makes biscuits, called catheads, that are too good to be described by mere words, and though she is never satisfied with them—"Lord," she will say, "I sure did let y'all down on them biscuits"—I cannot remember a single time in my life when there was one left.

She makes the best mashed potatoes I have ever tasted. Just butter, milk, salt, black pepper, and—for reasons I have never understood but know better than to argue with—a teaspoon of mayonnaise. Every Thanksgiving, I scrape the pan.

The legacy of the garden, and that hot summer, sits steaming on a side table. There are the green beans, cooked to death, with pork, and the corn, simmered with butter. The tomatoes my Uncle John threaded his way through months ago are now pickled in quart jars, bright green and heavy with dill. They look down from a high counter, waiting for someone with strong hands to pry them open.

And we will have macaroni and cheese, which is a vegetable in the South, and, one of the best things on earth, a big pot of pinto beans, a massive ham bone swimming in the middle for seasoning. The only fresh vegetable, the only cold thing except for the cranberry sauce, which is chilled, can and all, in the refrigerator, is cabbage slaw.

"Thank you, Lord, for this food for the nourishment of our bodies," my Uncle John will say, and every head is bowed.

Plates overflow. We drink sweet tea—this is a Protestant house, and the only alcohol is in the medicine cabinet. Dessert is pumpkin pies, pecan pies, coconut cakes, and chilled strawberry shortcake. I almost never eat dessert because I am never able. I live in big cities, in New York, Los Angeles, Boston, Atlanta, Miami, so I do not see this food for the rest of the year. I eat until it hurts, and my brother Sam will grin at me, because he lives here, works at the cotton mill, and can eat it all the time.

Kinfolks stop by, seldom the same ones every year. Everybody eats. Everyone says it was better than last year, and because of the gray I see in their hair, and mine, I suppose it is. This is not magazine-cover food. It is the food of my youth, my life. I guess I would live longer if I didn't eat it, but the life would be so bland. I would rather eat the pages of the magazines.

We sit and tell stories then because it is all we are able to do. Some of the people we talk about have passed on, like Grandma Bundrum, who I still miss terribly, and my Uncle John's daddy, Homer Couch, who was a live wire of a man, a storyteller who could make you feel good just standing in his shadow.

"Daddy used to tell this story," my Uncle John says, "about this man who wanted a turkey for Thanksgiving and every day the man would say, 'Lord, please send me a turkey.' And as the weeks went by, no turkey came. So finally, it was a week before Thanksgiving, and the man had to change his prayer. 'Lord,' he said, 'please let me go and get my own self a turkey.' And the Lord did. That might not be funny unless you knew daddy."

I would like to be the man trusted with the turkey some day, and maybe some day I will be. For now, I'll just be the man praying for one.

Potluck Traditions

JIM AUCHMUTEY

The first time my father made Brunswick stew for a hundred of his new neighbors, a woman took a suspicious peek into the pot and asked, "What kind of animals have you got in there?"

I wish a raccoon face had surfaced just then, if only to see how high she could jump. Being a gentleman, Daddy didn't crack any jokes about roadkill or missing pets. He patiently explained that while people used to put squirrel in their stew, he sticks to meats you don't personally have to stalk and kill, such as chicken, pork, and beef.

But I can understand why the woman was leery. Brunswick stew belongs to the Mystery Food branch of American cookery. No one can absolutely pinpoint the origins of stew or bog or muddle or chili con carne or any of the other one-pot wonders that dot the country's culinary topography. They all seem to have been born over some distant campfire in the days when people ate whatever they could lay their hands on. All of these hearty concoctions seem to be cooked in big black pots by men (almost always men) who approach their task with a shaman's sense of ritual.

The cooks are none too specific about what they put in there, either; at my family reunion, the stew men talk about "frog eyes," their inscrutable term for bits of soot that drift from the fire into the kettle and have to be fished out.

The South has more than its share of these single-pot folk foods. Many of them play sidekick to barbecue. In Kentucky, there's burgoo, a tangy stew that often contains barbecued mutton and is as much a part of the culture as horse racing. (In fact, a thoroughbred named Burgoo King once won the Kentucky Derby.) In South Carolina, there's barbecue hash, a gloppy pork or beef paste made from all sorts of offal and usually served over rice. In Virginia, there's a version of Brunswick stew that's different from what you find in the Deep South, having no pork but only chicken and vegetables. Virginians, not noted for their humility, claim to have invented Brunswick stew, but folks in Brunswick, Georgia, beg to differ.

Since men are doing the cooking, it follows that all of these dishes are endlessly debated. Which vegetables are appropriate? Is it burgoo if there's no sheep in the pot? Does hash have to contain organ meat?

Stan Woodward, a filmmaker from Greenville, South Carolina, asked these existential questions as he traveled across the South taping reunions and community get-togethers for a documentary on Brunswick stew. "It's a beautiful art they're practicing, and they get so passionate about it," he says. "There's almost a priesthood of stewmakers."

In the case of Virginia, it literally was a priesthood. Woodward found that many of the early stew men were Methodist ministers who took their pots along with their Bibles when they were assigned new parishes. Stew money has paid for many a choir robe.

There are no clergymen perched in my family tree, but I do descend from a long line of stewmakers. For a century, my kinsmen in north Georgia have been feeding the multitudes from black pots. My great-grandfather is said to have originated our recipe, which is trotted out every summer for members of our extended family at a reunion in Bartow County. His son, Robert Auchmutey, was a farmer who cooked stew and barbecue at gatherings throughout the Etowah River valley.

In 1954, after the *Saturday Evening Post* included him in a spread on Southern barbecues, he was invited by a community club near Chicago to lay on a Dixie feast in Illinois. He and some buddies drove up with their thirty-gallon cast-iron pots—the Chicagoans had only zinc washtubs—and gave them a taste of Georgia. "I imagine that was the highlight of his life," says my father, his eldest son.

The next generation carried on the tradition in more citified surroundings. My Uncle Earl, a career air force officer in Warner Robins, was so renowned for his stew that when he died his church sent out a memorial flier with a drawing of him in a chef's hat stirring a pot. He once made a videotape about stewmaking that had three cups of wisecracking for every cup of instruction. All the uncles and aunts and cousins watched it not long after his death, laughing and sniffling and getting awfully hungry.

Now my father is the only one among us who practices the old art. He's made stew for years, usually in the winter, giving all the kids Tupperware pints of it to take home and freeze. I've eaten his stew for so long that it didn't occur to me until recently that I had never cooked it myself. I am almost forty-three. My father is pushing seventy-eight. It was time to learn. He just happened to be cooking a batch for the Fourth of July dinner at his seniors' apartment complex in Decatur. "I'll see you at seven sharp Saturday morning," he said.

When I arrived around 7:15, my mother was still in bed and my father had been up more than two hours. Three pots were working on the stove, boiling chicken and cooking down ground pork and beef. The counter was crowded with cans of creamed corn and whole tomatoes, the only vegetables he allows in the pot. It's almost a commandment with him: Thou shalt have no onions, potatoes, or butter beans in thy stew.

This fundamentalist approach is typical of north Georgia stewmasters—they don't use many vegetables at Harold's Barbecue in southeast Atlanta, for instance—but I've always wondered why we observe this custom when Southern food authorities from James Villas to Craig Claiborne play fast and loose with the veggies.

"Daddy, why don't we use more vegetables?" I asked. He knocked back his baseball cap and thought a minute, then came back with an unassailable answer. "Because your great-grandfather didn't, your grandfather didn't, and I don't." He didn't have to spell out what was expected of me.

When the meat was ready, we loaded the pots into his truck and hauled them to the activities center. It looks pretty much like a rec hall at any other suburban apartment complex—a far cry from the antebellum schoolhouse in the country where the stew men at our family reunion set up a tripod cauldron on oak embers under the trees.

We were using stainless steel pots on an electric range in an air-conditioned kitchen. Except for a little smoke flavor, though, the taste wasn't much different.

"Daddy used to come home with that smell all over him," my father reminisced, "and Rags, our old bulldog, almost ate him up. I can still see that dog's nose twitching."

Once the chicken had cooled, we started the most time-consuming part of the process: picking the chicken from the bones. One of the secrets to stew is not letting it get too homogenized; you're supposed to see shreds of chicken and kernels of corn in the finished stuff. It took us almost an hour to clean the birds; then we threw everything together into a ten-gallon pot and started stirring and seasoning.

"I'll show you what I'm doing, but I'm the only one who gets to season," Daddy said. "I remember my father was making some stew for a fund-raiser one time—I think a church that had been damaged by a tornado—and he'd been stirring the pot all day. He went home to change clothes, and when he came back, some SOB had reseasoned the stew. Dumped a box of red pepper in it. I thought Daddy was going to kill him."

"That's what's wrong with this world," agreed Dutch Bucher, a military retiree who had been setting up chairs in the dining hall and was now in the kitchen paying his respects to the cooks. He shook his head sadly. "Some people have no respect for other human beings."

For the rest of the morning and into the afternoon, we took turns stirring with a 2-by-1 piece of hardwood. The stew turned from soft brown to a muddy red that resembled a clay road after a downpour. Every time my father left the kitchen, he'd return barking, "Don't fall asleep. Stir! We don't want that corn sticking."

After three hours of toil and tasting and seasoning, we finally had the proper flavor and consistency. We turned off the heat and covered the pot.

That evening, as I dipped the stew into bowls and hustled it out to the serving line, an elderly woman stopped me with a question. "Do you eat this with a fork or a spoon, or do you just pour it over the barbecue?" she wanted to know.

I thought she was joking at first, but she wasn't. The poor thing didn't know any better; she was from the far side of the stew line — New Jersey, I believe. So I thought of my ancestors, and the circle of stewmaking that would not go unbroken, and I took the opportunity to baptize her in the tradition.

"You've never had Brunswick stew?" I said, watching her try to balance a bowl on her plate. "Well, let me tell you about it. It's something of a specialty in my family. . . . "

The Peach Continuum

MM PACK

On the second Saturday in June, I went to the farmer's market for the first time this year. It's always a happy reunion—with the farmers who show up faithfully year after year, with Saturday-morning shopping friends I haven't seen in a while, and with the luscious, locally grown vegetables and fruit.

Among the heirloom tomatoes and peppers and herbs and varieties of squashes and eggplants, I was pleased to find Fredericksburg peaches. Could it be that time already? The older I get, the shorter the space of time between peach seasons seems to become.

I cruised all the peach vendors' stands and got in line at the one whose wares called out loudest to me. As I painstakingly picked mine out, my friend Carolyn walked up to see what I was buying. "I'm looking for really ripe ones," I told her. "I suddenly have a craving for peach pie."

The peach farmer pricked up his ears. "You want ripe? I'll sell you a bushel of seconds for five dollars." I mentally calculated everything else I had to do that day. I knew those peaches wouldn't keep. But there was really no question in my mind. "I'll take them."

Later that afternoon in my still-not-air-conditioned downtown kitchen, I spent a couple of hours peeling and slicing the peaches, visions of pies and cobblers and sorbets dancing in my head as I separated the sound flesh from the too-mushy destined for the compost. I thought about the miracle of seasonal fruit—that I could perform this exercise in Texas only in June and at no other time of the year.

Processing large quantities of produce can be tiring and tedious. Or it can become a meditation. As I worked my way through the bushel, I thought about long-ago summers when I was in graduate school, living on a hilltop farm outside then-rural Round Rock, where the land included an ancient and neglected but very prolific peach orchard. As I remember it, the entire crop became ripe and ready within about a week, and it was always a contest to get to the peaches before the birds did and a race against time to get them all

Cash crop. From Family Trees: The Peach Culture of the Piedmont *by Mike Corbin.*

processed before they spoiled. I could easily envision those long June after-noons in the farmhouse kitchen under that too-slow ceiling fan—peach goo up to my elbows, renegade flies buzzing, sweat trickling between my shoulder blades, wayward strands of hair in my eyes—as I endlessly stirred vast hot vats of simmering peach jam.

That old farmhouse (immortalized as the set for the movie, *The Texas Chain Saw Massacre*) and the peach orchard are only memories now, buried beneath somebody's suburban lawn. So are those myriad pint jars of peach jam that I so proudly put up in that high-ceilinged kitchen. But twenty-something years later, the catalyst of peaches remains. The peach continuum.

With half a bushel to go, I mused further back to some early childhood summers on the Gulf Coast, when four generations of Texas pioneer women (they all lived in the city by then, but they were still pioneers) perspired and gossiped on a big front porch as they worked through quantities of peaches or mayhaws or cream peas brought back from east Texas or purchased from black men in wagons on the streets of Houston. "I decLARE," my Great-aunt Jessie would say, marveling at some transgression or indiscretion of some-body. Her mother, my Great-grandmother Teke, her wrinkled and bent fin-gers working relentlessly, would purse her lips in disapproval, but she'd listen

MM PACK

anyway. So would I, although at five or so, I had no idea what Jessie was talking about. I probably wasn't much help with those peaches, either, but I somehow felt included in the proceedings, and I wanted to be part of the women's work and talk.

Peaches. I'm glad that I still want to do this—that despite my urban, high-tech existence, I feel compelled every June to repeat some form of the ritual. That patient peach ritual that is the legacy of my family and of women everywhere—the gatherers, not the hunters—who wait and watch and notice and then get busy responding to the fleeting but compelling bounty of the season. Peach ice cream, anyone?

Canning Time

ROBERT MORGAN

The floor was muddy with the juice of peaches
and my mother's thumb, bandaged for the slicing,
watersobbed. She and Aunt Wessie skinned
bushels that day, fat Georgia Belles
slit streaming into the pot. Their knives
paid out limp bands onto the heap
of parings. It took care to pack the jars,
reaching in to stack the halves
firm without bruising, and lowering
the heavy racks into the boiler already
trembling with steam, the stove malignant
in heat. As Wessie wiped her face
the kitchen sweated its sweet filth.
In that hell they sealed the quickly browning
flesh in capsules of honey, making crystals
of separate air across the vacuums.
The heat and pressure were enough to grow
diamonds as they measured hot
syrup into quarts. By supper the last jar
was set on the counter to cool
into isolation. Later in the night
each little urn would pop as it
achieved its private atmosphere and
we cooled into sleep, the stove now
neutral. The stones already
pecked clean in the yard were free to try
again for the sun. The orchard meat fixed in
cells would be taken down cellar in the
morning to stay gold like specimens

A stash to last the winter. Photograph by Marion Post Wolcott.
Courtesy of Southern Historical Collection.

set out and labelled, a vegetal
battery we'd hook up later. The women
too tired to rest easily think of
the treasure they've laid up today
for preservation at coffin level, down there
where moth and rust and worms corrupt,
a first foundation of shells to be
fired at the winter's muddy back.

Dead Men Don't Eat Brownies

JANET L. BOYD

The one true love of my life revealed itself to me at a funeral.

My grandfather died of heart failure in 1963. Papaw was young, only in his fifties, and by all accounts a fairly typical Appalachian man. A carpenter by trade, he worked hard, drank hard, smoked, and cussed. He was a womanizing prankster who was nicer to most other folks than he was to his own family. My mother once threw him out of the house for foul behavior during a live-in visit with us. But he was always sweet to the grandchildren. I have fond memories of licking cones outside the frozen custard stand with him and my brother. And once he helped me sneak out of bed to watch *The Lone Ranger*. But I was young when he died, and as an eight-year-old, I had little emotional investment in the stiff and unrecognizable body lying in Cousin Dellie's living room.

Appalachian funerals are intimate affairs. The loved one holds court, posthumously, from the main room of a relative's house. A coffin better than the family can afford is the centerpiece, with funeral parlor pole lamps and flower racks adorning either end. Teary-eyed friends and relatives show up bearing food: platters of fried chicken, potato salad, green beans cooked with bacon grease, hot rolls, and cakes. Oh, the cakes! Jam cake with caramel icing, fried apple pies, homemade angel food. Mmmmmm. The adults linger in the kitchen drinking coffee, reminiscing, and socializing with the relatives who have driven home from other states for the funeral. All the kids run around looking for entertainment, only to be chased away from the open coffin when they get a little too curious about what's keeping the dead man's eyes closed.

Mostly, funerals are family reunions. There's nothing like a death in the family to help adults reconnect with long-lost cousins who'd been childhood playmates. Or to bring alienated siblings back into the fold. Or, sometimes, to throw a divorced couple back together. Funerals can be great fun for children, resembling a holiday more than a time of grief. But not for me. My parents never lived in one state long enough for me to know my cousins by name, and

I was too shy to make new friends. My only consolation was the bounty in the kitchen.

Mountain folks make a three-day affair of a funeral, guarding the body every minute between death and burial. By the second day of Papaw's vigil, I'd had my fill of Dellie's overdecorated ranch-style house. I was hot and bored and tired of peeling my thighs off the clear plastic covers she kept on her furniture. The only excitement of the whole affair came when one of the kids saw Papaw's body twitch involuntarily and screamed out the news. Granny fainted. She was revived with just enough spirit left in her to fall, screeching, on top of Papaw to proclaim her undying love for a dead man she'd mostly despised when he was alive.

Having been engrossed in the jam cake at the time, I had missed the twitch. By the time I'd wiped the caramel off my hands onto my shirt, the preacher had control of the situation. Nothing to worry about, he'd said, and certainly not a sign from God, as some visitors had suggested.

Granny was escorted to the kitchen for a cup of coffee, a piece of cake, and probably a good shot of bourbon. I knew that by the time the adults finished giggling over Papaw's last bit of revelry there wouldn't be anything worth scavenging left in the kitchen, so, hoping for another twitch, I stayed in the living room with Papaw, squeezing my toes into Dellie's shag carpet and looking around the room for something that couldn't be ruined by the sticky touch of an eight-year-old's palms. A book on the table beside my chair caught my eye.

Dellie's twelve-year-old granddaughter, Dari, whose parents drove in from Virginia, had come prepared for the boredom. She was the thin willowy type who wore boots and miniskirts like I had seen on the pages of *American Girl*. Not inclined to entertain herself with the baked beans and coleslaw that had just been added to the dwindling kitchen stock, she had brought her own fun: the Nancy Drew mystery novel that lay on the table beside me. I had never seen one before, but the cover looked inviting—a young girl snooping around, seeming not to care if she was in danger or if she got caught. As Papaw hadn't tried to turn over again and no hysterical adults were leaning on the coffin, I opened up the book and began to read.

Stories of Dick and Jane and Spot were about as advanced as my school primers had gotten at the time. I'd never read a novel in my life, but soon I was steadily licking my finger to turn the pages as I snooped along with Nancy Drew—the girl spy of the 1940s—and her sidekick cousin, George. Before Papaw was sent to his final rest, I had devoured the *Mystery of the Old Clock*, along with about half a pan of Aunt Ruby's dry brownies—and I was as hooked on reading as Nancy was on sleuthing.

After the funeral, it was hard for me to find a fix for my new habit. We didn't have much in the way of third-grade reading material at my grandmother's house, where we were living in between moves up and down the Eastern Seaboard. We didn't have a car, so we couldn't just take off to the library. I don't even think I knew what a library was then. Certainly there wasn't one at the decrepit old elementary school I was attending.

Aunt Janie came to the rescue. My grandmother's sister, she was my great-aunt really. She seemed tough and brave to me, a real take-charge kind of woman who bellowed a lot but had a soft spot the size of Montana. I loved her fiercely, except for a brief period of hating her when, as my second-grade teacher for a few months, she wouldn't let me go out in the rain at recess with the other kids. She was always good for a fully stuffed sock hanging from her mantel at Christmastime or a trip to town on Saturdays. She'd pile me and my brother into her pickup truck and set off down the winding road to the county seat, where she'd conduct her business, which mostly involved lawsuits. Aunt Janie was so litigious, she'd sue anyone who crossed her. As we got out of the truck, she'd dust us off and hand each of us a crisp new dollar bill to be spent on anything we wanted at the dime stores in town. We would spend hours in the Murphy's and Hobbs stores trying to decide whether to buy marbles, candy, yo-yos, or paper dolls, while she took off to the courthouse, where she would dodge flying tobacco juice and chew the ear off her lawyer.

In addition to teaching second grade for longer than God had been in business, Aunt Janie owned a tiny store. I loved to go there. It had a candy counter laden with orange slices, mary janes, and maple goodies that were doled out in little white paper bags to girls who minded their manners. Shoelaces and cigarette lighters kept company with RC Cola and hunks of pickled bologna in gallon jars. Long, curling flypaper flapped in sticky spirals in the breeze that blew through the screen door. Her husband, Gene, ran the store while she went off every morning to teach hordes of dirty little kids how to read.

Her house, like the store, was full of every kind of junk imaginable, a child's paradise. Her beds were never made and the floors never swept, but guests were always welcome. The meals she conjured up were no less miraculous in her filthy kitchen than were the fishes and loaves our preacher said Jesus pulled out of his empty basket. Probably the only thing that kept us all free from ptomaine was the power of her love and the chemical content of her endless supply of icy Coca-Cola.

During one of her rare cleaning binges, she decided to purge some of her old college textbooks that had been taking up corner space for a couple of decades. For some reason, she carried one of them with her to my grand-

JANET L. BOYD

mother's house one day—a beat up hard-copy version of what I now know was the *Norton Anthology of English Literature*.

It had seen better days. The front cover was mostly gone and the spine flopped loosely. The pages were intact, though, and what pages they were! Silky smooth, thin, and covered with tiny print. What a treasure! My mother, whose taste in reading ran more to Erle Stanley Gardner than to Old English, built a new front cover for me out of cardboard and green duct tape. Thus adorned, that book became my constant companion.

No infant ever dragged a blankie to more places than I lugged my book. Every car ride, every grocery store trip, every Sunday to church, and, yes, every funeral saw me with my big green tome under my arm. Before turning nine, I had read "The Battle of Maldon," "The Dream of the Rood," and *Beowulf*. Although the meaning often escaped me, I was always entranced by the beauty of the words that I would repeat over and over, letting them roll around in my mouth like luscious ripe grapes. My initiation as a bibliophile was complete.

These days my home decor could be called *librairie moderne*. If it were available, I would dab a little Eau d'Ink behind my ears every morning. Bookstores exert a peculiar form of gravitational pull on me. My list of books to read is longer than my last will and testament. And I owe it all to a dead man and a pan of dry brownies.

You know, I think there were bean stains and brownie crumbs in that old Nancy Drew book by the time it made its way back to Virginia. No one ever complained about it, though. Years later as I ate apple butter stack cake and drank coffee at Aunt Janie's funeral, pregnant with what would turn out to be my own little bibliophile, I raised a private toast to Aunt Janie, Papaw, Beowulf, and Nancy. And, yes, to jam cake and Ruby's brownies. How dull my life would have been without them!

Passing and Repasting

ELIZABETH SCHATZ

My grandmother Nana died at a lunch table. She was eighty-six years old, and she laid her head down in the nursing home—undoubtedly beside a plate of mediocre roast beef and toast—fully satiated with life.

That Saturday in October, I boarded a plane from LaGuardia and flew home to Memphis, Tennessee, there to get into a car and drive south to the blink-you-miss-it town of Ripley, Mississippi, where Nana had lived most of her life. And the days that followed are best described as one elongated eating binge. If you feed a cold and starve a fever, you must gorge in grief.

My family, like many, has always come together around a dinner table. The conversation mumbled out of mouths full of food is always more jovial, the stories told over dessert always more touching. But the night my aunts, uncles, and cousins began to return to Ripley for Nana's funeral, there was no dining room table to accommodate our conversation. Nana's house had been sold years before, so instead we gathered around a musty, sway-back king-sized bed in room 108 of the Briarwood Inn. The room was dubbed "the bar" since it held the only alcohol to be had in dry Tippah County: a cooler of beer brought down from Memphis.

Seeing as how Ripley's greatest restaurateur was a man called Greasy who owned a catfish joint by the same name, our choices for dining that night were slim. There was Kentucky Fried Chicken, Subway, Pizza Hut, and several gas stations advertising turkey legs on billboards out in the parking lot. So we picked up dinner from the Pizza Hut (no delivery) and spent the evening before Nana's funeral swapping stories and slices of pepperoni.

The next day, I delivered the eulogy at the funeral, and not surprisingly, it began with stories of food. I've heard it said that olfactory memories are the strongest, and next to the smell of her Clinique moisturizer, my most potent memories of Nana originated in her kitchen.

For years as a child, I would wake up early for the honor of being dubbed "biscuit helper," padding across the brown and orange carpet of Nana's kitchen as if I had just been knighted.

Oleo was margarine kept in a crystal bowl on the counter, never kept cold in the fridge. Biscuit orders were always taken so we would know how many plain and how many cheese to make. Every meal was followed with dessert, and most contained one dish that had been fished out of the Fry Daddy, which sat on a throne of newspapers in Nana's back pantry.

But Nana's best asset in the battle of feeding our family was her deep freeze. God bless that frosty behemoth, full of meals that would probably taste just as good as the day they were half-sealed in an old Cool Whip container and labeled with masking tape. When we sold Nana's house, the freezer was still full to the gills. After the funeral, I became acutely aware that the ladies of the Methodist Church must have deep freezes just like my grandmother's. Those women were gracious enough to host a lunch after the service, and they carried on Nana's tradition of producing from the depths of their own freezers casserole dishes en masse and on demand.

Everything laid out on the folding tables in the fellowship hall was in a rectangle Pyrex and was either covered in a crust or congealed, true signs of a Southern luncheon. That and the fact that dessert, a dizzying array of pies, warranted its own table.

Something about a slice of chocolate cream pie, handed over by the powdery, wrinkled hand of an old friend with a story about "How wonderfully that grandmother of yours used to bake," simply heals the soul.

When the last glass of iced tea had been drunk, we headed back to our old neighborhood home in Memphis. The food found us. Each doorbell ring preceded a deposit of turkey, fruit, or cake on the kitchen counter. I haunted that counter, constantly being asked by my mother, "Are you still hungry?"

I would usually look up from where my fingers were nestled in a pan of cold barbecue and answer, "No." But for some reason I kept eating.

Maybe it was because barbecue in Manhattan is tasteless or scarce. Or maybe I'd created a belief that nothing assuages grief like a platter of cold cuts.

Reunion Time

REAGAN WALKER

"Daddy, where were you born?" Yvonne Fuselier shouted across pavilion number 1 at the Griffin city park.

"In a house, I reckon," shouted back Jessie Moore of Jasper, Texas, prompting an eruption of hee-haws from the menfolk who had gathered around to catch up with the retired tugboat captain. After all, Jessie, his wife, Flossie, and their daughters had driven more than fourteen hours to attend the Jackson-Moore family reunion.

"I've come to every reunion," Jessie, seventy-five, boasted just after Flossie, seventy-nine, let it be known that she "had to decide" to make the long journey. Sure, he was glad to catch up with the kin. But the real highlight of the day?

"The food, for sure," he said as he waved toward the thirty-foot-long brick island in the middle of the pavilion, crammed edge to edge with covered dishes, boxes of store-bought fried chicken, platters of home-baked hams, and coolers of iced tea. "It's out of this world!"

Sure enough. There were potato salads, every sort of bean from speckled to baked, stewed corn, deviled eggs, coleslaws of every style, sweet potato casserole, macaroni and cheese, cold pasta salads, old-timey congealed salads, pickled cucumbers, skillet cornbread, biscuits, coconut cake, angel food dream, cream puffs, and peach cobbler, just to name a few of the offerings.

In short, it was the classic family reunion potluck table—a smorgasbord of family culture and cuisine, history and geography, humor and eccentricities. And it's proof that even in this techno-time of faceless communication, the time-tested tradition of gathering for a family feast and gabfest prevails.

"With so many families living geographically so far apart, reunions are one of the ways of re-establishing ties with each other," said George Armelagos, professor of anthropology at Emory University. "A family reunion is all about re-forming the community, and food is a very important aspect of what you can share."

Dinner beneath the boughs. Courtesy of Bill Ferris.

We hear that even the Hatfields and McCoys, who launched the grand-daddy of all family feuds in Kentucky in the 1880s—one bone of contention between them being a razorback hog—recently met up to mend fences at a joint family reunion. The highlight? A pig roast.

Some worry that our growing reliance on such modernisms as e-mail and convenience foods is eroding the family reunion tradition. But others are using technology as a powerful tool to help bring the family together and plan the events. And, once gathered, many are opting for a blend of home-cooked, convenience, and catered foods that uphold the tradition of breaking bread but also fit into our new-millennium lifestyles.

One such gathering was of the Maxwell-Audley-Couper family, which met for the first time at St. Simons Island, Georgia, earlier this month. Farley Daniel-Cottrell of Athens found many family members through genealogical research on the internet. She helped organize the event, which included tours and a lecture on family history for about seventy-five folks.

And of course they ate, gathering for a picnic by the shore that combined catering with potluck and for a Sunday brunch that included sour orange punch, a recipe turned up in family research.

The recipe, which starts with three quarts of brandy and includes eighteen Seville oranges, was traced to Rebecca Couper, who lived on St. Simons until 1845. Family legend has it that Daniel-Cottrell's grandmother, Anne Couper, used to make it for her friend in Atlanta, Margaret Mitchell.

John T. Edge, a Southern foodways expert with the University of Mississippi's Center for the Study of Southern Culture, said that though some family reunion tables may be changing to reflect too-busy-to-cook schedules, the potluck is likely to thrive precisely because of the curiosity of those like Daniel-Cottrell.

"Our forebears didn't stand over the stove all day long because they wanted to, which is why we don't do it now," said Edge, author of the cookbook *A Gracious Plenty*. "But I think there is a countervailing influence of people who are getting interested in what their grandmothers cooked. A family reunion can be a way to reintroduce people to their culinary roots."

Those roots mean many potluck tables take on an ethnic or regional flavor. A reunion favorite of the Deacon John Hall family in North Berwick, Maine, is moose meatloaf. And when some 400 members of the Gazvoda family gather each August in Canonsburg, Pennsylvania, they feast on a roasted whole pig stuffed with Slovenian sausage and cabbage, sauerkraut, pierogi, potica (nut roll), and strudel—all part of keeping their Slovenian traditions alive.

In fact, reunion potlucks have been key to preserving and passing on family culinary history. There was some question at the Jackson-Moore family re-union in Griffin whether "Aunt Janet" McElwaney's coconut cake and maca-roni and cheese would be on the table.

McElwaney had been ailing, and all her effort went toward just making it to the reunion. But her cake and casserole were there, too. Daughter Bonnie Brown made the cake, and niece Samantha Mimbs made the macaroni and cheese. Both were coached by McElwaney.

"She always gets on me for not putting enough salt in it," confessed Mimbs before turning to McElwaney and assuring her she had done it right for the re-union. McElwaney cast a skeptical glance.

Debbie Gurtis of Parkersburg, West Virginia, said that when her mother died in 1998, family members made it clear they expected her to bring stuffed cabbage rolls to the family reunions, as her mother had done each year.

"I had never made them before, so I practiced several times during the summer before our reunion on Labor Day weekend," she said. "They were a hit. So now I'm the official cabbage roll maker for the family reunion, as my mother was before me."

Many a reunion-goer has become identified with a specific dish. "Aunt Ethel always brought the chitterlings, and Aunt Lily, for some reason we never understood, brought what she called Japanese fruitcake that always had a strange off-center tilt," recalled Tim Patridge, director of food and beverage at Morris Brown College, of the family reunions of his youth. "They were grand occasions."

Arnessa Holmes of Atlanta remembered those kinds of get-togethers, too. Her family still gathers every two years, but lately the reunions have taken a modern turn toward catered banquets and bus tours. She misses the old-style reunions with potlucks at the homesteads.

"I think I'll try to persuade them to return to Grenada [Mississippi] and do a potluck next time. I think reunions should be about the roots," she said. But she admits it may be a hard sell. With family gathering from across the coun-try, hotels are a must, which limits cooking.

Patridge said he regrets that his family no longer gathers regularly for fam-ily reunions—something he attributes to geography and technology. "Instead of getting together, everyone wants to talk over e-mail. But you can't touch, you can't smell, you can't feel anything over the cyber system," Patridge said.

Yet Patty Ledford of Blue Ridge said it was technology that spurred her to organize the Jackson-Moore family reunion, which used to be an annual event but had lapsed for several years. "I got a computer for Christmas; then I started surfing the Net and working on the family tree. And then I got some genealogy software, and things took off," said Ledford. "I decided it was time again for a reunion."

She kept family members informed on her web page and posted the reunion on family-reunion.com's registry. Bruce Buzbee, webmaster of family-reunion.com, said he started his site as a lark a couple of years ago but has found overwhelming demand for it. The site gets about 4,000 visitors a day during the summer season.

The T-shirt and banquet gatherings are popular, particularly with families in urban areas, Buzbee said, "but from the listings on our registry, my gut tells me that potlucks are still the favorite way to do a reunion."

It remains the popular way with the McCleskey family of Marietta, Georgia, which has held a family reunion nearly every year for more than a century. Most recently, the gathering has been at their namesake McCleskey Middle School in Marietta.

Last year, the potluck table took on some new dishes. Sylvia Caldwell Rankin, one of the organizers, and other family members located and invited descendants of a slave, Uncle Troup McCleskey, who research showed had been an important member of the family in the early 1800s. Several of Troup McCleskey's descendants were in the Atlanta area, so they joined in the annual food fest.

"We always have lots of fried chicken, sweet potato casserole, and four-layer cakes," said Rankin. "Uncle Troup's family brought some different food—big platters of ribs and the best homemade yeast rolls." Thus, new connections were made and old ones strengthened.

The food and fellowship were so good at the Jackson-Moore family reunion in Griffin this year that folks immediately started talking about the next one. "I haven't seen some of these family members in years," said Steve Moore of Carrollton. "Patty, are we going to do this next year?"

"Oh, I think we should!" said Ledford, as she watched folks wander away from the picked-over potluck table. Then she shouted, "No one better leave until I get everyone in family photos!"

Ode to *Joy*

SARAH FRITSCHNER

A huge hunk of pages from *The Joy of Cooking* fell to the floor as I reached for it the other day, reminding me that my 1975 edition is suffering the same fate that my 1946 edition suffered: overuse and, perhaps, abuse.

The 1946 edition didn't start out as mine. It was my mother's—the cookbook she learned to cook from when she married my father. She learned to make her quick lemon sauce from it (the one she poured over toasted pound-cake—the staple "company" dessert).

The book's "easy hollandaise sauce" page has disintegrated; only half exists now, and not the half with the recipe. The "round steak with onions and sour cream" has "good!" written next to it in my mother's handwriting, along with jottings about additions—2 tablespoons tomato paste, dry mustard, and sherry.

Her *Joy* was the cookbook I learned to cook from, when I checked it for a recipe for brownies and never looked back. My brother began making apple fritters from it one Saturday morning (Mother worked Saturdays), and that page is spattered with dry batter and egg yolk; crumbs and flour are still in the crease of the page. Making those fritters, we learned to separate eggs, beat egg whites until they were stiff, and fold them into the batter.

The *Joy* recipe style, written with directions between ingredient bundles and those ingredient lists in bold type, was easy to follow. And in the most spare but most specific and enlightening prose, directions were made clear for the beginning cook.

Unlike other "basic" cookbooks, which are often the creation of corporate entities and, though full of information, essentially personality-free, the *Joy* editorializes. Succinctly, of course.

Under the title "Beef Wellington or Filet de boeuf en croute," the 1975 version of the cookbook says, "If time is no object and your aim is to out-Jones the Joneses, you can serve this twice-roasted but rare beef incased in puff paste—but don't quote us as devotees."

And there is charm. "In response to many requests from users of the *Joy* who ask, 'What are your favorites?'" says the introduction to the 1975 edition, "we have indicated some by adding to a few recipe titles the word 'Cockaigne,' which in medieval times signified 'a mythical land of peace and plenty' and which we chose as the name for our country home." Hence: "Brownies Cockaigne," which were simply titled "Brownies I" in 1946.

Honestly, the most practical part of those old *Joy*s—authored by Irma S. Rombauer, first published by Bobbs-Merrill in 1936, and reprinted eleven times since then—is not the recipes. The abiding virtue of those *Joy*s is that they tell you how to cook everything you've ever wondered about cooking, everything you might cook once in your lifetime or once a year, and also practical things, like how to substitute ingredients (in the 1975 edition) and how much food a number 2 can holds.

You can find how to cook that standing rib roast you just spent $90 on and don't want to ruin or a saddle of venison. The *Joy* can walk you through roasting chestnuts or blanching almonds (and tell you how much a pound measures). It can tell you how to substitute all-purpose flour for self-rising.

Some years the books included the caloric content of common foods. The 1941 edition included recipes and strategies to deal with war rationing. Each book is a little different from earlier and later editions. Canned ox tongue did not survive the 1975 edition (though "about tongue" is there, along with five other related recipes).

And here's another important feature of the *Joy* for me: It led me through the kitchen door to many other classic cookbooks, especially Southern ones, some of which were no doubt inspired by the style and comprehensiveness of the Rombauer volume. Two of the best from the Deep South were written decades ago by Mrs. S. R. Dull and Marion Brown, but it would be hard to outshine the quirkily distinctive and authoritative works of three Louisville writers of the past half-century: Jennie Benedict, Cissy Gregg, and Camille Glenn.

The Joy of Cooking changed dramatically in 1997, when it was published by Scribner. What once had been a basic general cookbook (with chapters on canning, beverages, and equivalents) became a basic "gourmet" cookbook, representing cuisines and techniques from around the world.

Perhaps because I know as much as I need to about Parmigiano-Reggiano cheese and about Thai fish cakes and squash blossoms stuffed with cheese and herbs, I don't rely on the newer edition much (though I own it). Perhaps because I still want to know how to cook that prime rib, or substitute cocoa for chocolate, or make a punch for a party, I have ordered a newer copy of the

1975 hardbound *Joy*, which is, thankfully, still in print and available through bookstores.

The best basic cookbook is the one you grew up on—the one that made you feel comfortable learning to cook or reviewing what you know. For me, that happens to be *The Joy of Cooking*, and I'll be glad to get a familiar version that has all its pages.

Vacant Kitchens for Sale

LARRY T. MCGEHEE

A local shopping area has a large sign naming it "Historic Farmer's Market." There is a sandwich shop, a wildlife store, a home decor shop, a children's clothing store—but no farmer's market. Fifteen years ago, seasonal produce displayed in open-front booths filled the space, and on Saturdays a little old grandmotherly woman sold home-baked cakes she had brought from her own kitchen. Now, as the sign warns, that is all "historic," gone with the wind.

The nearest thing to a traditional farmer's market is seventy miles north, in Asheville, North Carolina. There one finds fifty or so booths in two airplane-size hangars. In season, they teem with corn, tomatoes, okra, beans, squash, apples, peaches, melons, pumpkins, gourds, jams and jellies, and homemade bread and pies. At Christmastime, the booths add greenery and wreaths.

In our growing-up days, there were produce booths around the courthouse square in our little rural town in Tennessee. Later, living in Alabama in our early adulthood in the 1960s, we frequented a farmer's market in Tuscaloosa.

The South used to be speckled with roadside markets, with plate-dinner restaurants, with high school home economics classes, with flour company bake-offs, and with festivals celebrating strawberries, bananas, pickles, watermelons, and even the lowly okra.

People used to "pig out" on fresh produce and home cooking, but today there are only the pigs, human and otherwise—no produce. Local fruits and vegetables are vanishing, and only occasional barbecue gatherings remain. Frozen foods and fast foods, and melons and strawberries from Mexico, have become staples. Folks aren't eating less (just look at the stomachs hanging over the counters at McDonald's and Taco Bell), but they are eating differently.

To get a "remembrance of things past," old people eat thawed country vegetables and cornbread at a chain restaurant such as Cracker Barrel or luck into a Mary Mac's in Atlanta or a Wade's in Spartanburg—those increasingly rare Southern restaurants where regional cookery is still done from scratch.

The worst thing about the Americanizing of Dixie may be that its farms and gardens are disappearing even as its fast-food restaurants and its population escalate. Southern tongues were tied to the land, and as long as the land was primarily rural farmland—which is to say, up through World War II—Southerners had a sense of taste.

We should have known, as early as the 1960s, that the end was near. When we started buying four Morton's chicken pies for a dollar instead of killing a chicken, picking and chopping some vegetables, and rolling dough to make our own, we drove the nails in the coffin of Southern cooking. When TV trays replaced dinner tables, taste had eroded too far to ever be reclaimed.

What was really happening was that people who had lived off the land with scarcely any hard cash ever passing through their hands moved to towns and then to cities looking for jobs the South had always lacked. Before the big changes began, almost every Southern family had a mule, a cow, a few acres, some cane-bottomed chairs, and some church fans.

But then it seemed that every family was moving "up" to having two cars and a ranch house, indoor toilets and running water, and air conditioning. The two-lane dirt roads of the counties were graveled, and then asphalted, and then four-laned, forming a gigantic spider's web that drew farm folk to the city lights. Progress, we called it. The South was finally catching up with the rest of the nation.

Some friends of mine blame the Republicans. The great change in Southern cooking coincided with the South giving up its Democratic Party and voting for Eisenhower, builder of the interstate highways, in 1952 and 1956 and persisting in pursuing peace and prosperity by GOP standards ever since. Al Gore could have won his home state of Tennessee in the last election if he had campaigned for home cooking.

As the South has aged, it has lost its sense of taste. As we old Southerners, survivors remembering repasts past, have aged, we find ourselves eating in a foreign land at dinnertime. We hang our hams in a willow and weep. Dixie has become America, and the flavor is almost gone from the stew.

In the Bible, Esau sold his birthright to Jacob for a mess of pottage. The South has sold its good tastes for a mess of progress.

I'd sell the whole mess of progress for a good mess of greens cooked with a two-year-old smokehouse-cured ham hock.

In Praise of Dinnertime

MARY JANE PARK

We love Thanksgiving because it lets us take time to be together to talk, to eat, to have fun. So why just on a holiday?

The Thanksgiving holiday begins the season when people traditionally gather at the table. Out come the tablecloths, the napkins, the good china, the silver—maybe even candles and a centerpiece.

It's not just National Gravy Boat Recognition Day. Regardless of where and how the meal is prepared, or by whom, it is likely that people will sit together, express appreciation for the food, the gathering, and whatever good fortune they may enjoy, and make an effort at conversation.

Extraordinary cooperation is required to bring such a group and such a meal to the table (not to mention getting the dishes washed and put away in time to watch football). But if we can achieve this monumental feat on Thanksgiving and Hanukkah and Christmas and New Year's, why can't we just sit down to dinner a few nights a week?

Many of us gulp breakfast bars as we race out in the morning. We eat lunch at our desks. We have soccer practice, dance classes, gymnastics lessons, pottery painting. And church services, civic meetings, and workouts at the gym. We have voice mail, e-mail, direct deposit, ATM cards, pagers and postage-stamp dispensers, answering machines. We don't have to talk with anybody unless we want to.

You have to wonder: How are we spending all the time we've saved by not walking to the bank or answering the telephone?

Eating together has become a special event, reserved for holidays and other celebrations, job interviews, business meetings, catching up with friends. Maybe the world would seem a little less out of control if we ate together more often.

So here's a modest proposal: Let us begin to observe dinnertime. At home, let the answering machine do its job. Turn off the television, the cell phone, the pager. When was the last time you got a suppertime call that couldn't have waited half an hour?

Set the table. Use a permanent-press tablecloth or place mats and fabric napkins. You'll be washing pizza sauce out of T-shirts anyway; might as well toss in the linens. No matter who cooks the food, serve it on plates. That goes for macaroni and cheese, Spaghetti-Os, pizza, burgers and fries, takeout Thai, even frozen TV dinners. No drinking from jugs, bottles, or cans. Juice, milk, soft drinks, and iced tea go into glasses.

If you can't have dinner at home, figure out a way to gather for the meal. How about a tailgate party in a park or parking lot before you split up for the evening's activities?

Show appreciation. Give thanks: to God, to the baker who rose early to make the buns, to the farmers who grew the wheat and potatoes and raised the livestock, to the fast-food worker who made change and handed you the bag of burgers, to the person who picked up the check.

Ask questions of your dining companion. What's the most important thing that happened to you today? What have you seen or heard that gave you a lift or made you laugh? Light a candle. Don't wait until there's a power outage. Here's why it's important to stop the merry-go-round, if only for a half-hour each day: These are the most important people in our galaxies, be they friends or family or both. Setting aside this special time, relaxing and nourishing one another with food and love, helps us draw strength. With all the commotion around us, this may be the closest we get to a sense of peace — in our lives and in the world.

THINGS

Iced Tea
A Contrarian's View

FRED CHAPPELL

There are people who eat cold pasta and salad. They enjoy despoiling their greenery with gummy, tasteless squiggles of tough, damp bread dough that are usually made palatable only when heavily disguised with hot tomato sauce and a stiff mask of Parmesan cheese. This salad does have the virtue of economy. Wednesday leftovers can be marketed to Thursday customers of perverse taste.

It is probably also perversity that accounts for the prevalence of ice tea in our American south. It was Edgar Allan Poe who first diagnosed this immitigable contrariness of human nature in his short story "The Imp of the Perverse," and he undoubtedly saw it as a normal trait of Dixie character. But please include me out. I am one southerner who detests that dirty water the color of oak-leaf tannin and its insipid banality. When I am offered ice tea by one of our charming southern hostesses, I know I'm in for a long afternoon of hearing about Cousin Mary Alice's new baby and its genius antics in the playpen.

Hot tea makes sense. It can relax as well as stimulate and in fact may be sipped as a soporific. It can offer a bouquet pungent or delicate and causes us to understand why the Chinese designated certain strains of flowers as "tea roses." It can be a topic of conversation too, as southerners revive the traditional English debate over whether the boiling water should be brought to the pot or the pot fetched to the water. Such palaver reassures us that all traces of civilization have not disappeared under the onslaughts of video games and e-mail.

But if you ice the stuff down, it cannot matter in the least whether the water or the pot has journeyed. Any trace of the tea's bouquet is slaughtered, and only additives can give the tarnished liquid any aroma at all. There is, of course, plenty of discussion about these added condiments. Even the mildest of southern ladies may bristle and lapse into demotic speech when they consider that a glass of ice tea has been improperly prepared.

Notice that we say "ice tea." Anyone who pronounces the successive dentals of "iced tea" is regarded as pretentious. And if you say "Coca-Cola" you will be seen as putting on airs, just as obviously as if you employed "you" as a collective pronoun. Down here we say "you-all," "CoCola," and "ice tea" and collect monetary fines from strangers who misspeak. Ignorance before the law is no excuse.

In recent years, some enterprising women have seen the futility of the pot/water controversy and have begun making "sun tea," a beverage that is acquainted with neither stove nor teapot. They simply fill a clear glass gallon jug with water, drop in a flock of tea bags, and set the container out on the back porch to brew in the broiling August sunshine. If this method does not make the kitchen more cheerful, it does at least lessen the hypocritical chatter about proper procedure. Ice cannot harm sun tea; it is created beyond the reach of harm or help.

Now as to the recipe for ice tea:

Lemons are essential and should be of the big thick-skinned variety, cut into sixths. They are never—repeat: never—squeezed but only plumped into the pitcher, four or five slices. Extra slices are offered on a cut-glass plate six inches in diameter. Mint may be added, but it is always submerged in the pitcher and never put into a glass where it would glue to the interior side like a Harley Davidson decal.

And sweetening is the soul of this potation. The sugar bowl passes from hand to hand at a pace so dizzying it is like watching the rotation of an old 78-rpm record. Southerners demand sweetness. The truly thoughtful hostess shall have already sweetened the tea for her guests with a simple sugar syrup that excludes the possibility of unpleasant graininess from bowl sugar. Sugar syrup for ice tea is concocted by adding one pound of Dixie Crystal sugar to a tablespoon of water.

In the south, sweetened ice tea is taken for granted, like the idea that stock car racing is our national pastime and that the Southern Baptist church is a legitimate arm of the Republican Party. If you order ice tea in a restaurant, it will arrive presweetened. If you want it unsweetened, you must ask for it. Actually, you must demand it with pistol drawn and cocked. And you will have to repeat your demand several times because tea unsweetened is as abstruse a proposition to most servers as a theorem of Boolean algebra. Even then you can't be sure. My wife Susan once ordered unsweetened, but it arrived sweet as honey. The waitress pleaded for understanding. "We couldn't figure how to get the sugar out," she said.

Why southerners are so sugar-fixated may be a mystery, but it is an indisputable fact. We are a breed who makes marmalades of zucchini, tomatoes, onions, and even watermelon rinds. Our famous pecan pie (puhKAWN pah) is a stiff but sticky paste of boiled Karo corn syrup studded with nuts. Since this is not sweet enough, it will likely be served with a gob of bourbon whipped cream dusted with cocoa powder and decorated with vegetable-peeler curls of milk chocolate.

"Do you want ice tea with that?"

"Oh yes. Sweetened, please."

Well, I'll confess that, though born in North Carolina, I make a poor example of a southerner. I don't even capitalize the name of the region. I'm a Democrat, a non-Baptist, and don't care what kind of car I drive. To me, adding broiled marshmallows to yams is like putting raspberry jam on porterhouse. I once spotted a recipe in the magazine *Southern Living* for "CoCola cake" and had to fight down a surge of nausea. I flee as if pursued from fatback, spoon bread, grits, and ice tea.

Susan tells me I need sweetening.

You Can't Eat 'Em Blues
Cooking Up a Food Song Movie

ROY BLOUNT JR.

One thing about being a Southerner in New York, you can't help but have certain areas of expertise, at least as far as New Yorkers can tell. When Krispy Kreme doughnuts came to Gotham a year or so ago, I was telling newspapers and TV programs right and left, "Oh yeah, I been eating Krispy Kremes my entire life. Which is one reason my entire life may not last much longer—but good, aren't they? And listen, here's what's crucial: get 'em when the neon sign outside says they're hot." I was like somebody in the seventh grade who has had sex.

So I chuckled authoritatively when, at a grocery store on the Upper West Side called Gourmet Garage, I came upon a tray full of cold Krispy Kremes for sale beneath a sign that read, "Fresh from the Antebellum South."

"Well, now," I said to the man behind the counter. "They can't be any too fresh."

The man behind the counter, whose English was limited to "cruller" and one or two other strictly job-related terms, just narrowed his eyes like a pestered zoo animal or a table dancer who has been asked to take a letter. Not wanting to be suspected of service-personnel harassment, I went on, "I mean, if they date back to circa 1859. . . . " I looked around for someone who might share my amusement, but the only thing I descried in my fellow shoppers' expressions was impatience.

Until a young woman leapt upon me from out of nowhere and demanded, "How does the tune to 'Ramblin' Wreck from Georgia Tech' go? We have the lyrics. How does the tune go?"

"Well, now, I'm not all that great at carrying a melody," I said, "but I've been singing that song my entire life. In fact—"

"I'm a rambling wreck . . . ," she prompted me.

"From Georgia Tech and a heckuvan engineer," I sang. "A heckuva heck-uva—"

"Helluva," she snapped.

"Well, I was raised in a Christian home," I said.

She narrowed her eyes like a cat that a dog has just barked at.

"What do you want to know for?" I asked, trying not to narrow my eyes at all.

"Shooting a film," she said, and after glancing around to make sure people had noticed what business she was in, she was out the door.

I followed, thinking that I might fill the filmmakers in on some of the great Yellow Jacket broken-field runners of my boyhood—Billy Teas, Leon Harde-man, . . . —but she was gone and there were no signs that any principal pho-tography, as they call it, was going on in the vicinity. She was probably a pro-duction assistant who had been sent running up and down Broadway to jump in and out of stores looking for somebody with my accent. No telling how many blocks she'd had to scour to find somebody from Georgia. The budget of this movie was probably millions. And I didn't get a nickel.

I haven't profited from my doughnut expertise, either. The Krispy Kreme people offered to send me a free dozen, but they'd be cold and I'd feel be-holden, and anyway I can afford doughnuts. What I need is a retainer.

I got to thinking . . . doughnuts and music. As it happens, I have the great-est collection of food songs anywhere in private hands. Forty-eight tape cas-settes comprising 183 food songs by 918 artists—including Andie MacDowell singing a little number that I wrote the words to: "Pie." She sings it in *Michael*, a movie with a big pie scene. People make whole food movies—*Soul Food*, *Fried Green Tomatoes*, and *Big Night*, that one about the Italian restaurant with the Louis Prima songs. I'll bet somebody, somewhere, is about to embark on a film project that could use a highly paid consultant in the field of songs involving food.

Say you want something on your sound track to help make the transition from nighttime to breakfast. Depending on the mood and what your charac-ters have been up to with one another, I could recommend Lee Wiley's "Chicken Today, Feathers Tomorrow," Zuzu Bollin's "Why Don't You Eat Where You Slept Last Night," Johnny Cash's "Beans for Breakfast," Lightnin' Hopkins's "Breakfast Time," Nicky Williams's "I Want You for Breakfast," or the Freight Hoppers' "How Many Biscuits Can You Eat This Morning?"

Maybe your movie is set in Memphis. I've got King Curtis's "Memphis Soul Stew," Dan Penn's "Memphis Women and Fried Chicken," Memphis Slim's

"Sweet Root Man," the Memphis Seven's "Grunt Meat Blues," and twelve different Memphis Minnie food songs, including "Good Soppin'" and "I'm Selling My Porkchops (but I'm Giving My Gravy Away)."

I don't claim to have every food song ever recorded. I don't even have Cecil Gant's "Owl Head Soup" — yet. But do I have Slim and Slam performing "Mama's in the Kitchen, but We've Got Pop on Ice"? Sure. Harry "The Hipster" Gibson's "Who Put the Benzedrine in Mrs. Murphy's Ovaltine?" Absolutely. "Chocolate Porkchop Man" by Pete "Guitar" Lewis? "Anyone Here Wants to Buy Some Cabbage?" by a group of anonymous women inmates of Parchman Penitentiary? Uncle Dave Macon's "Eleven Cent Cotton, Forty Cent Meat"? Yes, yes, yes. "Save the Bones for Henry Jones ('Cause Henry Don't Eat No Meat)," as sung by Ray Charles? Uh-huh, and also by Johnny Mercer.

And I have "Feast of the Mau Mau" by Screamin' Jay Hawkins, "Hamhark and Limer Beans" by Champion Jack Dupree, "Sal's Got a Sugar Lip" by Johnny Horton, "Pizza on the Ground" by the Austin Lounge Lizards, "Gimme Some of That Yum Yum Yum" by the Harlem Hamfats, "Who'll Chop Your Suey When I'm Gone?" by Margaret Johnson, "In the Garden Where the Irish Potatoes Grow" by Dr. Smith's Champion Horse Hair Pullers, "Got No Bread No Milk No Honey but We Sure Got a Lot of Love" by James Talley (remember him, from during the Carter administration?), Clyde Edgerton's "Quiche Woman in a Barbecue Town," Wynonie Harris's "Keep on Churnin' (till the Butter Comes)," Buster Benton's "Spider in My Stew," John Lee Hooker's "Onions," Louis Armstrong's "Big Butter and Egg Man," Jimmy Buffett's "I Wish Lunch Could Last Forever," Nellie Lutcher's "Princess Poo-Poo-Ly Has Plenty Papaya," Elvis's "Crawfish," Z. Z. Hill's "Home Ain't Home at Suppertime" (it'll tear your heart out), Slim Gaillard's "Avocado Seed Soup Symphony," Louis Jordan's "A Chicken Ain't Nothing but a Bird," Fats Waller's "Hold Tight (I Want Some Seafood, Mama)," and Gene Autry's "Methodist Pie."

I've got food songs sung by Little Richard, Little Milton, Little Jimmy Dickens, Little Feat, Little Temple, Little Sparrow, Mighty Sparrow, Little Joe and the Thrillers, Little Jack Melody and His Young Turks, Little Son Joe, Li'l Son Jackson, Li'l Ed and the Imperials, Bea Lillie, Lil Johnson, Lonnie Johnson, Robert Johnson, Luther "Guitar Junior" Johnson, Jimmy Johnson, Pete Johnson, Earl Johnson, Sherman "Blues" Johnson and His Clouds of Joy, Eddie Johnson and His Crackerjacks, the Chips, the Box Tops, Buckwheat Zydeco, Gravy, Greasetrap, Stringbean, Peaches and Herb, Biscuit, Cracker, and Cake.

Is it a family picture you have in mind? I've got the Andrews Sisters, Boswell Sisters, Chenille Sisters, McGuire Sisters, Pointer Sisters, Sister Carol,

Sister O. M. Terrell, and Sister Rosetta Tharpe. The Holmes Brothers, McGee Brothers, Mills Brothers, Neville Brothers, Carson Brothers and Sprinkle, Big Wheeler with the Ice Cream Boys, Famous Hokum Boys, Happiness Boys ("I've Never Seen a Straight Banana"), Sweet Violet Boys, Blue Scott and His Blue Boys, Bob Wills and the Texas Playboys, Johnny Lee Wills and His Boys, Jimmy Revard and the Oklahoma Playboys, A. E. Ward and His Plow Boys, and Rude Girls.

That was a good group, Rude Girls. I have their "Chitlin Cooking Time in Chatham County." Not to mention "Peach Picking Time in Georgia" by Jimmie Rodgers (and by Willie Nelson, and by Kenneth Threadgill), "Honeycomb" by the other, lesser Jimmie Rodgers, and the bluesman Jimmy Rogers's "My Last Meal." And speaking of pickin': "Pickin' Peas (down the Long Pea Row)" by the Carlisles, "When It's Tooth-Pickin' Time in False Teeth Valley" by Homer and Jethro, "Pickin' Wild Mountain Berries" by Conway and Loretta, and "Pickin' Off Peanuts" by Seven-Foot Dilly and His Dill Pickles.

I've got "Good Jelly Blues," "Jelly Whipping Blues," "Jelly Jelly Blues," "Hot Jelly Roll Blues," "Jelly Bean Blues," "Fine Jelly Blues," "Sugar Blues," "Sugar Mama Blues," "Ration Blues," "Food Stamp Blues," "Red Cross Store Blues," "Grocery Blues," "Fort Worth Hambone Blues," "Stewmeat Blues," "Grunt Meat Blues," "Meat Cuttin' Blues," "Butcher Shop Blues," "Sweet Potato Blues," "Yellow Yam Blues," "Bakershop Blues," "Bakin' Powder Blues," "Rice and Gravy Blues," "Vitamin A Blues," "Plain Food Blues," "Your Greens Give Me the Blues," and "I've Got the Yes! We Have No Bananas Blues."

The great majority of food songs are Southern. Southern Culture on the Skids has recorded thirteen that I know of, including "Fried Chicken and Gasoline" and "Too Much Pork for One Fork." I also have "Hambone Am Sweet" by Four Southern Singers. And both Asleep at the Wheel's and Phil Harris's renditions of "That's What I Like about the South." And Moon Mullican's "Southern Hospitality," "Southern Deep-Fry" by someone named C. McAlister, and Margaret Johnson's "Folks in New York City Ain't Like the Folks Back South," which is full of food references, for instance:

The horses and the numbers keep most of them alive.
All they eat is hot dogs when eatin' time arrives.

Maybe you're making a Southern movie about what folks in New York City are like. I could help you on that.

But not on a pro bono basis. I ain't giving any more of my gravy away. I can't afford to—I live in New York.

Summer Feeding Frenzy

DEBBIE MOOSE

The North Carolina Farmer's Market in Raleigh on a Saturday in July is like Crabtree Valley Mall in December.

By 9:30 A.M., even the perimeter gravel lot is stacking up. Volvos and minivans troll for brake lights in the spaces next to the shed, stalling traffic back to the main entrance. There's a line twelve deep at the ATM.

Under the shed, undulating waves of people are broken by the prows of two-seater strollers. T-shirts flash by: the Confederate battle flag, a church camp, National Public Radio. Grown adults climb over each other for samples of cantaloupe or peaches. A man walking fretfully beside me swings around and bellows his son's name directly into my right ear, then reaches across my path and grabs the boy's plump forearm.

Southern accents stretch by, wrapping around a rat-a-tat of Japanese conversations, a peppery burst of Spanish, and some sounds I can't recognize. A stately, dark woman with a musical African lilt sells me nectarines grown in the North Carolina foothills.

It's the height of the feeding frenzy of summer. Everyone's out at once, intent on consuming what has arrived all at once. As if we've never tasted watermelon so sweet, tomatoes so juicy. Myself included. I cannot walk past a fresh peach or resist diving into a cascading green mountain of corn in a pickup truck bed.

After tempting weeks of nature doling out the goodies in dribs and drabs, hoarding them like Halloween treats at the beginning of the night, it's all out there now, overflowing the bounds of baskets and good sense. Buy a dozen ears of corn for $3, you get fourteen. Pick out a basket of peaches, they toss a couple more plump ones into the bag. Ask about an unfamiliar kind of eggplant, and the farmer says, "Try you one," and tosses it into your already-paid-for sack.

I just can't stop myself. Every week, I waddle home to my two-carnivore household with more vegetables and fruit than an army of invading vegans could consume in seven days. I could never become a vegetarian (I can sum up my reasons in three words: soft-shell crabs), but I could come pretty close during the summer, when everything is so fresh and good—and, frequently, free. Farmers aren't the only ones who are dealing with a garden glut.

Tom invited my husband and me for dinner recently, warning that everything he served would have tomatoes in it because the tomato plants in his backyard were bursting. "I've had tomato sandwiches every day for lunch," he said gleefully. Red orbs perched on the windowsill and by the sink. A bowl of a dozen or so round things wrapped in newspaper sat nearby: green tomatoes that he was ripening. "Storm knocked down the Celebrity," he said, referring to one of the varieties. "So I picked these up." He used some in a fried green tomato sandwich, which he described in lip-smacking detail.

We ate angel-hair pasta tossed with tomatoes and basil and black bean roll-ups with tomato salsa. I'd looked around my kitchen for something to contribute that would also use some of my fourteen ears of corn from the farmer's market. I found a corn salad recipe from *Joy of Cooking* but didn't bother to cook the corn: corn kernels, onions, basil, vinaigrette (olive oil, vinegar, garlic, and Dijon mustard), and, continuing the theme, tomatoes. Tom sent us home with as many tomatoes as we were willing to carry away, promises (threats?) of more.

There is an unwritten rule of summer: You cannot throw away fresh tomatoes—any fresh vegetable, really—nor can you allow them to go to waste. When I was growing up, most of the houses in my neighborhood had backyard gardens—many, like my father's, of considerable size. He set out maybe twenty tomato plants, plus the "volunteer" cherry tomatoes that came up on their own. This was in addition to the cucumbers, squash, butter beans, crowder peas, bell peppers, October beans, new potatoes, green onions, carrots, radishes, lettuce, cabbage, and several rows of corn.

Every year, around July, the same phenomenon would take place in our neighborhood. I call it the Boomerang Vegetable Toss. This is how it worked: I'd announce that I was heading up the street to play with a friend. Mama would shout, "Wait!" Then she'd grab a paper bag, throw in some tomatoes (only ten or so), and say, "Take these up yonder for 'em." I'd hand the bag to the friend's mother, saying my Mama had sent them. She would offer a pinched smile, thinking of her own groaning tomato vines. When I was ready to leave, she would meet me in the carport with a sly smile and a bag of her own, say, squash. Destination: My house.

One of the rules of this game was that you couldn't send back the same vegetable that was tossed to you because it would look like you were returning the original vegetables, which would be a major neighborhood faux pas. It was risky to toss to anyone who lived close enough for you to see their garden because you would know what they were growing and couldn't say, "Oh, I didn't know you'd put out tomatoes this year. I guess you didn't need those fifty tomatoes I sent over." It was also considered bad form for the tossee to tell the tosser that she had plenty of the vegetable sent.

The round would end when I delivered the return toss to Mama, who would harrumph and roll her eyes, declaring that we had plenty of whatever the bag contained and wondering why she sent it to us. Why, indeed.

One house on our road did not have a garden. So when everyone got tired of the Boomerang Vegetable Toss, particularly at the end of a long, strained summer, they aimed their veggie volleys at this little family of three. Nobody knew the couple and their toddler very well, except that they came from Someplace Else (as in a foreign country) and their last name was unpronounceable to our red-clay tongues. Their vegetable deliveries were addressed as "Take this over to them up there."

These poor folks got it from all sides, a torrent of zucchini, squash, and tomatoes that I'm sure they appreciated, at least at first. By mid-August, signs of tension would appear even on their faces at the sight of another sack of zucchini for thirty.

Now I am one of the people with no garden, thanks to a yard shaded by too many tall pines. I am a target for the produce patrol. Neighbor Bill sends over squash and zucchini to say thanks for my husband's help with his computer. Treva uses me as a home for wayward banana peppers. I don't even wait for Tom to offer—I call up to raid his Italian parsley or whatever else I need. (It would be so much easier if he'd just cut a hole in his back fence for me.)

But hey, I'm not complaining. I say, bring it on. To paraphrase Shakespeare, summer's vegetable lease hath all too short a date.

The Gospel of Barbecue
for *Alvester James*

HONORÉE FANONNE JEFFERS

Long after it was
necessary, Uncle
Vess ate the leavings
off the hog, doused
them with vinegar sauce.
He ate chewy abominations.
Then came high pressure.
Then came the little pills.
Then came the doctor
who stole Vess's second
sight, the predication
of pig's blood every
fourth Sunday.
Then came the stillness
of barn earth, no more
trembling at his step.
Then came the end
of the rib, but before
his eyes clouded,
Uncle Vess wrote
down the gospel
of barbecue.

Chapter one:
Somebody got to die
with something at some
time or another.

Bedspring barbecue.
Courtesy of North Carolina Collection.

Chapter two:
Don't ever trust
white folk to cook
your meat until
it's done to the bone.

Chapter three:
December is the best
time for hog killing.
The meat won't
spoil as quick.
Screams and blood
freeze over before
they hit the air.

HONORÉE FANONNE JEFFERS

Chapter four, Verse one:
Great Grandma Mandy
used to say food
you was whipped
for tasted the best.

Chapter four, Verse two:
Old Master knew to lock
the ham bacon chops
away quick or the slaves
would rob him blind.
He knew a padlock
to the smokehouse
was best to prevent
stealing, but even the
sorriest of slaves would
risk a beating for a full
belly. So Christmas time
he give his nasty
leftovers to the well
behaved. The head ears
snout tail fatback
chitlins
feet ribs balls.
He thought gratitude
made a good seasoning.

Chapter five:
Unclean means dirty
means filthy means
underwear worn too
long in summertime heat.
Perfectly good food
Can't be no sin.
Maybe the little
bit of meat on ribs
makes for lean eating.
Maybe the pink flesh

is tasteless until you add
onions garlic black
pepper tomatoes
soured apple cider
but survival ain't never been
no crime against nature
or Maker. See, stay alive
in the meantime, laugh
a little harder. Go on
and gnaw that bone clean.

Welcome to Livermush Land

KATHLEEN PURVIS

Every Southern state has grits. All of them have biscuits. Most states—yes, even Texas—have something that could pass for barbecue. But when it comes to foods that define the Carolinas, there is one that is completely our own.

Livermush.

Oh, we hear you. Right about now, some of you are saying, "Yes, and you can keep it." Livermush is like that. Love it or hate it, it's guaranteed to inspire something. "I don't ever remember seeing a dish called livermush anyplace else," says John Egerton, the Nashville-based author of *Southern Food.* "And I hope never to see it again."

See?

But that's ok. Because people from around here know that whether you call it livermush or liver pudding—and we'll get back to that—those pan-fried slices of spare pig parts are right up there with vinegary barbecue sauce in announcing to the world that a Carolinian has pulled up to the table. Livermush does tend to attract attention.

Remember the Bhagwan? In 1985, when Shree Rajneesh left his ashram in Oregon and tried to flee the country, he was arrested in Charlotte. But what really grabbed national attention was his breakfast at the Mecklenburg County jail: livermush and grits.

More recently, Jan Karon's Mitford books have inspired livermush questions in newspaper food sections from Asheville to Arkansas. Set in a fictional version of Blowing Rock, Karon's characters eat livermush for breakfast, leaving her fans craving information.

Well, here's what we can tell them: Livermush is, by law, at least 30 percent pork liver, plus other pork meat—usually including meat from the head—cooked until it falls apart. Then it's ground, mixed with cornmeal, seasoned, and chilled in a block.

Sliced and pan-fried, it's a breakfast meat. Sliced cold, it's a sandwich filling. Any way you slice it, it tastes like country sausage with a hint of liver.

Some people say liver pudding is South Carolina's version, thickened with rice. Others say livermush is just called liver pudding east of the Yadkin River, probably because it sounds nicer.

If you're from Pennsylvania, all this might sound familiar. Both liver pudding and livermush are believed to have derived from scrapple, brought down through the Appalachians by German settlers. Scrapple, says Fritz Blank, a Philadelphia chef with expertise in his native Pennsylvania Dutch foodways, is cooked pork and pork liver thickened with cornmeal or—more authentically—a mixture of buckwheat and cornmeal. Made into a loaf, it is sliced, dipped in seasoned flour, and pan-fried in lard.

"These things all have a commonality," says Blank. "Much of it has to do with the availability of the ingredients and the climate." In other words: If you have pigs and you have corn, you can have livermush.

Some people think livermush's real time has arrived. Ron McKee of Mack's Livermush in Rutherfordton says consumption is up "because people are watching their cholesterol, calories, fat. In a class of breakfast meats, nothing can compete with livermush." High in protein and about 8 percent fat in a two-ounce slice, he says, "it's hard to beat the nutritional factor."

Don Jamison wouldn't know about that. But he does know how to make livermush. For forty-two years, starting when he was seventeen, Jamison has made livermush twice a week. Although there are a half-dozen or so livermush makers left in the Carolinas, including Mack's, Greensboro-based Neese's, and Frank Corriher's of Landis, R. A. Jamison on Lawyers Road is the last in Charlotte. Don and his brothers Arnie and Ronnie continue a sausage and livermush business started by their grandfather in the 1920s.

To watch, you have to get up early: Livers and boneless pork are put on to cook about 10 P.M., so they're ready about 2 A.M. "It was something started a long time ago," he says of the early hour. "We used to do same-day wrapping and we just never did change it."

The cooked meat is ground, then mixed with salt, black pepper, red pepper flakes, and sage. Then, in a vat-sized mixer, a motor stirs it while Jamison or his son-in-law, Butch Allen, mixes in about 100 pounds of cornmeal. Mixing slowly is key. You can't dump the cornmeal in all at once or add it too fast or it will clump.

Wearing a white butcher's jacket and a racing cap, Jamison stands at the mixer tossing in handfuls of meal in a steady motion, like feeding chickens, then waiting until the lacy pattern of meal is absorbed into the brown soup before adding more.

When the cooking mush has gotten Jamison's approval—a little soupier than warm peanut butter—he and Allen use a chain to raise the beater, which looks like a ship's anchor. They clean it off, then start filling metal pans. Using a ladle as long as a boat oar, Jamison scoops about sixteen pounds of liver-mush into each pan, then fills in the corners and levels it off with a metal bar.

"I have a friend who's a brick mason," he says, smiling. "He told me I would make a good one."

The night's batch fills forty-four pans. There's no alternative to filling the pans by hand, he says. Every machine they've tried just gets clogged. Jamison is obsessive about cleanliness. The small plant is inspected regularly, he says. He shows off the cooler, where the walls, floor, and ceiling are scrubbed with bleach. He watches the temperatures through the process: Cook it to 190 degrees, cool it to 130 degrees, then down to 80 degrees within an hour. Then it's chilled to 45 degrees within five hours. After that, it's sliced and wrapped: four-pound blocks for restaurants, one-pound vacuum-wrapped blocks for supermarkets.

It's not exciting, he admits. Not much changes in the livermush business. "It has to be done the same way every time. There's nothing to change."

And that's just how North Carolina likes it.

Aspiration

LYNN POWELL

Further south they call it hog jowl.
Up north they call it salt pork.
But we called it streakéd meat
the one Elizabethan elegance
in a lexicon of liberries, chimbleys,
y'alls, might coulds, and sherberts.

On New Year's Day, my mother would slice it ten times
the thickness of bacon, the salt in one slice
enough to make a mouth shrivel for days.

Faraway, others were igniting sauces,
shaping the daily tortilla or boiling
mussels from the river in coconut milk . . .

But we were counting on a mess
of black-eyed peas, a fried slab of pig fat,
and the charm of a name, perfected.

Here's One for the Birds

DONNA PIERCE

Next time an error in judgment forces you to "eat crow," don't worry. I've found recipes.

Drop a plucked and cleaned bird into a kettle of boiling water and simmer until tender. If you're not counting calories, split blackbirds in half lengthwise, dredge in flour, and fry in hot oil. *Miz Jessie's Gatherin' of Old-Odd-Unusual Receipts* is just the sort of prize that keeps me setting my alarm for garage sales. There's no publication date inside the pink construction paper cover, but there's a typed note signed by "Miz" Jessie Lanphere, followed by her address in Bull Shoals, Arkansas. A photo shows Lanphere in a sunbonnet enjoying a long draw from a corncob pipe. Think Granny from *The Beverly Hillbillies* TV show.

Directory assistance couldn't pull up a Lanphere in Bull Shoals or any other Marion County hamlet, but when my call to the library interrupted a morning board meeting, the librarian had a chance to poll board members. "No one here ever heard of her," she reported back. She did offer the name and telephone number of one Bob Harper, who is finishing a book about the area. Harper, who said his wife's family has lived in the area since the Louisiana Purchase, was happy to discuss local history. In 1946, the Southwest Power Authority brought in 1,500 men to build the Bull Shoals Dam. "They arrived to find nothing but dirt roads coming into town." Stores went up quickly; Bull Shoals earned a dot on the Arkansas map.

Had he heard about Jessie Lanphere or the cookbook?

"I have a copy," he said. "It's very rare. When I got hold of that cookbook, I spent three hours reading it. It's a classic."

Harper, an Oklahoma native who moved to Bull Shoals in 1983, discovered Lanphere in newspaper archives. "She used to go out to the Mountain Home Court House square and make corncob jelly," he said. "I don't know how long she lived here before the fire, but I'm pretty sure she moved out of town when her home burned to the ground in 1964."

When I reminded him that her address in the book included a zip code, we narrowed its printing to either 1963, when zip codes were added, or shortly before the 1964 fire. Chances are, some of the books went up in flames in the house Lanphere shared with her "mister," whom she called Grandpa Hyar.

I asked Harper about the colloquial language used in the recipes because this book seemed different from plantation-style cookbooks I collect, where dialect, often used as a colorful device by writers other than the cook, seem mocking and insensitive. Lanphere's instructions seem more authentic. "Rat good cooked with any vegetable like beans, peas er meats such as chicken," she writes about "Riffles," a homemade noodle. "Ifen ut gits too dry, ya kin add a little cold milk ta ut in your bowl."

"I understand that's just how she talked," Harper said.

Like many old cookbooks, this one offers much more than recipes. It's about resourcefulness in the face of empty pantries and keeping a sense of humor— and pride—while making do with what's at hand. Miz Jessie's little book is like a survivor's manual, a handbook on hard times. I learned about coffee brewed with dried sweet potatoes. "A pinch of salt brings out the flavor better." For farkleberry pie, "bake 35 minutes until the crust gets a purdy brown." And it doesn't get any more direct and simple than "Poor Boy Oyster Soup": "Drain off one flat tin of sardines packed in oil, crumble into one quart of milk and heat."

At some time in Lanphere's life, she had been desperate enough to serve groundhogs—which she called whistlepigs—raccoons, and rattlesnakes at her table. And when life dealt her a cupboard almost bare, she celebrated birthdays with "Eggless, Butterless, Milkless Cake," to which she added this note in the margin next to the recipe that called for water, sugar, lard, raisins, nutmeg, cinnamon, and cloves: "What's left is good."

My Blue Heaven

JULIA REED

For almost a quarter of my life, I was so madly in love with a Cancer, it almost killed me. No wonder they are represented in the zodiac by a crab. Just like their crustacean counterparts, Cancers move mostly sideways, and they change directions with no notice—or worse, they simply retreat into their shells. They can indeed be "crabby," which Webster's defines as cross or ill-tempered, and "crabbed" (morose and peevish), and they are very adept at "crabbing" (making sour) what were, just moments earlier, the best of times. They are moody and sensitive and vulnerable, and you want to kill them, but they are saved by the fact that they also share the crab's more irresistible nature. Once you have had a taste of what lies beneath that hard and occasionally difficult shell, you find that it is more than worth the patience and the hassle. And that it is damn near impossible not to keep coming back for more.

What lies beneath the blue crab, found along the Atlantic and Gulf coasts, is, to use one of my father's favorite expressions, "a little piece of paradise"— or, actually, several pieces. In fish stores, the best of what the blue crab has to offer, the solid chunks of sweet white meat from the back fin, is marked "jumbo lump," but it should be labeled "food of the gods."

Mary J. Rathbun of the Smithsonian Institution knew what she had on her hands when she gave the blue crab its scientific name, *Callinectes sapidus* Rathbun. In Greek, *callinectes* means beautiful swimmer (which this crab is), and *sapidus* means savory in Latin. Rathbun identified and described 998 crab species in her time, but the only crab she named savory was the blue.

Given the blue crab's scientific status and the gorgeous appearance of its pristine white lumps, not much should be added to it when cooking except those ingredients that highlight its already rich goodness. One of the most irritating things on a plate is a crab cake full of bread crumbs or mayonnaise or some other filler that has turned the noble crab into a patty of mush. Holding a crab cake together is a problem, though. Georges Perrier, the brilliant French chef who presides over Le Bec-Fin and Brasserie Perrier in Philadelphia, has an elegant solution. He purees raw shrimp in the food processor until it is shiny (it looks exactly like boiled seven-minute cake icing) and stiff enough to act as a binder for the crab. He adds seasonings, makes cakes, sautés them, and serves them with a warm mustard sauce. They are light and lush at the same time and definitely good enough to go to Philadelphia in search of (or you can buy Perrier's wonderful and accessible *Georges Perrier: Le Bec-Fin Recipes*).

My own favorite crab cake recipe came to me from the great and gifted book editor and equally gifted cook Jason Epstein. He can no longer remember where the recipe came from or even what it contains, but I can. I have been making these crab cakes regularly since the first time he made them for me, on my birthday years ago. The crab is mixed with not much more than scallions, butter, and cream; the secret is in the refrigeration. The cakes, when first formed, are almost runny, but they are immediately chilled until the butter and cream harden completely. Then they are quickly dipped in beaten egg, rolled in crumbs, and pan-fried. People always go crazy over these, and they can never figure out why they're so much better than other crab cakes. It's because by the time they are crisp and brown on the outside, nothing but pure crab is melting on the inside. They are so rich that I serve them with a tangy tomato vinaigrette, but small ones, passed as hors d'oeuvres, can be accompanied by traditional homemade tartar sauce.

Not that richness is necessarily a problem. When I was growing up, there was a famous restaurant in Memphis called Justine's. It was in a lovely old house, the flowers on the table were roses from the garden, and the thing everybody always ordered as a starter was Crabmeat Justine. Where I lived was about three hours away by car, but people would start talking about Crabmeat Justine, and the next thing you knew, somebody would volunteer to drive. I recently came across the recipe in an ancient copy of *The Memphis Cook Book*, published by the city's Junior League, and figured out why it was so incredibly good. It consists of only seasoned crabmeat sautéed in lemon and butter and topped with hollandaise sauce.

James Beard's favorite crab dish was Crab Louis, a recipe that originated on the Pacific coast, which means it was probably first made with Dungeness crab, but it is equally popular made with lumps of blue. The recipe appears in Beard's first cookbook, *Hors D'Oeuvres and Canapés*, and at least two subsequent ones, and he always played around a bit with the recipe (sometimes adding chopped green olives, sometimes using grated onion instead of chopped green onions). Beard insisted that the "finest" Louis he had ever had was at the Bohemian restaurant in his hometown, Portland, Oregon, though the recipe was served earlier by the chef at the Olympic Club in Seattle.

When the Metropolitan Opera touring company played that city in 1904, Enrico Caruso kept ordering the salad until none was left in the kitchen. It's too bad that Caruso didn't make it to New Orleans, to Galatoire's, where the signature crab salad is Crabmeat Maison, a lump crab salad with mayonnaise, capers, and a bit of green onion. I love it on saltines topped with anchovies (a homey and weirdly delicious presentation created by the late, lamented waiter Cesar), but at cocktail parties, I dress it up by serving it on toast points, without the anchovies. Once, at a particularly grand party, I filled a friend's enormous silver punch bowl with about ten pounds of the stuff. It was so over the top that people sort of stood and stared at first, but within an hour, it was gone.

Galatoire's is very big on crabmeat. If you ask them to, the waiters will top any fresh fish of the day with lumps that have been lightly sautéed in lemon and butter, and for serious crab lovers, they will even pile it on top of softshells. They serve crabmeat hot, bound with a bit of béchamel and topped with bread crumbs and Parmesan in an appetizer known as Canapé Lorenzo, and cold, tossed into Godchaux Salad with boiled shrimp and Creole mustard vinaigrette topped with anchovies and hard-boiled eggs. However, the best tossed salad featuring crabmeat is at another New Orleans institution, Mosca's, a roadhouse started by Provino Mosca, a favorite chef to the don of the New Orleans crime family, Carlos Marcello. Mosca's salad is simply iceberg lettuce, lump crabmeat, wine vinegar, olive oil, and an olivey antipasto salad (available by mail order from Central Grocery in New Orleans). Not long ago, I served it for lunch to a group of folks who included a French photographer, an English garden designer, a young woman from Arkansas, and a photographer's assistant from Manhattan. None of them had ever tasted anything like it before, and none of them could get enough. You would have thought each was Caruso. They had discovered the curse of the crab—once you've had a taste, you must keep going back.

The Green Bean Conundrum

JANN MALONE

"It's a generational thing."

That's the standard explanation in our household for strange behavior and off-the-wall opinions from people who are either older or younger than we are. I guess I should define those terms. Strange behavior is doing things differently from our way. Off-the-wall opinions run contrary to our way of thinking.

Now that that's clear, let's move on to the latest example of strange behavior: cooking green beans to death. I'm against it. I like them tender-crisp. But one night last week, I cooked them beyond tender-crisp all the way to—well, let's just call them uncrisp—because we had a guest for dinner who wanted them cooked that way. And, of course, the guest is always right.

Besides, he bought the beans. He also bought the steaks and the fresh corn to go with them, so he had more say than dinner guests usually have. I don't want to use this person's real name because it might embarrass him. He lives out of this paper's circulation area, but he has a lot of friends here. So let's just call him Dad.

I knew there was going to be trouble when Dad asked, "Got any salt pork for the beans?" As far as I know, the words "salt pork" and "cook until tender-crisp" have never appeared in the same recipe.

"Noooo," I said. "I don't think so."

"Well, that's OK," Dad said. "Sometimes when I don't have salt pork, I just use bacon."

By now, all you smart readers are no doubt saying, "Mabel, this woman is an idiot. She doesn't use salt pork. She eats raw beans. It's not a generational thing. It's a Southern thing. She must be a Yankee." Wrong, I'm a Southerner, so it must be a generational thing. Anyhow, I started looking through cookbooks for a green bean recipe that could make everyone happy. I found one in *Jane Brody's Good Food Book* with three ingredients that have universal appeal in our family: garlic, onions, and tomatoes.

Three circumstances forced me to fiddle with the recipe: It was a very hot day, so I decided to use the microwave to keep the kitchen cool. I didn't have a can of regular tomatoes, so I had to substitute Italian-style stewed tomatoes. And I also had to disregard the "cook until tender-crisp" instructions.

When I thought the beans were done, I asked Dad to taste them. "They need to cook more," he said.

"You don't like them still a little crisp?"

"Yes, but these taste like they just jumped off the vine."

So I cooked them five minutes more five minutes more five minutes more, until Dad said they were done.

They were wonderful, probably the best green beans I've ever eaten. Could've used a little bacon, though. Maybe even some salt pork.

A Butter Lover Spreads the Word

MARY E. MILLER

Regarding butter's comeback, let me just say, on behalf of the right-headed, faithful foodies who heeded not the fat hysterics who stacked their cabinets with canola oil and refrigerators with plastic vats of that whipped, sickly yellow substitute: Ha! We knew it!

We knew it all along, even while the fat police chastised us about our imperiled cholesterol levels or, heavens to Mergatroid, the slippery slope to cellulite. Butter remains, and always shall be, our friend.

So sing it, brothers and sisters: "Make new friends, but keep the old; butter's tasty and it feeds your soul."

Remember a few years ago when *Saturday Night Live* comedian Mike Myers said Barbra Streisand was "like buttah"? The phrase was immediately adopted by the masses at the very same time they were shunning butter. How ridiculous. Finally, the fanatics have had a meltdown. Butter, they now timidly put forth, is fine—in moderation. For that, let's give them a little pat and say "welcome back."

When America abandoned butter, my refrigerator remained a safe house, even as the low-fat salad dressings sat cranky and ignored, like skinny old maids, on the shelf. Margarine, child of darkness, was unwelcome, even wearing a garlic necklace.

This is not to make light of people with eating disorders or those whose medical conditions truly require a low-fat, butterless diet. They have true reason for concern.

I am relatively young, slender, and definitely blessed with good health. Many who know me well say I'm a tad hedonistic, though sybaritic sounds better. It's true, red meat and liquor have a mortgage on my digestive system. But I could abandon beef or even (gulp) eighteen-year-old Macallan if I had to. Butter? No way.

Not coincidentally, all my favorite recipes begin with the phrase, "Take one stick of butter." I don't use it every time I cook, and I do use it judiciously. For

Working the churn on a spring day. Photograph by Dorothea Lange.
Courtesy of Southern Historical Collection.

example, I do not slip a pat of butter on a bacon-wrapped filet mignon. That would be excessive. But some dishes simply require large amounts of butter. Anything that qualifies as comfort food contains copious amounts of butter — enough, as a rule, to change the color of the dish.

I make mashed potatoes that have brought tears to grown men's eyes. And I have more than a few friends who would pitch out on the floor if they saw how much butter I chuck into those bad boys. (Recently, I attempted "skinny mashed potatoes" using chicken broth. To say the dish was less than delicious would be inaccurate. Even the dogs turned away in disgust.)

Like most of my friends, I work out. Unlike them, I don't do it for my butt, but for my butter. Attaining the perfect body is not my goal. I work out so that I can eat whatever I want, whenever I want.

Most of my friends my age are perfectly healthy. Probably a lot more healthy than women of my mother's generation. But these women have been programmed to believe that butter is evil incarnate. They look longingly as the dessert tray passes by. They run miles on treadmills, sweat gallons three and four times a week. For what? To spend an extra ten years eating bowls of grass?

If that's what I get for giving up butter, forget it. Whip me up some mashed potatoes, baby. And while you're at it, a hot buttered rum. If I've gotta go, I'd rather dig my grave with my teeth.

MARY E. MILLER

What the Angels Eat

JIM HENDERSON

Somewhere on my desk is a folder containing everything you would ever want to know about a watermelon. I glanced at it once, just long enough to learn that the watermelon is a vegetable (relative of the gourd) and not a fruit, that it came originally from the Kalahari Desert of Africa and has been cultivated for more than four thousand years, and that it contains abundant vitamins, scant calories, and lots of water.

What else? When the colonists arrived in North America in the 1600s, they consumed watermelons with a waste-not efficiency—eating the pulp, drinking the water, pickling the rinds, and roasting the seeds. Eventually, watermelons were used in—or their taste and scent called on to provide inspiration for—a variety of marketable products, including candy, sorbet, lipstick, candles, incense, soap, and, of course, wine.

Enough continuing education. Everything I really need to know about watermelon I learned before kindergarten. Well, I learned *something* a few years later. To my great surprise, I learned that watermelons weren't free.

There was a time in rural America—particularly in the Southern states, where watermelon patches have long been part of the landscape—when you could easily reach puberty before you realized that these things were actually sold in stores and were not, in every instance, appropriated from some moonlight market at the edge of town.

At every family get-together in spring and summer, an uncle or cousin—whoever had a reliable car—was designated the official watermelon producer. He would cruise the section lines out beyond the cemetery, spot a likely patch, and return after sundown to . . . well . . . produce.

Stealing watermelons was common, guiltless, and socially acceptable. Look, these things are 92 percent water, and the rest is almost pure sugar. How could they have commercial value? Until the age of ten or eleven, I imagined that the kindest and gentlest farmers had neon signs over their crops: *Watermelons for Steal.*

What I knew about watermelons back then—and it was enough—was that they were mandatory at picnics and cookouts, they were intended to be eaten outdoors (preferably standing up and leaning forward), they were best eaten cold, spitting the seeds was half the fun of the indulgence, and slicing the melon was a ritual (like carving the Thanksgiving turkey) presided over by a wise and skillful family elder.

The iceboxes of that day tended to be too small to accommodate a twenty- or thirty-pound melon, so the chilling was usually accomplished with the aid of a galvanized washtub and a timely delivery from the local icehouse. Refrigeration works okay, but an ice bath is still the better method.

Because chilling was not always practical back then, I learned something else: Warm melon, sprinkled with a small amount of salt, is a delicacy worthy of its own place on the picnic blanket.

But no matter how watermelon was eaten, mamas rarely imposed limits on their children. Unlike other family-gathering standards, such as rich, hand-turned, homemade ice cream or mountainous pies oozing fresh berries, watermelon was thought to be downright wholesome.

Yesterday's folk wisdom turns out to be today's scientific fact: A two-pound wedge—a modest portion, once the weighty rind is discarded—contains a little iron and potassium and half the daily adult requirement of vitamins A and C. The pulp has nothing to clog the arteries, and the juice is as innocuous and refreshing as a frosted glass of mint tea.

The watermelon, Mark Twain once allowed, is "king by the grace of God over all the fruits of the earth. When one has tasted it, he knows what the angels eat." Lavish praise for such common vegetation. American farmers produce more than 4 billion pounds of watermelon a year, and supermarket bins overflow with the melons from May to September. But I prefer to procure mine from the farmer's market or, better yet, a roadside stand. It's more like getting them straight from the patch.

Except I do have to pay for them.

Dueling Steaks

DENISE GEE

"This *is* chicken-fried steak," the waitress insists, ready to pop me with a ketchup bottle if I pipe up again.

"But it's not battered and deep-fried," I implore (politely, of course, seeing as how her grip on that bottle is tightening). "This is *country-fried* steak. Smothered steak. Good, but not what I wanted. I wanted *crispy*."

"Well, you've got *this*," she says, setting down my plate (and that ketchup) and putting a lid on the aggravation. "Besides, everybody knows they're both the same anyway."

Gasp! Such mislabeling mayhem needs an explanation. And I am not to find it here in this sleepy diner smack-dab between chicken-fried and country-fried territories. So I hit the road. What I found beneath all that gravy was enough ammunition to blast another Grand Canyon between the South's east and its west. In defending these savory steaks, people are either fierce chicken-frieders or country-frieders. They aim to protect and, of course, serve.

First I went to Texas . . . home of the world's best chicken-fried steak. It's also home to Eddie Wilson, owner of the legendary Threadgill's in Austin—a mecca for chicken-fry fans. The original Threadgill's location, opened in 1933 on what was then the dusty northern frontier of the state capital, is still a bustling café and watering hole. Inside are hefty helpings of comfort food, friendly servers with tattoos here and there, neon beer signs, and photos of such music legends as Janis Joplin, who frequented the place back when musician-founder Kenneth Threadgill threw hootenannies. When Eddie came along later, he morphed this colorful roadhouse-diner into a music hall he whimsically called the AWH (for Armadillo World Headquarters). Then, in the 1990s, Wilson opened a second Threadgill's near downtown Austin.

"I'm not shy. I'll tell you what I think," Eddie says in pure Yosemite Sam fashion. "You won't find any country-fried steak on *this* menu. People like to

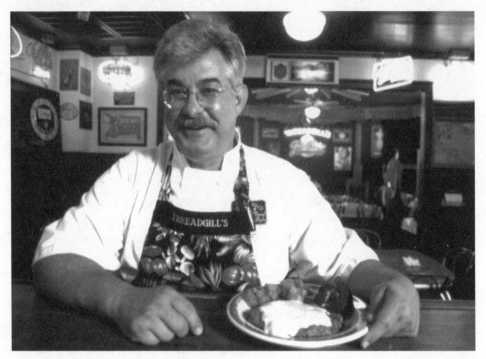

Eddie Wilson, proprietor of Threadgill's in Austin. Photograph by Charles Walton IV. Copyright 1998 Southern Living, Inc.

eat here," he says with a wink. "They want something they can really sink their teeth into—not wimpy food."

Exhibit A: The star of Threadgill's menu, chicken-fried steak, is deliriously crisp and tender (but not, of course, cuttable with a fork—it still holds its own). Its milky gravy, rich and creamy, is seasoned to perfection.

"It's like this," Eddie says. "Chicken-fried has something going for it that country-fried doesn't: crispness. Yet the irony is, the gravy covers it up. And because the crispier it is, the fresher it is, a lot of true chicken-frieders order their gravy on the side just to see how much effort was made to make it right."

But what about all that grease? (That's *juice* to a Texan.) "I don't see too many people worrying about it; they just don't eat it every day," Eddie reasons. "Fifteen years ago we sold so much chicken-fried steak it was almost sinful. Now folks eat more of that chicken-fried *chicken*, which to me is a lot like drinking a bourbon and Diet Coke."

As for chicken-fried's country-fried cousin? "I associate it with bad grade-school cafeteria food or an old Salisbury steak TV dinner," Eddie bristles. "I simply have no use for it."

DENISE GEE

Lynn Winter, impresario of Lynn's Paradise Café in Louisville.
Photograph by Charles Walton IV. Copyright 1998 Southern Living, Inc.

Off to Kentucky . . . for country-fried steak in paradise. Actually, to Louisville and Lynn's Paradise Café. In this neck of the South, country-fried is king, and decidedly, Lynn's is as good as it gets. It has been since the artist-wood-worker got into the restaurant business in 1991 after moving back home from California.

Lynn's has a wonderfully kitschy decor. Outside, an eight-foot coffeepot perpetually pours "coffee" (colored water) into a giant cup and a gargantuan wall mural accentuated with colored corncobs has passersby gaping in awe. Inside, 1950s lamps, Formica dinettes, a children's play area, and flea market treasures keep drawing patrons not just to Lynn's eclectically varied food but also to the funky surroundings. There's something for everyone, from "Boursin Grilled Rib Eye" to the widely praised, home-style country-fried steak.

Lynn's skillet-cooked steak is often featured at breakfast, lunch, and dinner. "It's a big hit here," she says. "Kentuckians love tradition and especially enjoy comfort food in a fun setting. Our country-fried steak is pretty straightfor-ward, but cornmeal, cayenne, and garlic give it an updated twist."

Lynn's recipe was adapted from her good friend, cookbook author Ronni Lundy (*Shuck Beans, Stack Cakes, and Honest Fried Chicken*). Ronni adapted *hers* after a visit with country singer Emmylou Harris, who shared her ideal: "To stop at a roadside diner and tie into a real nice piece of country-fried steak and creamy gravy," Emmylou said. "Of course, that's not something you can eat all the time, but every once in a while, it's awfully good. And eating it almost feels like being back home."

"That's exactly how I feel about it," Lynn says. "It's one of those cherished foods that reminds me of why I came back home too." Her well-seasoned version, with just a hint of crust, is fork-tender yet firm. With a dab of cream gravy, it's a joy to eat. Patrons agree. "Lynn's country-fried steak is awesome," says college student Jim Ames. "It reminds me of my mom's." But what about that chicken-fried steak? "Don't fast-food places sell that stuff?" he asks. "I don't like to gnaw on my meat." In Kentucky, country-fried *rules*.

At that point, Lynn hears Eddie Wilson's thoughts on the subject. "*Wrong,*" she laughs. "When I think of chicken-fried, I think of frozen patties with cheap, packaged gravy. *Country-fried,* on the other hand, is total cast-iron comfort. Give Eddie our recipe, will ya?"

Then, we got busy cookin' . . . and the winner was . . . undecided. "I like country-fried steak better," said one test kitchen staffer, remaining anonymous for fear of chicken-fried retaliation. "No way," replied a dyed-in-the-wool chicken-frieder. "You obviously haven't lived."

The battle continues. "Meanwhile, beyond our borders," muses Texas writer Jerry Flemmons, " . . . horror stories keep coming in." In Oregon, for example, a Texas businessman discovered "Real Texas Chicken-Fried Steak" on a small-town restaurant menu and quickly ordered it.

"Yes sir," said the young waiter, adding expectantly, "and how would you like that cooked?"

The South's Thirsty Muse

BRIAN CARPENTER

Long before William Faulkner declared that civilization began with distillation, Southerners knew it had achieved a genial and ruddy perfection in the South with the creation of that velvety smooth distillate of sour mash and sparkling limestone water known as bourbon. I refer not to the rotgut, wildcat corn that every child of calamity ever raised to his lips in countless southwestern tales, nor to the old "white mule" or "baldface" John Barleycorn, or even the smooth-sippin' Tennessee Black Jack that Faulkner kept within reach while he wrote, but to good "old bourbon," the Kentucky thoroughbred, the crown prince of whiskeys, and the eponymous spirit of "Old Bourbon" County, Kentucky.

The distinction is not a matter of mere connoisseurship but of tradition. It is by now a cliché that any writer who may be regarded as being connected in any way to the South—by birth or by temperament or by earnest affectation—that is, any writer whom we may without hesitation call "Southern," must have, at the very least, a general acquaintance with, if not a genuine affection for, the peculiar charms of John Barleycorn's genteel cousin. That is, if he doesn't have the said spirits pocketed away—presumably in Grandfather's antique hinge-topped hip flask—somewhere on his very person right now.

So goes the myth, but what of the literature? What have Southern writers themselves had to say about bourbon—its history, its merits, and its restorative and aesthetic influence on the writer and his work? And whence its enduring reputation as the South's thirsty muse?

Between the bear hunters and bootleggers, the Johnny Rebs and dissipated gentlemen, there is whiskey enough to be found in the pages of Southern fiction. But of bourbon proper, one finds mostly isolated anecdotes. Walker Percy's preference for Early Times. Twain's recollection of sharing his grandfather's whiskey toddy, his delight at being presented six cases of bourbon during his stay at London's Savage Club, and his dismay at having to leave the last two cases behind when called back home on business. These anecdotes aside, however, there are few revelations beyond what one might discover at the bottom of a shot glass, julep cup, or snub-nosed bottle. Bourbon, after all, if we are to cite again the common myth, is what the Southern writer turns to when the book is finished or when the words no longer come. We do find a few exceptions, however, like "Colonel" Irvin S. Cobb, the Kentucky humorist, whose novel *Red Likker* stands to this day as the only American novel to chronicle the rise and fall of Kentucky's "bourbon aristocracy," and William Alexander Percy, whose Mississippi memoir, *Lanterns on the Levee*, includes a recipe for mint juleps guaranteed, he says, to bring about "half an hour of sedate cumulative bliss." They, like Will's nephew Walker Percy, who conducted his own personal survey on the aesthetics of bourbon drinking in the South, are among those rare Southern writers who managed to set habit aside long enough to decipher the message in the bottle.

In 1920, Irvin Cobb took his own stand against the New South by writing a novel that found in bourbon's rich history the spiritual sustenance lacking in an age of doubt. Written during the era of bathtub gin and bootleg liquor, Cobb's novel is both a celebration of good honest bourbon and an elegy for the culture that produced it. *Red Likker* traces the fortunes of Colonel Attila Bird, a fictional patriarch of the bourbon belt and descendant, says Cobb, of that "big-boned, fair-skinned, contentious, individualistic breed" who first sprang from the cradle of civilization deep in the heart of Kentucky. The first settlers, we are told, were the first distillers, that "hardy breed of early American argonauts" who first discovered that a bushel of corn could make three gallons of whiskey and that those three gallons were worth more than a man could ever expect to make from corn alone. And so, we learn, bourbon became a respectable business, and the gentle art of distilling was born.

Cobb's Bird is of that particular species of "unregenerate" Southerner, a backward-looking, progress-fearing guardian of agrarian tradition. Though bourbon is his business, Bird remains a son of the soil, distilling from the corn and grains raised in his own fields and from the sparkling water taken from his own limestone springs the liquor that he mellows in barrels cut from the tall oaks at the edge of his property. The distillery itself, says Cobb, sits "right on [the old] home place," with the heavy scent of the sour mash wafting through the curtains of the family parlor. Bird knows that in the language of his Scottish forebears, whiskey was the word for "water of life," and it is through his family's "Old Blockhouse" brand of bourbon that their "sanguinary flood" continues to flow "throughout the history of the land."

History, of course, has long been part of bourbon's appeal. As Gerald Carson notes in *The Social History of Bourbon*, even some of the earliest distillers capitalized on national pride, manufacturing bottles in the shape of log cabins and commemorative flasks bearing the impressions of historical figures like George Washington and "Old Rough-and-Ready" Zachary Taylor. After the Civil War, these same distillers sold canteen-shaped decanters to old soldiers and introduced new labels like "Rebel Yell" and "Lost Cause" (the latter, says Carson, "decorated with a mourning border in heavy black") that traded on bourbon's Old South origins. "Every brand you heard of," says Cobb, "was the 'Old' This or the 'Old' That brand." "A traditional reverence for what was aged or what passed for being aged or was so labeled," he continues, "came literally to be a part of you. Likewise and inevitably, whenever men grew eloquent or women grew poetic, Kentucky was 'Old Kentucky,' the words being spoken with lingering and affectionate cadence."

Looking back, Cobb saw that what bourbon barons like Bird were really fighting against was not Prohibition but progressivism. A good example is the rhetorical "campaign of education" the colonel undertakes in the last days before Prohibition. In sketching out the details of this particular scene, Cobb drew upon the example of the real-life bourbon distiller, George Garvin Brown, who in 1910 published, at his own expense, a tract titled *The Holy Bible Repudiates "Prohibition"* that included, says Carson, "all the verses from Genesis to Revelation containing the words *wine* or *strong drink*," as well as "interpretive commentary" suggesting that the drinking of alcohol, and of good Kentucky bourbon in particular, was indispensable to those seeking the revelation of Christ.

Cobb's Bird seeks to win Southern conservatives back to "the true faith . . . the hallowed standards . . . theories . . . [and] prejudices of the Old South — good land, good family, the Democratic Party, White Supremacy and Old Line Sour Mash whiskey" — things as true, says Bird, as "gospel writ." It seems to him "a sheer moral impossibility" that bourbon, having survived war and reconstruction, should succumb at last to the teetotaling rhetoric of progress. And yet, succumb it does. The final chapters of Cobb's novel are a sober account of Bird's last days — the coming of Prohibition, his betrayal by family and friends, and his final heroic act: burning down the old distillery before the federal occupation. In the end, Bird's plea, says Cobb, is "a cry in the wilderness," the invocation of an old man in a dry country.

Cobb's veneration of bourbon and his patriotic attachment to its Southern heritage place him in the same class of Southern gentlemen as William Alexander Percy, the planter's son from Greenville, Mississippi, who forever associated bourbon with the defenses of honor and noblesse oblige he heard

Civil War veterans sipping mint juleps. Courtesy of Vanishing Georgia Collection.

as a boy. Percy was himself a confirmed julep drinker, having acquired a taste for that "delicious mess of ice and mint and whiskey" from his father and the other "Delta sages" of his youth, who routinely gathered on the front porch of the Percy home to philosophize and debate over mint juleps. As Percy recalls in *Lanterns on the Levee*, those anxious moments he spent eavesdropping

BRIAN CARPENTER

while waiting to drain the sweet nectar from his father's julep cup were his first exposure to the "relentless striving" and "sense of duty" that would later form his own character. And yet, he explains, what impressed him most when he looked back on these occasions a half-century later was not *what* his elders discussed there but *how* they discussed it, sipping their juleps, he says, like the "patriarchs of Chartres," with his mother in her summer dress "shedding immortal grace" over them like "the Queen of Sheba."

The family's traditional julep recipe becomes, in Percy's memoir, a kind of liturgy detailing the julep's precise preparations, from the proper way to powder the ice (a tricky procedure involving a towel and a wooden mallet) down to the last dash of nutmeg. The novice takes first the cup—presumably of solid silver, bearing his father's initials or, better yet, the family crest—and then the sacraments: a spoonful of sugar dampened with a drop of cold spring water; a sprig or two of mint handpicked from the garden behind the house; then the ice, powdered dry and packed tight down to the brim to soak up the whiskey—not Scotch, not rye, says Percy, but good Kentucky bourbon, "the older the better," its superior pedigree lending to the mixture that particular refinement of character that instills in the julep drinker a "calm rapture" of contentment. To waver from the ritual—to add a slice of orange or lemon or "one of those wretched maraschino cherries"—would be, he says, a "sacrilege," as sure a sign of deficient breeding as if you had stumbled in the presence of ladies with liquor on your breath. As Irvin Cobb once said of his friend H. L. Mencken: "Any guy who'd put rye in a mint julep and crush the leaves, would put scorpions in a baby's bed."

In the novels of Walker Percy, Will's nephew and literary successor, the julep myth is little more than a tired cliché perpetuated by the social-climbing nouveaux riches who bought the old home place and paid cash, dead set on restoring the South to a glory it never knew and a grandeur that never was. Yet so pervasive is the myth that almost anyone might submit to its charms, stopping on occasion "to pour a whiskey from crystal decanter into silver jigger—the way Southern gents do in the movies."

Walker Percy's last word on the subject comes in a brief essay simply titled "Bourbon" that addresses, he says, the "aesthetics of Bourbon drinking in general." Today's bourbon drinkers, Percy says, are the sons of the Sunbelt, the residual gentry of the South, languishing in the suburbs of Memphis and Montclair, where they return each day at 5:30 to nurse their feelings of transcendental homelessness with a shot of "Kentucky sunshine." They are not necessarily connoisseurs, says Percy; on the contrary, they may drink bourbon only "because too many Houston oilmen drink Scotch." But the pleasure they derive from knocking it back neat—beyond the obvious anesthetizing effect of that "little explosion . . . in the cavity of the nasopharynx"—owes less to the "sedate cumulative bliss" that inspired Will Percy's rhapsodies in *Lanterns on the Levee* than to what Walker calls that "evocation of time and memory" that induces in the drinker the realization of a "kind of aestheticized religious mode of existence."

Percy imagines William Faulkner post *Absalom, Absalom!*, "drained, written out, . . . hunkered down in the cold and rain after the hunt," flat-footing a third of a pint of bourbon and shivering, but not from the cold. For Percy, bourbon evoked memories of sneaking a snort from a "proper concave hip flask" at a UNC-Duke football game; of the "prolonged and meditative tinkle of silver spoon against crystal" resonating from Uncle Will's sunporch on late summer afternoons; and of his late father "aging his own bourbon in a charcoal keg" in the garage of their suburban home. What his survey tells us, in the end, is that even in this, the same South that defeated Cobb's agrarian dreams and exasperated Will Percy's noble pretensions, one might still find cause to invoke the amberish spirits of that "real uncorrupted essence, the true and uncontested fruitage of the corn," whose soul, as Colonel Bird reminds us, "goes on perpetuating itself, and reincarnating itself, world without end."

BRIAN CARPENTER

PLACES

Dinner at Darrington

ROBB WALSH

Benny Wade Clewis is fixing me dinner. Watching him assemble the ingredients, I'm not very hopeful: a pair of frozen hamburger patties, two potatoes, flour, a stalk of broccoli, that's about it. For spices, there's salt and pepper. "We gotta make do with what we got," smiles Benny, holding three huge pots with long handles. "We never had any skillets at home either, just ol' stewboilers like these, so this is gonna be real authentic soul food."

Benny Wade Clewis is a convict at the Darrington Unit, a Texas penitentiary. He is also something of a legend in the food world. He writes long letters to editors of food magazines, and his recipes have turned up in several cookbooks. He learned to cook from his grandmother in Palestine, Texas. He has been cooking in the Texas prison system for forty years. Benny remembers the days when black prisoners supplemented their meat ration by bringing the cook a rabbit or a possum they had caught in the cotton fields—in short, Benny is a culinary time capsule.

I'm getting a tour of the prison kitchen as I follow Benny around looking for cooking oil. A Texas Department of Corrections officer goes along wherever we go to protect my safety. As an avid student of Southern cooking, I've eaten in strange circumstances before. During my career as a cab driver, I used to stop and buy barbecue sausage in a vacant lot late at night where the rest of the crowd played a loud game of craps. I've eaten at shade-tree barbecue stands and catfish camps where you could watch the proprietor wade into the pond to catch your fish. But this was the first time I'd ever gone to prison for dinner. Unfortunately, it's the only way to taste Benny Clewis's remarkable cooking.

Black Southern cooking is a dying art. Integration ruined many restaurants where it once flourished. Outstanding black eateries like the Southern Dinette on East 11th Street in Austin were once popular with blacks and whites. They were the meeting ground of the races in the days of segregation. But these bustling black restaurants lost their steady clientele when segregation ended and the black middle class moved to the suburbs. Today, the last of the inner-city black Southern restaurants are fading away, despite a resurgence of interest in regional cooking.

Benny throws a bunch of flour into a bowl, adds some oil, a pint of milk that mysteriously appeared when a friend of his walked by, and some baking powder. He makes no measurements, and he mixes the dough with his hands. It's obvious that Benny could make biscuits in his sleep. Since he is isolated from modern trends in commercial kitchens, his cooking is unique; he has never heard of many conveniences and shortcuts. He uses few mixes, and he has no microwave. In fact, today, he can't even find a skillet. He isn't cutting down on fat or red meat—the people he cooks for do backbreaking work in the fields all day and don't have much trouble keeping their cholesterol low. He carries on the traditions of his grandmother, who taught him how to clean a possum, smoke a hog, and find sassafras in the east Texas woods. Benny is a down-home purist; he cooks like he lives on a Southern cotton plantation—which he does. Darrington sits in the middle of 8,000 acres of cotton fields, and the inmates still pick cotton by hand.

Benny is busy at the stove now, stirring a roux, heating oil, blanching the broccoli, preheating the oven, and patting out his "catheads" all at the same time. The enormous kitchen is bustling and noisy; black men in clean, white clothes sing while they carry potatoes and stir broccoli in sixty-gallon pots with paddles the size of boat oars. There are bars and cages on the windows, barbed wire out the back door, and every scrap of food is padlocked. But Benny doesn't mind. He is the king of the prison kitchen. The other men who work there stop by to observe his technique as he chicken-fries my hamburger. He sometimes teaches classes in commercial cooking for other inmates.

Benny tried applying for a cooking job at the Hilton Hotel in Fort Worth once when he got out. When asked about his experience, he would only say, "I cooked here and yonder." He didn't think he'd get hired if they knew he'd been in prison most of his life—but without references, the Hilton wouldn't hire him anyway. So he tried a few chain restaurants, but the instant mixes and modern commercial kitchen apparatus intimidated him. He felt he couldn't compete. "I just know how to cook from scratch," Benny says, showing me his brown roux.

He calls my attention to the change of water he gives the broccoli. "Gotta 'bleach' your broccoli in berlin' water first to raise the bugs—lookit here," he says, fishing a green winged insect out of the first pot. "Tha's a 'stinky Jim.' If you crush it, it gon' stink like a skunk." This broccoli is obviously fresh from the field. Like most of the ingredients in the Darrington kitchen, it was grown on a prison farm. "Back in the old days, we only ate what we grew on the farm. We'd grow peanuts and send them to 'Bama, and they'd send back peanut butter. We'd grow sugarcane and send it to Imperial Sugar, and they'd send us back our sugar." Benny recites the names of the ten Texas prison farms clustered in the fertile flatlands south of Houston and tells me which crop each produces.

Pounding out his dough, he begins cutting his "catheads" with a plastic glass. I asked him what catheads were, and he told me that catheads were what got him started cooking at the Gatesville School for Boys in 1952. "When I got to Gatesville, I seen all these little black dudes running around in the kitchen. They had they little blue jean pants on and they little blue shirts and they was clean, they was real clean.

"I said to one of the dudes, 'What is that right there?' He said, 'That's a cathead.' I had them catheads on my mind all night. They called them that because they looked like a cat's head. They was tight and round across the top just like this." He shows me the biscuits as he slides them into the oven.

In the reform school, the fifteen-year-old Benny did everything he could to get transferred to kitchen duty, where everyone wore clean clothes and biscuits were free for the taking. Eventually he got his chance, working under a retired cook from Fort Hood named Tucker. "He was one hell of a cook," says Benny. "He taught us how to cook soul food—ham hocks, pinto beans, oatmeal, grits, greens, corn, rice, and catheads."

Benny batters some french fries in egg, flour, salt, pepper, and an ingredient he makes a show of concealing. "Us chefs always got to have our secret ingredients"; he winks as he throws the fries in the hot oil. Benny's first adult prison was Central Unit Number 2 in Sugarland, one of the oldest penitentiary complexes in the Texas prison system, the "Sugarland" made famous by Leadbelly's song, "The Midnight Special."

One day, Captain Montgomery, a warden there, observed Benny in the kitchen standing for hours diligently fanning the flies away from a pot of beans he was cooking. Montgomery was so impressed that he arranged to have Benny transferred to his house for duty as his family cook. Over the years, Benny has worked for a long line of wardens' families, learning "fancy cooking," as he calls it, along the way.

Benny has borrowed some yellow food color from the bakery, and now he is making a "cheese sauce" for my broccoli out of flour and butter and yellow dye, which he adds to my finished plate with a flourish. He serves me my dinner in the warden's dining room. He has battered the hamburger patties and chicken-fried them. They are served smothered in brown gravy with battered french fries and broccoli in "cheese" sauce with biscuits on the side.

The catheads are among the best biscuits I've ever had. The hamburger, fried while the patties were still ice cold, is crunchy on the outside, moist and pink in the middle. Since Darrington raises its own beef, the meat is very fresh, flavorful, and more coarsely ground than commercial ground meat. The battered french fries are excellent; I guess the secret ingredient is cayenne. The "cheese" sauce can only be appreciated by someone who hasn't eaten real cheese in a long time, and the gravy could use some herbs. But considering the limited ingredients, the cooking is sensational.

The genius of black Southern cooking has always been to turn the most common ingredients into bold, flavorful dishes. Benny remembers a time when catfish were too expensive for his family and they had to learn to cook carp. He remembers making a stew to feed twenty out of one rabbit.

"Soul food is called soul food because the cooks had to make do with what they had. They made up for the missing ingredients by adding some of their soul," says Benny.

While I eat, Benny talks about how different it was learning how to cook for the wardens' families. "One time Mrs. Montgomery told me she was having some people coming over for the weekend and she wanted me to cook a good meal. She told me to write down what I would need from the store. I didn't know but a few things to cook, so I told her to get some rice, neck bone, sweet potatoes, mustard greens. When she saw this list she said, 'This is nigger food! I don't feed neck bones to the dog.'

"She gave me the cookbook put out by the Chicago Institute of Cooking. This was my first cookbook. I carried it everywhere I went. It was like a Bible to me. Most of the inmates would sit around the tank and talk about girls, getting drunk, stealing cars. I would sit around the tank and talk to Smokey and the rest of the cooks and steal cooking knowledge from them."

Benny worked for a long succession of wardens in his ten trips to prison. His cooking and his manner made him a coveted "houseboy" in their eyes. "I know how to do the shuffle. I know how to please white folks. Cooking is about pleasing folks," says Benny. Mopping up gravy with a cathead, I am inclined to agree. Benny Clewis is a charmer.

But Benny has also been convicted of a murder he committed while in prison. "Yeah, we was mixin' it up and I cut a guy up pretty bad," he says. With ten convictions and three life sentences, Benny is considered a career criminal.

I told Benny that I wished I could eat his cooking in a restaurant, and I asked him if looking back over his life, he didn't wish all of this could have been different. I asked him if society or the prison system couldn't have gotten him back into the mainstream somehow.

"I've been asked this question often, and I've analyzed it," says Benny Wade Clewis. "I never woulda knew how to turn a spoon if I wasn't forced to cook in prison. I wasn't really forced—I had a choice. I coulda tried to been a good cook—or went out into the fields with a cotton sack on my back, from sunup to sundown, rippin' and a-runnin' up and down those turn rows. I seen blacks dragged, I seen 'em beaten, I seen 'em stomped, I seen 'em die out in those cotton fields. I chose cooking."

Benny's eyes fill with tears as he tells me about the kindness of the wardens' families and the other black prisoners who taught him to cook. Kindness that he never found in the free world. "I think this was my life," says Benny softly. "I think this was the best thing."

Dirt Rich

RONNI LUNDY

Once Steve Smith believed in the biggest, newest tractor money could buy. He thought that was the key to making his family's farm thrive. He found out otherwise. Now Steve Smith believes in community.

You can find Steve's community any Thursday from late April to the end of November in the parking lot of St. Matthews Episcopal Church in a bustling Louisville, Kentucky, neighborhood. The buzz of the traffic from busy streets nearby can't compete with the lively conversation as individuals from some eighty-five families swap recipes and stories and meander rows of fresh produce, filling a half-bushel basket each.

In the spring, the baskets are bright with green onions, asparagus, sweet peas. By July, they are weighted with juice-filled crimson, pink, and purple tomatoes, ivory and golden kernel corn, cucumbers, crookneck squash, green beans. Watermelons have to be carried separately, as do the fat pumpkins that show up later, just in time for jack-o'-lantern and pie season. Standing around talking, cradling these, people will sometimes pat the curved bottoms absently, as if they were holding babies. Indeed, there is something almost parental in the pride you see on the faces here when a bumper crop appears.

That pride is not misplaced. Although it is Steve and his wife Karen who actually plant the seeds and tend the fields at Ewingsford Farm, forty minutes away in Trimble County, these Louisville folk have a significant part in the operation. All are shareholders in the community-supported agriculture (CSA) cooperative that provides the literal seed money and pays a part of the operating expenses for the farm. Each Louisville household pays $425 a year and for that receives fresh, organic, regionally grown vegetables for thirty weeks.

Members also have the pleasure of knowing their equity is invested in land that is being cultivated organically and sustainably for the long haul. And for many, theirs is also an investment in what they perceive is a valuable but endangered species: the small family farmer. More than once during the season, someone in the group will nod to the church that provides them space for their weekly exchange and note that those who gather in the parking lot are also a congregation of believers.

Ewingsford Farm covers 324 acres, 70 of them bottomland tucked in a curl of the Little Kentucky River and flanked by steep hills. Steve has lived there all his life; Karen came three and a half years ago when they married. One early spring Saturday, over lunch of creamy winter squash soup garnished with toasted seeds, homemade pickles, and bread, we discussed the yin and yang of successful small farming. Karen poured from a mason jar filled with deep coral liquid and said, "It's the last of the homegrown tomato juice." It made for a merry communion.

Karen is a landscape designer and thus land-focused by profession, but her connection to this particular geography has deepened as she has lived here. She's become actively involved in the local watershed-watch organization. She points to the Little Kentuck, as Steve calls it, which runs past the farm on its way to connect to the "Big" Kentucky River and the Ohio.

"I have been transfixed by this river," she says. "It has been my teacher. The first year I was in this house, it crept up to the porch, it was that full and overflowing. The next year there was not enough water in it to irrigate the crops. The following year, I was baptized in this creek."

As both Karen and Steve speak about the land and their purpose in relation to it, there is a delicate interplay between hard reality and the spirit. Steve cautions about the common tendency to romanticize the small farm or a cooperative venture such as theirs. He notes there is a risk for the members just as there has always been a risk for farmers who must try to predict and cope with the unpredictability of nature. He says that the reality of the farmer's job is simply "a whole, whole lot of hard work." But while he describes his journey to becoming an organic vegetable farmer for a CSA as one of continuous hard knocks, he makes the point that it has also been one of revelation and grace.

Steve's grandparents came to this land during the Great Depression and, despite the economic desperation of the era, were able to raise ten children — along with tobacco, corn, hay, and a garden that, with a small dairy, hogs, and chickens, sustained them through the seasons.

Steve has strong memories of the harvests of his childhood, when kin would gather to bring in the crops and preserve the produce for the winter. As kids will do, he, his cousins, and his siblings groused about the work, but he says, "We liked feeling useful, and we liked the security of being together, of being united by important work. And we liked the tomato fights."

His grandparents used draft horses to plow the land, and while his parents modernized some with the times, Steve describes them as "good small-farm

Steve and Karen Smith, home from the fields. Courtesy of Dawghaus Photography.

advocates." They, too, canned and cooked from the garden, made the clothes their children wore to school, sustained the family by their labor. But growing up in the 1970s, Steve says he was also influenced by the images of mass media, made to feel ashamed of "homemade" goods, defensive about his choice to be a farmer. He recalls a high school teacher telling him that "farming is for people who can't do anything else." He recollects the embarrassment he felt even among his FFA peers who tended to have newer farm equipment at home to brag about.

"I was buying it. I was dreaming about shiny tractors," he says with a rueful laugh. "I said, 'You just wait! I'm gonna farm big!' So I went into debt in 1986 and proceeded to farm as big as I could. Lord God a-mercy, I was justified! I had payments, and the more payments I had the bigger I needed to farm, and the bigger the farm, the more payments."

Interest rates were high, and prices for tobacco—which has for generations been the cash cow of most small southeastern farmers—were low. Following the prevailing agricultural philosophy of the time (then–Secretary of Agriculture Earl Butz said farmers should either "get big or get out"), Steve planted more tobacco and bought more fertilizers, pesticides, and equipment to increase yield.

But as the debt and the farm got bigger, Steve realized the rewards were growing less: "I was wearing out the farm, myself, the equipment."

Quixotically, he'd planted a two-acre truck farm along with his tobacco, hoping that vegetables might provide a way back to the farm of his childhood and provide a future when the bottom fell out of tobacco farming, as it looked sure to do. The vegetable farm was failing as well.

The first summer, he sold vegetables from a roadside stand and enjoyed the interaction with his customers but made no money. Then he tried trucking cantaloupe and tomatoes to stores and wholesalers in Louisville, where he had to compete with corporate produce, a doomed proposition. In the winters, he read everything he could get his hands on about small farming. He was an easy convert to organic and sustainable methods—those were in keeping with his raising. But growing food wasn't the issue. "I could *grow*," he explains; "I just couldn't *sell*."

It was in the winter of 1989 that he had the revelation that changed everything: "I was in the process of failing miserably at farming, and a friend who had been watching me flounder gave me Elliot Coleman's first book, *The New Organic Gardener*." The coastal Maine author/grower has been a leading advocate of organic farming.

"His ideas on farming resonated," Steve says, "but what caught me was a chapter on marketing." Steve thinks that because Coleman's background was not in farming, he was able to think about marketing produce in unconventional ways. "As soon as I read that chapter, I called him up and told him about my situation. He was very encouraging, very helpful. He was the person who mentioned the idea of a CSA, although he wasn't doing it himself."

Steve spent that winter planning a cooperative such as the ones Coleman described. By early 1990, he had built a greenhouse and root cellar and planted three and a half acres in thirty varieties of vegetables. It was enough to feed forty families, but word of mouth had garnered none. So he sent a letter explaining his concept to the *Courier-Journal*. The following Sunday, a story appeared in the Louisville paper with his phone number in it. By day's end, he had his 40 families—and 100 more on a waiting list.

It hasn't all been cauliflower and turnip greens since. Steve describes the first few years as constant trial and error. Some crops proved more amenable to growing than they did to the members' palates (longtime CSA members still recall "beet summer" with a little shiver). There were failures along with the successes, many in the early years due to depletion of the land. But as he has shifted to appropriate small-scale technology, replaced chemicals and manufactured fertilizer with manure and compost from the farm, and begun farming crops and grazing animals in a rotation that he brags "has the potential to confuse even the potato beetle," the land has improved visibly and dramatically and the crops have responded in kind.

Nowadays the farm grows some fifty varieties of vegetables, herbs, and flowers. This year's lineup will include newcomers globe artichokes, mustard greens, bok choy, early Bodacious sweet corn, and heirloom cabbages—if the Lord is willing and the Little Kentucky don't rise. Ewingsford Farm not only feeds some ninety families but also supports itself, netting approximately $6,000 per acre. Two other farm families, Den and Billie Berry and Steve's parents, Gus and Mabel Smith, also participate at the supply end. And as of this spring, Steve owns the farm free and clear and says, "There will be no tobacco grown on it and virtually everything will be organic."

And there are wider ramifications of success. At least one other CSA has been established in Louisville since the Smiths started, and by demonstrating there is a clientele for fresh, regional produce, Steve has had an impact on the burgeoning farm market scene in the city, providing other small farmers with an outlet for their product.

"We're not just cultivating crops, but this is also about human relationships," he explains. "Those are what we are trying to nurture and depend on in the most realistic way possible. This cooperative is about mending divisions in people in a time when we are isolated from one another and the land. We can't separate ourselves from the land and get away with it."

Then he laughs and adds that one of the most important lessons he's learned in the process is to use a different scale when measuring success. "It's not really about who's got the biggest tractor," he says. "My land's getting better. My life's getting better. I'm getting happier. There are other ways to get your benefits than cash on the barrelhead. One of the best is by growing a community."

In the 'Ham, the Hot Dog Rules

TARA HULEN & THOMAS SPENCER

The scene: St. Louis, Missouri, the 1904 Louisiana Purchase Exposition. Vulcan, the newly cast iron-ore giant, soon to become Birmingham's symbol of industrial might, is first shown to the world.

Somewhere in the Great Iron One's shadow, a Bavarian concessionaire named Anton Feuchtwanger is having a problem. He's selling piping hot sausages, and to allow his customers to eat the sausages without burning their fingers, Feuchtwanger is loaning out pairs of white gloves. But the customers keep walking off with them.

So he asks his brother-in-law, a baker, for help. The baker improvises long, soft rolls that fit the meat—and thereby invents the hot dog bun. According to the National Hot Dog and Sausage Council, that technological breakthrough made possible the true modern hot dog, the American classic. And it all happened on Vulcan's first watch.

That was the beginning of a cosmic kinship between Birmingham, Alabama, and the hot dog. Yes, New York can claim that its Coneys were the original hot dogs; Chicago is a sausage town, and no doubt its dogs are special. Birmingham, though, is a hot dog town in its own right. The BellSouth Internet Yellow Pages lists fifty-seven local restaurants under the title "Hot Dogs."

As summer begins, as the smell of sizzling dogs wafts from grills, as the vendors at the Hoover Met cry out, "Get your red hot hot dogs . . . ," it is fitting to salute the Birmingham hot dog. And there's no better place to begin than the cradle of Birmingham hot dog civilization, known far and wide as Pete's Famous Hot Dogs. The earliest chapter of Birmingham's hot dog history opened there not too long after the coining of the term "hot dog."

A sports cartoonist named Tad Dorgan is generally credited with giving hot dogs their name in 1906. According to the story, Dorgan saw vendors peddling hot sausages nestled in warm rolls during baseball games at the Polo Grounds, home of the New York Giants. The artist's rendering, apparently meant to convey both the shape and content of the sausages, bore an uncomfortable resemblance to the widely popular dachshund, and the name "hot dogs" caught on quickly, in spite of efforts by the local chamber of commerce to ban the name and its inference that the sausages contained dog meat.

Whatever the truth of the origin of hot dogs, they were widely known and loved by 1910, and they got to Birmingham soon thereafter. In about 1913, a Greek immigrant named Theodore Gulas opened a hot dog stand on Second Avenue North between 19th and 20th Streets. In the coming years, the narrow little stand—7 feet wide by 20 feet deep—would bear many names: Hole in the Wall, Louie's Place, Pete's Dining Room. But most famously, it would be celebrated as Pete's Famous.

"Pete" was Pete Koutroulakis, who in 1939, with a partner, bought the store and renamed it Pete's Famous. Pete's nephew, Gus Koutroulakis, started working there in 1948, and he's never stopped. In fact, he's rarely paused. Pete's Famous is open seven days a week from 11 A.M. to 7 P.M. Gus's first vacation was in June 1995 when he and his wife closed the shop for three weeks to visit Greece.

A few things have changed at Pete's since the early days. Back then, the floor was covered with sawdust that was swept away every night. The entrance used to be a set of swinging doors, the kind you'd see in old saloons.

Today the crowds still come, as they've been coming for decades. At lunchtime, people pack the standing-room-only restaurant. Half the space is taken up by the silver metal counter and grill, manned for the past half-century by Gus.

Still spry at seventy, he's slightly stooped from years of bending over the grill; his hair is a thin, wavy wisp of white. He can be polite, especially to ladies and children, or he can be gruff. He has a low threshold for nonsense. He also has an amazing memory for names and biographies—and especially whatever your regular order might be.

"No onions, heavy kraut, pint of milk?" he asks, peering over his glasses.

His customers crowd the small bulge of space right by the front door and stand shoulder-to-shoulder along the white tiled wall facing the silver counter. The low counter in back is the top of an icebox that was converted into a refrigerator after folks stopped using block ice.

There are construction workers coming in from the heat and bankers with their ties thrown over their shoulders or tucked into their shirt to avoid a dribble of sauce. "You'll see tuxedoes and cut-off blue jeans," says customer Rick Green. "It's just a unique atmosphere."

Green has been coming to Pete's since he was a boy. "I used to cut my grandparents' and my parents' yards during the week to earn enough to come

Birmingham's temple of haute dogs, Pete's Famous. Courtesy of Steve Kimble.

down here," he says. "I'd ride my bike in from Fultondale, catch a movie, and eat at Pete's."

If you've been to Pete's, you've likely noticed a sign promising that if you eat twelve hot dogs, you'll get the thirteenth for free. Green is one of the few brave souls to take Pete up on the offer. How'd he feel after he ate thirteen hot dogs?

"Full," Green said, bulging his eyes. "Very full."

The loyal customer base for Pete's Famous has enabled the store to survive the tide that has swept most of retail business out of downtown.

"Ain't as many people down here as there used to be," Gus says. A number of other downtown hot dog joints have disappeared completely, including the Hot Dog King and the Downtowner. And many that started downtown have migrated to the suburbs. For various reasons, a lot of those hot dog places out there have "Pete" or "Gus" or "Famous" in their names. All Gus will say to that is: "Everybody wants to get into the act."

"A hot dog tends to be a very regional thing," says Pete Graphos, who founded Sneaky Pete's with his brothers Jimmy and Sam and partner Gus Fifles. New York likes them with mustard, Texas with chili, Chicago with vegetables.

In Birmingham, the classic formula is a grilled dog, mustard, kraut, onions, and special sauce—oh, that special sauce—on a soft, steamed bun.

Jimmy Graphos says the Birmingham hot dog's peculiarity begins with grilling the dog, a much better technique than steaming or boiling.

At first, everyone used the locally produced Zeigler hot dogs and the Birmingham-made Home Baking Company buns, that is, before the company stopped making hot dog buns. Pete's Famous still uses Zeigler hot dogs (the red Zeigler wiener is the best-selling in Alabama). Zeigler began making hot dogs in 1927 with a plant in Bessemer; the family-owned plant is now in Selma. But the crowning glory on the unique Birmingham hot dog tradition is the secret sauce. And there are four principal lineages to Birmingham's hot dog sauces.

The earliest was developed by Theo Gulas at his stand on Second Avenue North. He passed the recipe on to his son, Aleck Gulas, who used it when he started his chain of Dino's Hot Dogs, named for Aleck's brother-in-law and business partner, Dino Jebeles.

Years later, when Pete Koutroulakis had moved into Theo Gulas's old location, he created the sauce for Pete's Famous, which remains imitated but never copied.

A third strain of sauces comes from Gus Alexander, who for years operated the Hot Dog King on 20th before starting the Gus's Hot Dogs on Fourth Avenue North (still open today). Gus shared his recipe with his nephew, George

Pappas, who opened the Gus's location in Crestline Village. Pappas also sold the recipe to a few other authorized vendors.

According to Rick Davis, owner of the Gus's in Inverness Corners, his shop has the original recipe, but early on, Alexander didn't trademark his name and sauce, so there are some faux-Gus sauces.

The fourth strain is Sneaky Pete's sauce, now dominant because of the proliferation of the chain. It came from a recipe used by Pete and Jimmy Graphos's father, Ted, and their uncle, John Collins, who ran the Lyric Hot Dog stand downtown. The Lyric is still open in a different venue and with different owners.

"It's a Birmingham-style hot dog sauce," Pete Graphos says. "It's a tomato-based product; it's not hot like Mexican products, but it's spicy, very tasty."

Don't think you'll get the secret recipe, but Graphos and others offer a few hints. The sauce is sort of a Greek-influenced spin-off of the barbecue sauces favored around Birmingham—tart, not sweet, and a bit hot. There's a dose of cumin, like chili, and the sauce is thickened with flour or cornstarch, depending on who's stirring it up.

There are fans of the great sauce traditions who have tried to create their own imitations. Phil Locasio, who owns Phil's Famous and used to be a Sneaky Pete's franchisee, says the Birmingham sauce is elusive. "The sauce doesn't have any taste until you put it on the dog; I don't know why," Phil says.

Locasio will readily 'fess up that his own sauce isn't his favorite. That honor belongs to Pete's Famous, whose sauce is more vinegary. Phil has tried and failed to copy it. (Vinegar and cayenne pepper are the only two ingredients Phil will reveal about his own sauce.)

Once dominated almost completely by the Greek community, the Birmingham hot dog business is now passing into other hands. Money made selling hot dogs sends the next generation into the legal profession, into medicine, into high-powered business. The story of Jimmy's is a prime example.

"It was the smallest place in town," owner Jimmy Sarris says, describing the original location of Jimmy's, where for twenty-four years he served as many as 500 dogs a day out of a 12-foot-by-7-foot slot in the old City Federal Building.

This truly was a hole in the wall. "It was supposed to be for an elevator but it wouldn't fit," explains son George, a college student at UAB.

In 1966, like many other local Greek restaurateurs, Jimmy Sarris emigrated from Greece and went to work at his brother's popular restaurant, Ted's Old Hickory Barbecue. "It's more easy for me, because I don't speak English," the friendly Jimmy explains in his very-bruised-if-not-broken English. "You don't have to have an education to make hot dogs or mop the floor."

In the downtown Birmingham of the 1960s and early 70s, things were buzzing. Jimmy rattles off the theaters and stores that used to draw people downtown until late into the night—the Melba, the Empire, the Alabama, Loveman's, Pizitz. All kinds of people waiting for buses would rush in for a hot dog—quick, cheap, and easy to eat on your feet. You had to stand at most places, like a narrow Jimmy's and Pete's Famous.

"I used to stay busy all day, *all* day. Was open 7 to 7." He got his four kids an education that way; the oldest is now an accountant, but he's still in the family business, working for Empire Seafood and Niki's restaurant downtown.

"My kids now, they can do anything they want," Jimmy says proudly. But through all the years and all the transmutations of the hot dog lineage, the question remains: Why are hot dogs so hot in the 'ham?

"I think it's because they were all available, and it was a good, hot product that was very tasty," Pete Graphos says. "You can depend on them being the same. It's almost like a snack instead of a meal."

Brother Jimmy Graphos, who still runs his own place—Jimmy's on Sixth Avenue South, not to be confused with Jimmy's on Fourth Avenue North—says Pete's Famous and Gus's downtown were so good they started a tradition.

"It all stems back to Pete's Famous. . . . Everybody grew up on Pete's Famous," Jimmy Graphos says.

Parents who worked or shopped downtown took their kids; now those kids go back for nostalgia. When Pete's is gone, that will be the end of that style of shop, Jimmy Graphos says. Today's building codes wouldn't allow that design.

Eventually, the hot dog joints expanded, mostly over the mountain and around other residential shopping areas where the people and traffic were moving. The franchised Sneaky Pete's sold out to Benny and Frank D'Amico about 1990. Sam Graphos now operates Sam's Super Sandwiches in Homewood, and Pete sells real estate for Brigham-Williams Realtors in Mountain Brook.

Sneaky Pete's is now a corporate-culture chain, with more than thirty stores in the Birmingham area and sixty total, including at least one out of state in Mississippi and with more expansion planned, says Kevin Gustin, marketing agent for the company. Ironically, the corporate dog is keeping the tradition alive, he says.

"At a time when it probably would die out, Sneaky Pete's came along and expanded it . . . to the suburbs. And it's something the somewhat insecure Birmingham is proud of and celebrates for being different from its Southern sisters. I think people, for all our jealousy of other cities . . . I think they like it that it's our little culture here. It is a part of day-to-day life."

Stalking the Wild Hog

DAN HUNTLEY

In the grainy half-light of dawn, Craig Sasser paddled his duck boat silently up a winding tidal creek deep in South Carolina's low country. A pelting winter rain had slowed to a sprinkling mist. Sasser slowly turned from the boat's bow and gave the no-talking sign by pulling his fist across his lips—we were entering wild hog country.

Soon he was tiptoeing along a narrow boardwalk through a bald cypress swamp to his homemade hunting cabin hidden in the trees. On the porch, he slid a 3-inch .280-caliber shell into the chamber of his rifle, strapped on a .44-caliber Magnum pistol, and grabbed a 12-gauge auto-shotgun, then headed into the woods.

Sasser, a wildlife biologist and low-country native, was leading nine people on a wild hog hunt on his land. Each year after duck-hunting season, he kills a wild hog to use in a family-style barbecue at his hunting cabin on an island about fifteen miles northeast of Georgetown, South Carolina.

The rain had left misty pockets on the heavily wooded island, and visibility was limited. Spanish moss lay draped like tattered flags on the leafless trees. In his camouflage jacket and tan-colored waders, Sasser soon became a blur as he crept along the mushy forest floor.

A few minutes later, Sasser held up his right hand to halt all movement. From somewhere deep in the bush came a single guttural snort, like a fat man's snore. Sasser slowly raised his rifle to his shoulder and flipped open the plastic lid on his high-powered scope. BOOM! His shot cracked through the woods like a sledgehammer smashing a board.

The thirty-two-year-old Sasser is an easygoing guy who likes to sip a cold one while telling a good dog tale by the campfire, but on this morning, he was all business. He was concerned about the rain and whether the wild hogs were on the move. He calculated that his only chance might be to get onto the island without making any noise and be downwind before sunrise, when the hogs would be feeding.

Craig Sasser (left) and childhood buddy Todd Browning (right) share a joke and a cold brew while roasting a wild hog. Photograph by Layne Bailey. Copyright 1998 Charlotte Observer.

His friend Furman Long had told him the night before about some poachers spotted in the area. They'd been capturing the wild hogs with pit bulls and then illegally selling the animals to inland hunting clubs. "I'm pretty sure we can scare up some hogs, but they're wild animals and you never can tell what'll spook 'em in this weather," Sasser said as he cranked up his outboard and headed out into the tidal creek. The rain looked like BBs hitting the water's surface.

Sasser felt extra pressure to kill a wild hog to feed the crowd that would be arriving the next day. "A wild hog is not something you can just pick up at the neighborhood grocery out here," he said with a grin. "If we're going to cook one tonight, I'm going to have to kill one today."

He looked out toward the marsh and said that with the water up high from the rain, we'd have to be on the lookout for submerged logs floating down the river. Sasser snaked down one unnamed creek after another; the marsh grass parted like a curtain and then closed in the sweeping wake of the boat.

The water widened and Sasser increased the boat's speed. He held his right hand up to the brow of his sou'wester rain hat to block the rain so he could see a fork in the creek. Suddenly, the boat slammed into a log. Sasser and his two passengers were thrown to the floor of the boat, along with gun cases, life jackets, and cameras. The prop kicked up and the engine conked out.

"Didn't see that one," Sasser said while lowering the outboard and restarting the engine. A purple bruise of light was just beginning to glimmer over the marsh grass on the eastern horizon.

We approached Sasser's island, which is surrounded by a swamp grove of knobby-kneed cypress and tupelo gum trees. We began to cross over into a no-man's zone that is neither land nor water. This unnamed spit of spongy high ground does not exist on navigation charts or county maps.

The Sasser family owns about 600 surrounding acres—mostly wetlands, with about 100 acres of uplands. The land was part of a 1730 land grant from the king of England. It was later at the heart of the rice-growing aristocracy that flourished in this region before the Civil War. Remnants of the old rice dikes still exist on the Sasser land.

Sasser slowed the boat and began to explain some of the lore, history, and behavior of our prey. "The Vanderbilts imported Russian wild boars in the early 1900s for their hunting preserve," he said. "During Hurricane Hugo in 1989, I think a good many were washed down the river. And that's when we really started seeing them here among the old rice fields."

Wild boar meat historically has been considered a royal delicacy in Europe, going back to the thirteenth century, when England's King Henry III reportedly served 200 boars at a feast. The Spanish explorer Hernando de Soto brought thirteen domesticated pigs with him to America in 1539. Over time, feral pigs and wild hogs became plentiful in the Southern woodlands, and they remain so to this day.

Whatever you call these porcine creatures, they have developed an unsavory reputation among some landowners and environmentalists. Hunting clubs imported the hogs at the turn of the twentieth century in western North Carolina and along the South Carolina coast. And due to their ability to adapt to their environment, their numbers quickly multiplied.

In the Carolinas, wild hogs are not considered game animals; in most regions, they can be hunted anytime, with no bag limits. Hogs have been a major problem in the Great Smoky Mountains National Park, rooting out endangered native plant species and competing for food with native game animals such as deer and wild turkey.

"The best place for a wild hog is over a bed of hot coals or in a skillet," said Mark Bara, a wildlife biologist with the South Carolina Department of Natural Resources. "In the wild, they can be very destructive creatures. They don't back down to anything in the woods, and they can go through a forest floor like a Rototiller." Environmentalists generally do not object to hunting hogs because they are so destructive to other animals and habitats, Bara said.

With the exception of bobcats—and man—wild hogs have no predators in the Carolinas. Consequently, they're fearless and will not hesitate to charge a human if cornered or if their young are threatened. Most wild hogs weigh between 100 and 225 pounds. A 565-pounder was killed near Fort Motte, South Carolina, in 1996, and what was thought to be a state-record 890-pounder was later killed near Coward, South Carolina. It was later determined the monster hog was pen-raised and had escaped.

Biologists say domesticated hogs will revert to the wild and grow tusks after several generations—quicker if they interbreed with Russian boars. Wild hogs have long, upturned snouts that they use to dig up tubers and plant roots. The tusks can grow up to four inches and are used to rip and maul their enemies. The curved tusks have a razorlike edge. Hunters have described hearing the tusks clicking just before a charge. When threatened, the boars toss their heads and tusks in a slinging motion and have been described as "nature's own food processor."

The male hogs also have a layer of tissue up to two inches thick on the front of their shoulders that works like armor plating. Biologists say the thick skin can stop small-caliber bullets. Sasser warns his visitors about the possibility of

Thrill of the hunt. Photograph by Layne Bailey. Copyright 1998 Charlotte Observer.

the hogs charging. We should quickly look for a tree to shinny up, not necessarily the biggest tree but one big enough to hold our weight.

"A skinny tree is a lot easier to climb than a fat one," he said. "Particularly when you're in a hurry." To say nothing about having on a pair of waders caked with marsh mud and slick as goose poop.

One of Sasser's first hunting memories is of his father hunting doves and him helping retrieve the birds from a cornfield. It was on a farmer's land, and the farmer had penned up some wild hogs to fatten them.

"I was running with our golden retriever and came around some cornstalks. And there was a mama hog with her babies and she took off after me. I knew she would tear me up if she could catch me," he said. "I was wearing a pair of my dad's too-big boots and just as she was about to get me, a friend of ours snatched me up and threw me across the fence. And my dad stared her down with his gun."

Sasser's father and grandfather were both low-country physicians. His great-grandfather, Phillip Sasser, moved to the area from Lake Waccamaw, North Carolina, in the late 1800s, helping to extend the railroad southward.

On the island, Sasser moved with the stealth of an assassin, frequently stopping to listen. The wild hogs continued rooting up the black earth and snorting, but they remained partially hidden in the bush. Sasser braced himself against an oak, waiting for one to step out for a clean-kill shot to the head. Sasser had warned us about the dangers of chasing a wounded wild hog into the marsh grass. "He'll be able to see us but we won't see him until it's too late."

After more than a minute with his finger on the trigger, Sasser squeezed off the shot. In front of us, a snarling wild hog lay still on the ground. Other hogs continued to mill about, rooting in the damp earth and clicking their ivory tusks like pairs of dice. The animals were oblivious to the downed 185-pound sow or even the approaching hunter. Amazingly quick and thick-shouldered, the hogs finally trotted to the shore and swam out of sight into the waist-high, wheat-colored grass.

"Whooooo! That's about as easy as it gets out here," said Sasser as he leaned his rifle up against a tree and examined the hog. Steam began to rise from the wild hog's black-bristled back. "With the rain and not much wind, I figured they'd be out here at first light on the high tide. But we could have just as easily been out in the mud all day and not seen them. We're lucky. . . . Let's get this hog ready for the pit."

Later, when we were sitting on the back porch of his cabin at dusk, Sasser idly stroked the Labrador asleep at his feet and looked around at his guests. "I love hunting and fishing," he said, "but lots of times I just like being out here. No phones, no honking cars. . . . It's a wonderful place. Please don't tell anyone how to find me out here."

The Watermelon Market

AMANDA HESSER

Americans have become familiar with things like blueberries from Maine and tomatoes from New Jersey, but there is some produce, like watermelon, that seems to have no origin. Watermelons are just something that you know will be there, piled high in your grocery store throughout the summer. Every day, tons and tons of them arrive in the city, just hours out of the field, and as they are dispersed to grocery stores, markets, and bodegas, all traces of where they came from disappear.

Such mystery piqued my curiosity. I set out to find some answers—to find a watermelon farm that was in the middle of its harvest. Watermelons are grown in most of the southern half of the country, but the harvest moves around, beginning in the Deep South and moving north. Pinpointing its location felt like chasing a wave, which would expand and shrink, altering its course and collapsing into froth just when I got near.

Finally I chose a spot and got on a plane headed for Savannah. I drove north from there, about sixty miles, into South Carolina. And when I pulled into Coosaw Farms, a large white block of buildings just off of a dart-straight country road near the town of Fairfax, I felt like I was right on the wave's crest.

Tractor-trailers were rumbling all around, sending up clouds of dust as they lurched back to the loading dock. On the other end of the building, old school buses, which had had their tops cut off and their seats scooped out, were domed with watermelons, waiting to be unloaded. One bus was lined up next to a conveyor with two men on top of it moving up and down like pistons as they bent over and lifted the watermelons one by one onto a carpeted conveyor belt. The melons tumbled and spun down the belt and were swallowed up by the building.

"It's cooled off a bit in New York, huh?" asked Bradley O'Neal, the owner, with his wife, Louise, of Coosaw Farms, as I entered the offices. I nodded. Indeed, the night before, a rainstorm had hit New York, extinguishing a week of blistering heat. When I left the city that morning, temperatures were in the

50s. "Yeah, we had a dip in sales this morning," O'Neal said. "We're totally dependent on the weather."

As if it were not bad enough that farmers have to worry about the weather when their crop is growing, in the watermelon business, the weather during harvest is just as critical—not only in the grower's region but in the market areas as well. South Carolina was the eighth-largest producer of watermelons in 2000 (Florida, Texas, and Georgia topped the rankings). But as the harvest sweeps northward, South Carolina is a major player in the industry, producing 150 million pounds of watermelons in a five- or six-week period. By July, fields in Florida and Texas are stripped bare, and Georgia and Arizona are skidding to a halt. By mid-July, North Carolina starts to harvest, then Missouri, Delaware, and Virginia. Then the season turns back around and heads south. In the fall, Georgia and Florida begin a second harvest.

While it seems a perfectly logical journey, in the throes of the season it couldn't be more chaotic. The watermelon industry faces an unusual paradox. It has become so large and systematic as to resemble that of a commodity crop like corn. Hybrids and advances in farming techniques have increased yields tremendously. And yet the harvest is still incredibly primitive, with melons plucked from the earth and packed by hand and each and every sale made by a series of phone calls coordinating buyers, truckers, and the weather.

O'Neal, fifty-three, a fit man with thick salt-and-pepper hair brushed to the side, took me back to his paneled office. It was abuzz with phones ringing, faxes beeping, truckers coming in to fill out forms, and Brad, the O'Neals' son, keeping a running check on sales as he guided the flow of watermelons into and out of the packinghouse.

Things seemed very busy, even overwhelmingly so. But there is a saying in the business: you never see anyone with a watermelon in one hand and an umbrella in the other. The cool weather in the Northeast had turned sales sluggish. O'Neal said, "We've got to move some melons." Buses full of fruit were pouring in from the fields, and the packinghouse, stacked with pallets of watermelon bins, was getting cramped.

He got on the phone and began working through his list of buyers, scratching notes on a pad. After an hour or so, the owner of Double Green Produce, a distributor that sells fruit to stores in Manhattan's Chinatown, took the bait, ordering a truckload. It had warmed up after the rain.

"You've got trucks moving at 10 miles per hour, your fruit's moving at 2, your buyers are moving at 50 miles an hour, and your labor is at 20," O'Neal said. "And you have to make sure they all come together at exactly the same point." If you do, shoppers can get their melons just a day and a half after

Bounty of summer. Courtesy of Vanishing Georgia Collection.

being cut from the vine. If you don't, you have rotting melons, unhappy laborers, stubborn buyers, and idle trucks.

Suddenly it began raining. O'Neal stared out the window and sighed. Louise O'Neal said, "He can handle a drought better than he can handle the rain." Trickle irrigation has allowed watermelon farmers to finely control the amount of water and nutrition a plant gets. But if it rains during harvest, the vines can get wet and rot. In fact, everything stops.

"You can't harvest when it's wet," Louise explained, "because sand sticks to the melon and scratches the skin." It seems like an odd concern. But the watermelon industry has suffered, much like tomatoes and apples have, from the American obsession with perfect produce. If the watermelons are scratched, misshapen, or blemished—even if they have a little sunburn, which they get on their top side in hot weather but which has no effect on the flavor—stores will reject them. This has given a lot of control to the stores buying the fruit. Each day, a store or distributor can pick and choose the farm they buy from and send back rejects at the grower's cost. "When the load is rejected," Bradley said, "that's the last thing you want to hear. You're lucky to get your freight."

When O'Neal's father and grandfather had watermelon farms, watermelons grew to all different shapes and sizes; they all had seeds, too. Every day, a train would pass through town. Each grower was assigned a section of the train, which they would fill by driving wagonloads up to the train car and then tossing the watermelons one by one to men in the straw-lined car who arranged them in overlapping rows like bricks in a wall. Then the train would move north to terminal markets in cities like New York.

O'Neal studied agriculture at Clemson University, where he was a split end on the football team, then spent ten years working at a bank that dealt in farm loans. When he and his wife bought land in 1980, they began with about 30 or 40 acres. Now they have 1,200 acres, a quarter of the land in watermelons and the rest in soybeans, cotton, wheat, Napa cabbage, and corn.

The trains are gone, and so are the terminal markets, at least in the O'Neals' minds. Now they deal primarily with chain stores like Costco, Wal-Mart, Stop & Shop, and Harris Teeter, where profit margins are greater. All the melons are shipped by truck, mostly in thick corrugated cardboard boxes, rather than in rows on hay.

On his father's farm, it cost $50 to $60 to produce an acre of watermelons. Now it's $1,200 to $2,000, and the prices stores pay for melons have barely budged in twenty years. Seeded melons are selling for about 8 cents a pound, plus shipping. It costs the farm 5 to 7 cents a pound to produce. "Now we've got so much invested," O'Neal said, "it's scary."

"One of the problems in the watermelon industry now are all the other competing products," said Wilton Cook, a horticulturist who had stopped in on his weekly rounds. That means everything from peaches to plums, nectarines, and guavas.

Coosaw Farms is one of South Carolina's largest growers, producing 12 million to 15 million pounds of watermelons a year. The O'Neals recently began a venture with a tomato grower on St. Helena Island, just off the state's southern shore, where the watermelon season parallels Georgia's. And next year, they may join forces with a grower in Florida. The O'Neals will deal with the sales, so that to a store like Wal-Mart, there is the impression of working with Coosaw Farms from the time the harvest begins in Florida until it reaches South Carolina.

The next day, O'Neal pushed aside a shotgun on the front seat of his truck to make room for me. "I got one this morning," he said, referring to crows, which are a big pest to watermelon crops. They peck their beaks into the fruit for a little taste and then leave it to rot. Deer are another. "It's like a salad bar for them," he said. He hunts them during season; we ate venison lasagna for lunch.

The farm runs along the Coosawhatchie River, which is where the name Coosaw came from. As we drove, we came upon a small, scruffy field, where

AMANDA HESSER

an old tenant house teeming with ivy sat in one corner and plumes of pigweed dotted the rows of vines. The field was penned in by dark loblolly pines. Though there are about 300 acres of watermelon, the fields are scattered around. "Out West," O'Neal said, "I like it out there because everything is flat and square and simple."

But the land here is perfect for watermelons, which need a sandy soil and a base of clay. For this reason, it was once a large asparagus-growing area. Commercial production of watermelons began in South Carolina in the 1870s, Cook said. There are now about 7,500 acres in production in the state. At one time, he said, there were two to three times as many acres.

The O'Neals grow three varieties. Red seedless watermelons and a classic variety called Tri-X Brand 313, which is smaller and rounder—about 16 to 20 pounds each—make up about 70 percent of their crop. Red seeded watermelons, which are oblong and a little bigger, about 20 to 25 pounds, make up the rest, with less than 1 percent consisting of yellow seedless.

We hovered over a sprawl of ruffled leaves, fuzzy vines, and watermelons. "Every watermelon has what we call a twirl," O'Neal said, pointing to a green curl of vine, much like a pea shoot. "If you see that that twirl is dried up, there's a pretty good chance it's ripe. Another way is to look at the yellow belly to see how yellow it is." He turned over a melon, which had a butter-yellow patch of skin where it sat in the dirt.

"If you tap it," O'Neal said, "and it kind of echoes, then that's a good, fresh melon. If you hit it and it sounds dead, you look for another one." Darker-skinned watermelons generally have a redder flesh, but dark-skinned melons are also more susceptible to bruising, and the color of the flesh has nothing to do with its sweetness.

To harvest a field, one crew is sent out to cut the ripe fruit. A group of twenty, some of them women, walk along, large kitchen knives in their grip, inspecting the vines and bellies. If a watermelon is ripe, they cut the vine near where it meets the melon and flip the melon over so its yellow belly is facing upward. This signals the next crew, the loading crew, to pick it up.

The loading crews, which are paid more than the cutters, are mostly Haitian and Mexican. They work in groups of nine. One man drives the shaved-off bus (which O'Neal pointed out works best because it sits low so the men do not have to toss the melons as high; it also holds a lot of fruit). It creeps along at a stroll while three men on each side spread out like the wings of a bird picking up all the yellow bellies they see and fluidly tossing them to the next person until they reach the men on the truck, who catch the melons and set them down, building a mountain at their feet. About 25 melons a minute make their way to the truck. There are about 30 such trucks on the farm, and about 80 workers.

When the melons come into the packinghouse, they spill down a conveyor belt. One man slaps stickers on as many as he can, while a row of sorters first separate seeded melons from seedless, and then sort each by size. They are placed, stems still moist, into the boxes they are shipped in and often stay in those boxes even at the grocery store.

On a catwalk above the sorters are men who assemble the boxes and drop them down as needed. On the floor of the packinghouse is a heart-stopping frenzy of forklifts, gliding in and out of one another's way at top speed, beeping and buzzing, hauling 700-pound boxes as if they were feathers.

Back in his office, O'Neal, who was just halfway into his fourteen-hour day, was rubbing his forehead with a phone to his ear. He was on hold. "Man, things are slowing down for the holiday," he said. "We thought we'd have six or eight Costco's, and only two came through. It's going to be a struggle."

The person picked up. "Hi Ken. You ready for some watermelons?"

He hung up the phone without an order.

East of Houston,
West of Baton Rouge

COLMAN ANDREWS

Me and two gorgeous Texans—a long, tall, redheaded location scout and a bright-eyed brunette photographer—are doing 75 miles an hour up Highway 59 in a dusty, white, year-old Buick Regal with the sunroof open and the ashtrays full, three six-packs of Lone Star in a cooler in the trunk, and Chris Gaffney on the stereo singing "East of Houston, West of Baton Rouge"—which, as it happens, is exactly where we are.

Bill Johnson, a lanky, fast-talking Houstonian who was born and raised in Lake Charles, Louisiana, got me into this. Johnson used to own a restaurant in Houston called Sabine, named for the Sabine River, which forms much of the Texas-Louisiana border. Though the cooking at Sabine, which closed last year, was modern American in tenor, the accents and many of the ingredients came from the territory on both sides of the river—from an area stretching from Lake Charles into the so-called Golden Triangle, defined by the Texas towns of Beaumont, Jasper, and Orange (and named, some say, for the color of the region's ubiquitous rice fields).

"A Cajun can look at a rice field and tell you how much gravy it'll take to cover it," Johnson observed to me one day over pecan-crusted pork chops at Sabine—where I found myself eating every time business took me to Houston. Then he reminded me that there are Cajuns on both sides of the river and that "gravy is what we call everything that comes off the meat: the juices, the drippings, everything." He used to tell me things like that all the time. "We ate rice at every meal," he'd say, "but potatoes were so rare, I grew up thinking they were a delicacy." Or, "Any time you stop by someone's house around Lake Charles, they'll offer you something to eat because they cook such big portions, they always have leftovers." Or, "You haven't tasted peaches till you've tasted Jasper peaches. And have you ever tried mayhaws? No? Cher, you have *got* to come down to the Sabine with me." His enthusiasm always seemed so genuine that I was sorely tempted to say yes—especially when he added that he'd bring the bourbon.

But first we sent that redhead to reconnoiter. She spent a weekend prowling around eastern Texas and western Louisiana with Johnson, ducking in and out of smokehouses, sampling everything from mayhaw jelly to crawfish étouffée on our behalf. Her report: Don't expect some entirely new and different, undiscovered version of Cajun cooking; do expect to eat lots of simple, irresistible food. That sounded pretty good to us—which is how we ended up in that Buick, on our way to join Bill Johnson.

We're cruising along somewhere outside of Livingston while Lyle Lovett reminds me musically that I'm not from Texas but Texas wants me anyway when it dawns on me that this is not like any Texas I've ever dreamed of. The terrain is mildly hilly and crowded with dense stands of pine trees, accented here and there by dogwoods, magnolias, oaks, maples, and mulberries. This isn't cattle-drive territory, Alamo-land, or cosmopolitan Austin—and it's certainly not the vast, flat plains of the western reaches of the state. This is the Texas of the Big Thicket National Preserve and the 114,500-acre Lake Sam Rayburn, where bass fishing is more cult than recreation. The Texas where the stench that drifts through the air now and then comes not from cow manure but from the local paper mill. The Texas where, in towns like Woodville, where we stop for the night, the only place to eat after 8 P.M. is apt to be the Sonic Drive-in—and this is precisely where we pick up chili dogs and jalapeño poppers for dinner, which we wash down with a few of those Lone Stars, sitting in the warm, damp air by our motel pool, talking about love and life and music.

The next morning, with Dave Alvin singing "East Texas Blues" in the background, we drive out to Jasper, where we meet up with Bill Johnson at his friend A. L. (Leon) Sunday's Magnolia Hill Peach Orchard. Sunday grows twelve varieties of peaches on about 600 trees, harvesting them from early May through mid-July, beginning with split-pit flordakings—which are glowing on the branches as we arrive. Virtually everything he and his family and friends pick is sold from the farm stand out front at $27 a bushel or $14.50 a half-bushel. (A bushel averages about fifty pounds.) "We cull them in the fields," Sunday says, "then I cull them again when I box them up in front of the customers. My theory is you don't sell anything you wouldn't buy yourself." The flordakings, he admits, are not the most flavorful of peaches, "but they get people started." They sure do: Biting into a piece of the juicy fruit, my first fresh peach of the year, I think I'm tasting paradise.

Then it's on to Gaskamp's Orchard Creek Farm, a few miles from Sunday's. Regina Gaskamp and her daughter and son-in-law, Ginger and Tracy Hillebrandt, grow blackberries, blueberries, two kinds of muscadine grapes, elder-berries, and Christmas trees, but their biggest crop is mayhaws. The Texas and Louisiana mayhaw (*Crataegus opaca*) is a small red- or yellow-skinned, yellow-fleshed fruit that tastes like a very tart apple. It makes a luminous jelly (Gaskamp's is delicious) and a sharp-edged wine, and Bill Johnson used its juice as a glaze at Sabine—but like its northern counterpart, the cranberry, it's not a fruit you'd want to just pop into your mouth.

Gaskamp's husband, Harvey, who was the county agricultural agent in Jasper for thirty years (he died in early 1999), helped develop the domesticated mayhaw in Texas, grafting it onto hawthorn roots, so it didn't have to grow in wet soil like wild mayhaws do. We watch Gaskamp's friends and relatives sort-ing mayhaws—among the last of the season. "Mayhaws come in around mid-April," says Johnson, "and the local joke is that they ought to call them april-haws because they're all gone by May."

Later that afternoon, as we pull into the parking lot outside the Lazy H Smokehouse in Call Junction, just south of Kirbyville on Highway 96, Flaco Jimenez and Ry Cooder are rumbling the door panels of the Buick with "The Girls from Texas." *These* girls from Texas—and the rest of us, too—are hun-gry, and we've come to the right place. The Lazy H—run by Velma Willett with the help of Marie Johnson and Willett's son and daughter-in-law, Paul and Jodee Willett, and her daughter, Rena Flowers—was named one of the top fifty barbecue places in Texas (where the competition is steep) a few years back by *Texas Monthly*. And when we get out of the car, the air is thick with fragrant smoke.

The political climate at the Lazy H may be gauged by a couple of bumper stickers by the cash register: "Whitewater is not over until the First Lady sings" and "If Clinton is the answer, it must have been a stupid question." The gas-tronomic climate, on the other hand, is defined by the yards and yards of smoky beef sausages and racks of pork ribs stacked on one side of the place and by the Sunday-only buffet of vegetables on the other. The day we visit, the selection includes yellow squash casserole, fried okra, fresh corn off the cob in butter, pan-smothered garlic potatoes, a mess of greens, fresh purple-hull peas (Willett brags that she can pick a bushel in sixteen minutes), cooked car-rot rounds, and Thanksgiving-style stuffing.

The main attraction at the Lazy H, of course, isn't vegetarian in nature: It's the pork sausages and barbecued beef brisket and unparalleled jerky—which is long, thick, squared-off, smoky as a smoldering campfire, and unbelievably delicious. Willett, who took over the Lazy H in 1975, is also famous for her long-smoked ham and bacon. "If I go visiting," she says, "I always take my own bacon. Everybody invites you over for breakfast if you bring your own bacon."

We sit down and basically eat everything in sight, including homemade peach cobbler and vanilla ice cream for dessert, with big glasses of lemonade on the side. I ask Willett for some recipes, for her greens, for instance, which are ingeniously plain but full of flavor. She looks at me and smiles and says, "Hell, any old one-eyed idiot can cook greens." Well, yes, I reply, but could we have the recipe anyway? Willett, who was once described in print as "a brass-mouthed woman whose witty tongue is as sharp as the knives she uses to cut wafer-thin slices of delicacy," squints down a little and says, "The only reason you might have a chance to get any recipes from me is because I don't know nobody around here who reads your magazine." Then she tells us how she does it.

It's late afternoon when we cross the Sabine River on Highway 12 out of Vidor. (East Texas joke: Why is a hurricane like a divorce in Vidor? Somebody's gonna lose a trailer.) It's hot and dusty and the beer is getting warm, but when we stop at a bait shack on the Louisiana side, they're out of ice, so we push on, cutting down to Interstate 10. Lucinda Williams is singing "He had a reason to get back to Lake Charles . . . " as we pass that town's city limits and head toward the hotel portion of one of its big casino complexes, the Isle of Capri (known over in Texas as the Pile of Debris for its mock-castaways'-island design). We check in, fortify ourselves with some of Bill Johnson's bourbon, then head for the slot machines. The gorgeous Texans must be bringing me luck: I win $230 in a couple of hours' time and, after some injudicious reinvestment of profits, still manage to walk out with $90 of it. We celebrate in the casino's restaurant, with salads all around.

We have a rendezvous the next morning with Glenn Daigle at Rabideaux's Sausage Kitchen in Iowa (that's "RAB-a-dooze" in "Io-way"). Daigle was in the home construction business until 1992, when he bought Rabideaux's from its original owners, and he now constructs a remarkable variety and quantity of smoked and otherwise prepared pork products: His twenty-five or so employees process as much as 100,000 pounds of boneless meat per month into sausage, boudin (Cajun pork-and-rice sausage), bacon, ponce (stuffed pork belly), tasso (spicy smoked pork), cracklings (fried pork rind), stuffed pork chops, and "cushon d'lait" (cochon de lait—whole roasted suckling pig). He also produces crawfish boudin and stuffed deboned chickens and turkeys (including his version of the legendary turducken—a chicken and a duck stuffed inside a turkey) and turns about 50,000 pounds of fresh-shot deer into various venison products every fall.

"Everything is smoked with oak," says Daigle. "I get it from the prison, cut by the inmates." He benefits from the law in another way, too: The county sheriff grows green onions for him for his boudin. "When I was a boy," Bill Johnson interjects, "we called it ' 'dan,' as in 'Want some 'dan, cher?'" Real boudin, cautions Daigle, isn't very spicy. "Cajun food shouldn't burn," he says. "If you taste the hot pepper while you eat it, it's too hot. If you taste it after you eat, it's just right."

Outside Rabideaux's, we find two teenagers sitting sidesaddle out the sliding door of a minivan, blithely eating boudin squeezed right from the casings. We sit down at a nearby picnic table ourselves and dig into boudin balls (skinless boudin meat formed into rounds, dipped in milk and flour, and deep-fried) and plump, crisp, lightly spicy cracklings until we feel not unlike stuffed pork chops ourselves.

On the counter at Rabideaux's we'd noticed a pile of sweet potato turnovers ("sweet-dough pies") wrapped in aluminum foil. These, we'd learned, are made for Daigle in the nearby town of Lacassine by Delsie Vital, whose daughter Helen works for him. Through her intercession, her mom agrees to show us how she does it. We pull up to Vital's neat little house, where she welcomes us into her kitchen, not sure what all the fuss is about. "What I know comes from my mom," she tells us. "She'd make pies in a cake pan. I try to make them small, but sometimes they come out bigger. I don't use a knife. I'm old-fashioned all the way." As we watch, she rolls out her dough, her hands cloaked in surgical gloves, trims the excess with the side of a fork, then uses the same fork to crimp the edges. "Mostly I just make these for my church," she adds.

We ask what else she cooks. "Weekends," she replies, "I make jambalaya, chicken, roast, corn or peas, rice with gravy . . . " We start wondering whether we could somehow talk her into showing us how to prepare one or two of these dishes, but our faces must give us away because she quickly adds, "Don't even *think* about it."

Terry Allen sings "Gone to Texas" as we cross back over the Sabine and head for Beaumont, where Melanie Dishman, a friend of a friend, has promised to make us a traditional crawfish étouffée.

Dishman, who has a degree in speech communication from Beaumont's Lamar University and years in the catering business, is now development director for KVLU, her town's public radio station, and lives in a handsome, art-filled town house that could be situated in any good-size city in America. But her family owns a farm in nearby China, where they grow soybeans, blackberries, and rice, and Dishman grew up eating "great fried chicken, Sunday roast with rice and gravy, and lots of crawfish. Around my house, if

Delsie Vital at work on a sweet potato turnover. Courtesy of Laurie Smith.

you didn't peel crawfish fast enough, you didn't get any. If you had a sore thumb, it meant you'd had a great afternoon." Texas Cajuns eat pretty much the same food as their Louisiana counterparts, she tells us, as she starts chopping celery, green peppers, onions, and the tops of some green onions for her étouffée. ("What do you do with the white parts?" I ask her. "Oh, I just put them in the refrigerator until they get rubbery, and then throw them away," she cheerfully replies.) But a good étouffée, Dishman adds, isn't easy to find. "When I started ordering it in restaurants," she remembers, "I thought it would be like my mother's. But so many people use tomato products in it, which is just wrong. I can look across a room and tell if an étouffée is one I want to eat." (Hers, as it turns out, is most definitely the one we want to eat, and eat it we do, blissfully.)

Later, outside Dishman's house, my roadworthies and I say good-bye to Bill Johnson, punch up Johnny Copeland rhetorically asking, "Houston, won't you let me come home?," and drive off together toward that very city, happy and full.

Isleño Pride

GENE BOURG

For much of the thirty-mile drive south from New Orleans to lower St. Bernard Parish, the sensation that prevails is one of descent—even though the terrain is iron flat. Rising from the mists along the Mississippi River, which runs parallel to and mere yards from the road, are live oak, dwarf palmetto, mimosa, and bald cypress. The air is different down here—damp and heavy, with smells that evoke the memory of old things: weathered wood, attic-cured paper, decayed vegetation. Every so often, a landmark resembling some vestige of a forgotten civilization materializes—a bare brick chimney standing starkly in an overgrown field, a sagging house tangled with muscadine grapevines.

We're headed to the marshy homeland of one of the least-known ethnic groups in this country: the Canary Islanders of St. Bernard. Even though the Isleños—"islanders"—have lived near New Orleans for more than two centuries (roughly as long as one of the state's most familiar cultures, the French-descended Acadians or Cajuns), few people in the city know that the Isleños are Louisiana's largest Spanish-based culture and have made rich contributions to its culinary heritage.

The cooking that thrives within the frame bungalows and ranch-style homes of St. Bernard is based partly on foods brought here long ago in the holds of Isleño ships—olive oil, garbanzos, rice, potatoes, garlic, cheese, olives, honey, almonds, mirliton (chayote), lemons, and wine. The region's marshes, part of the richest fishing grounds in North America, yielded shrimp, oysters, crabs, and turtles, as well as ducks; rabbits and deer were hunted on higher ground. The Isleños became superb farmers, too, growing exceptionally flavorful fruits and vegetables—notably tomatoes and citrus—in the fertile soil and near-tropical climate of the Mississippi River delta. All this bounty was also transported to the bustling French Market in New Orleans, where it was to prove indispensable to the creation of south Louisiana's cooking.

Today, pots on Isleño stovetops simmer with recipes that reflect the influences of the region's surrounding cultures, including Cajun and Creole. A few

Isleño staples have a direct Canary Islands provenance, and others, like paella, trace their lineage to mainland Spain, having been brought to Louisiana either by the Isleños themselves or by the generations of Spaniards who emigrated to the region beginning in the mid-eighteenth century.

In south Louisiana, the cultural-culinary stew is a rich mix of all the communities that have settled the region for centuries. For instance, Creoles (the New World–born descendants of Louisiana's original Spanish, French, and African populations) brought their culinary traditions to bear on locally grown ingredients like Native American corn and filé (ground sassafras leaves), okra from Africa, and cayenne chiles from the Caribbean to create their famous gumbos. Jambalaya, another hallmark regional dish, may have West African roots; it may also have been inspired by Spain's paella—which likely arrived during Spanish rule in Louisiana (1763–1803). French-speaking Acadians from Nova Scotia, or Cajuns, who began coming in the 1760s, borrowed ideas from other communities, too, producing such south Louisiana specialties as étouffée. (In general, Cajun cooking is affiliated more with the countryside than with the city and tends to be simpler than Creole cooking.)

The Isleños were just as open to the exchange of ideas as the Creoles and Cajuns and today cook gumbo and jambalaya, too—but with an Isleño spin: both dishes are likely to contain more seafood than they do elsewhere in Louisiana. Overall, Isleño food uses olive oil, not butter or lard. Certain dishes are common, many of them a blend of French Creole, Canarian, and mainland Spanish influences. Chayote stuffed with shrimp or crab, marinated shrimp, and arroz con leche (rice pudding) all have Iberian or Gallic roots. Caldo, the hearty Canarian-style vegetable and meat stew that is the flagship Isleño dish, has changed very little over the centuries since it was first made on Louisiana soil.

In the St. Bernard Parish town of Poydras, inside the small, tidy house that Irvan Perez shares with his wife, Louise, the kitchen is fragrant with the scents of rice, tomatoes, shrimp, and crab, elements of a cuisine Louise inherited a half-century ago from her husband's grandmother. Louise is Sicilian American but has been immersed in Isleño culture since she married Irvan at seventeen, almost sixty years ago, and she is known as one of the best traditional cooks in the community. "She's not really Italian anymore," says Irvan with a grin. "We sort of adopted her as an Isleña." Around their simple wooden table one afternoon, we taste Louise's potato-onion omelette—an obvious offspring of Spain's tortilla de patatas (except that Louise adds shrimp, too). She hasn't quite finished the other dish, the classic Isleño stew called caldo, so we cluster around her stove to watch.

A hearty bowl of caldo. Courtesy of Chris Granger.

The recipe serves thirty-five "or more," says Louise as she raises the lid of an enormous stockpot filled to the brim with onions, carrots, corn, green beans, turnips, and potatoes that have been simmering with white beans and pickled pork. "I spend all morning chopping and slicing and cleaning up. Then I spend all afternoon dividing the caldo among my daughters, their kids, and our neighbors." The recipe, says Louise, is also Irvan's grandmother's—"only they couldn't afford so many vegetables, and usually had only corn, white beans, potatoes, and cabbage." She gently adds cut-up yams, explaining, "I cook these separate and put them in last because they kinda break up."

The caldo looks ready—but no, there's one more thing to do. "I'm talking, an' I'm forgetting," says Louise. "The last thing you put in is green cabbage." She sprinkles in a bowlful of coarse shreds and gives the pot a stir. Later, at the table, Louise serves the meat and vegetables on a platter, the broth over steamed white rice in individual bowls; then we pile the meat and vegetables on top. A forkful of pork, a bite of turnip, a hot slurp of rich broth: Louise's caldo is a carnival of bright colors and soul-warming, diverse flavors.

As we eat, Louise and Irvan tell us about a lunch they had while visiting the Canary Islands years ago at a restaurant on Lanzarote, where they were served a specialty called puchero, a stew of meat and vegetables, including corn on the cob. "The hosts told us they were going to feed us something we'd never eaten before," chortles Louise. "And it was caldo! Down here, we've been eating that since the 1700s."

The Perezes are unofficial ambassadors of Isleño culture. Louise gives demonstrations of Isleño cooking at fairs and festivals in New Orleans and once even gave one at the Smithsonian. Irvan, a retired shrimper and aluminum-plant worker, has become the Isleño spirit incarnate, fluent in Spanish dialect, an accomplished woodcarver, and one of the few remaining singers in St. Bernard of the ancient Spanish narrative ballads called décimas, which he has performed at Carnegie Hall. Like many in their community, Irvan is determined to keep alive a heritage whose connection to the Canaries had, at one point, nearly vanished.

Between 1778 and 1779, more than 2,000 Canarians were dispatched from their homes, a cluster of seven Spanish-ruled islands lying forty-five miles off the coast of Morocco, to south Louisiana by the Spanish government. Their mission: to strengthen the Spanish presence in a region newly ceded by France. (Another, smaller group of about fifty Canarians had been sent to found San Antonio, Texas, in 1731; many of their descendants still live there.) The new immigrants, as well as later Canarian arrivals, created several settlements in southern Louisiana, but their Spanish heritage slowly blended with the French Creole, Acadian, Native American, and Anglo-American cultures that swirled around and into the Canarian communities; surnames like Dominguez and Rodriguez became Domingue and Rodrigue. Only St. Bernard, the most isolated of the communities, kept aspects of its culture — particularly the (un-Spanish-named) towns of Yscloskey (wye-KLOSS-kee), Reggio, and Delacroix (DEH-la-crow) Island.

Yet by the early 1900s, even this remote area was beginning to lose its identity. The Spanish-speaking Isleños had no written tradition, only an oral one, and when English was mandated in schools in 1916 — and Isleños went to work in the burgeoning oil industry of the 1920s, run by English-speaking Texans and Oklahomans, and fought in the country's wars — their own language, customs, and culture began to erode. Bertin Esteves, now sixty-nine, comes from a family of farmers, hunters, and trappers and grew up without ever realizing he was an Isleño. "It wasn't until I went to Spain and Portugal, in my thirties, that I learned to pronounce my own name — it's 'es-TEH-ves,' but at home we used to say 'es-TEAVES.'" By the early 1970s, fewer and fewer Isleños in the parish spoke Spanish. And although the old Canarian dishes — puchero (caldo) among them — were still being cooked, their origins were gradually being forgotten.

In the late 1960s, Frank Fernandez, a school principal and the newly appointed St. Bernard Parish historian, who had researched the region for years, traced the Isleño community's origins to the Canaries. To help preserve that link, Fernandez urged Irvan Perez and several others to form the Los Isleños Heritage and Cultural Society in the town of St. Bernard. "Even as a kid at the age of ten," explains Perez, "I could see that our way of life was changing. We needed to keep our heritage." The society formed in 1976; soon afterward, Fernandez contacted the regional government of the Canaries, which invited him and a small group of society members — including Perez — to visit.

Today the society has hundreds of members, runs a museum and cultural center, and hosts several events a year at which local folk wear the brilliantly colored costumes of the Canaries. A second society, the Canary Islands Descendants Association, formed five years ago, with Perez among its founders, and has just opened its own museum in Caernarvon, in the northern half of the parish. The Canarian government has shown great interest in the Isleño community, sending representatives to visit St. Bernard and even giving the parish the gift of a Spanish teacher for several months. Steadily and surely, people here are becoming fascinated by Isleño history, genealogy, customs, and language (Isleño is in effect an eighteenth-century Canarian dialect of

Spanish, with borrowings from American Spanish, Cajun French, English, and Portuguese).

The new Isleño pride is especially evident in the kitchen. St. Bernard matrons vacationing on Grand Canary or Tenerife are hopping from restaurants to shops there, seeking out new dishes to sample or cookbooks to take home. An across-the-fence conversation today might touch on papas arrugadas ("wrinkled" potatoes) and whether a cabbage leaf should be placed atop the little new potatoes as they cook to help them steam or whether they should be served with a red mojo (a hot sauce made with red chiles) or a green one (of green chiles and cilantro or parsley). Last year, the Los Isleños Heritage and Cultural Society even published *Los Isleños Cookbook*, a collection of community recipes.

As you drive farther down into St. Bernard, the land gives up more of itself to water. Birds are everywhere. Snowy egrets and elegant blue herons flutter up from the tall, deep green marsh grass. Curved-bill ibises and long-necked cormorants wind-sail overhead. Birds for eating—gadwall, mallard, and teal ducks—glide through these waters, too. Trapping for muskrat, otters, mink, and raccoon, once a well-paying winter mainstay, virtually disappeared when the market for furs dried up, but hunters still go after the deer and rabbits inhabiting the sparse woods.

At Yscloskey, on the banks of Bayou la Loutre, dozens of vessels—for fishing, shrimping, crabbing, and oyster farming—bob along the piers: canoelike pirogues, used by trappers and duck hunters; Delacroix skiffs, shallow-draft boats with butterfly nets for scooping up shrimp; and tall-masted trawlers, big enough to carry several tons of iced shrimp.

Near the bayou, Charles Robin Jr. and his wife, Celie, live in a small cottage built on stilts to withstand flooding. The front rooms are festooned with Charles's intricately detailed models of boats like the ones outside, mementos of his years of shrimping and oyster harvesting. A couple of years ago, Charles retired and gave his trawler to his son, Charles Robin III, but Celie still says proudly, "He was a fisherman at eleven years old, taken out of school and put on the boat." Both Charles and Celie feel rejuvenated by the revived interest in their Spanish heritage. During the Blessing of the Fleet in August—an event meant to ensure the fishermen's safety—Charles helps his son string marine flags from deck to mast top. And Celie has thrown herself into her work as a docent at the Los Isleños Museum: "I think it's great. I tell them what I experienced in my life as an Isleño, how my husband used to build boats and how we used to go trapping, and what the marsh was like—and I think they learn from that." Celie cooks Isleño specialties like the marinated shrimp she learned to make from her husband's Isleño father. It's a wonderful, tangy jumble of fat pink shrimp, minced garlic, herbs, and olives, with a simple dressing of olive oil and vinegar.

The marinated shrimp—or escabeche, as current parish historian William Hyland says the elders of the community used to call it (although Celie doesn't recognize the term)—is one of the dishes she brought to the Los Isleños Heritage and Cultural Society's unveiling of a new community center last August. Scores of locals arrived in the showy striped skirts and crimson vests of the Canarians. A group of teenage girls skipped and bowed in the traditional dances of the islands, the *isas* and the *folias*, and fisherman Jerry Alfonso sang a *décima* or two. Arranged around everyone were tables covered with hand-sewn, Canarian-style textiles and laden with papas arrugadas (and both red and green mojos); mirliton halves stuffed with shrimp and topped with a buttery blanket of bread crumbs; steaming cauldrons of caldo; a paella strewn with bits of chicken and string beans; ensaladilla, a Spanish-influenced potato-tuna salad; chunky mugs of arroz con leche; and squares of turrón, the Spanish almond-honey candies. For libations, William Hyland ladled out a dazzlingly good sangría made with a recipe he coaxed from a Spanish consular official. And Dorothy Benge, the society's president, mentioned with immense pride that references to the Isleños were finally being included in state-approved school history textbooks.

Somewhere, the ghosts of a multitude of long-deceased Isleños had to be smiling.

A Sweet and Soulful
South Carolina Tour

. . . .

MATT LEE *&* TED LEE

It started nearly ten years ago, when we left our native Charleston, South Carolina, to attend colleges in the Northeast. New England's fall colors were dazzling, but not enough to distract us from the fundamental questions that came to mind whenever our stomachs growled: Where are the briny boiled peanuts? The lemony fig preserves over hot biscuits? The watermelon-rind pickles? The Goo Goo Clusters?

We sent home for care packages but soon exhausted our parents' patience and budget — two children in college was bad enough, they said. We joked that upon graduating we'd become mail-order grocers to expatriate Southerners.

Then, five years ago, we both found ourselves in New York City, suffering postcollegiate doldrums. Ted was on the run from two years in book publishing that felt like twenty. Matthew was using his art history degree to fetch iced lattes for a talent agent. And we were still hungry. So with the printer Ted had been given for graduation, paper we hand-cut from shopping bags, and Matthew's 1952 Singer sewing machine to bind the pages, we put out the first issue of the Lee Bros. Boiled Peanuts Catalogue.

Passport-sized and personal, it's an insider's sourcebook for authentic Southern foods, especially roadside staples: the sometimes homely, always earnest and boldly flavored condiments, candies, and canned items found at fewer and fewer country stores, farm stands, and grange fairs. We've been hustling to keep up with orders ever since. To us, there's nothing more satisfying than sending Southern treats to people in far-flung places. Tell a Minnesotan who thought she'd never taste anything like her grandmother's pickled peaches that two quart jars will be on her doorstep the next day, and you've made a friend, okay, a customer, for life. Perhaps the best part of our job, though, is the research — exploring South Carolina, rooting out undiscovered delicacies, touching base with suppliers, and finding material for our book, tentatively titled "Endangered Foods." In it, we hope to spotlight some of our favorite things to eat, such as cane syrup (especially in its purest state, as produced by farmer Robert Layfield of St. Matthews, South Carolina); canvasback duck, a particularly tasty species; and the state's famed Carolina Gold rice, recently saved from extinction by Savannah ophthalmologist Richard Shulze.

Our home region, the coastal low country, is rich with the bounty of the sea, salt marsh, and farm. But one of our favorite areas to explore is the rich, mysterious, and underappreciated interior, the up country of South Carolina, where roads trace old cowpaths through tobacco fields and you can pass six sensational barbecue stands in less than an hour. Last fall we set out on a road trip for business and pleasure. Here's how it went.

We always want car snacks, so on the way out of town we stopped at our favorite boiled-peanut stand, Harry's, on Johns Island, fifteen miles south of Charleston. There we bought a couple of pounds of this hot, wet delicacy—simply raw peanuts boiled in saltwater. People in South Carolina, Georgia, and northern Florida adore the beanlike taste. Aside from their addictive flavor and beguiling aroma, boiled peanuts are associated with a particular outdoorsy, take-life-as-it-comes, often anticommercial attitude that is endangered in the New South, with its Wal-Marts, nationally televised golf classics, and gated communities. We're convinced that boiled peanuts still have an important cultural role to play, crossing both racial and social lines and reminding us that the best things in life can come in slippery, messy packages.

Eating a boiled peanut is a bit like eating lobster; it releases its brininess when you crack it open, so have some napkins or a towel on hand to mop up. Just about the only way to get boiled peanuts is by spotting a roadside vendor. So if you ever see a sign for HOT BOIL'D P-NUT or the like, hit the brakes. And if the opportunity never arises—or, better yet, if you develop an addiction—we're always happy to take an order.

It's difficult to say where, exactly, the upstate begins. As children, we thought it was anything fifteen miles beyond Charleston. There's a point on rural Highway 52, about an hour and a half northeast of Charleston, where you notice that the sand-swept roadsides have given way to thicker stands of pine and broader vistas of open, leafy tobacco and scrubby cotton fields. In another hour and a half, you're in prime tobacco country, and the air is rich with the heady fragrance of the fields and curing warehouses. Several times we got stuck behind trucks piled high with tobacco bales shedding leaf fragments right and left.

A spunky network of small towns in this tobacco corridor have banded together to turn their brick downtowns and long history of tobacco farming into a draw for road trippers. Latta has a bright, diverse collection of galleries on a revitalized Main Street (don't miss Eddie Watson's Different Strokes gallery or RJK Frames & Things café and art store). The town of Mullins recently opened the Tobacco & Farm Life Museum in a restored train depot. We were surprised to find ourselves so intrigued by the displays of planting and harvesting implements, gorgeous archival photos, and a six-foot-tall wax tobacco plant in full flower. But after all the luxurious smells in Mullins, what we really wanted was to taste the "sweet scotch" snuffs we kept spotting on convenience store shelves. We chose three brands in beautifully labeled tins: Peach, Rainbow, and Tube Rose. We thought snuff was sniffed, until we read the warning: "This product may cause lip cancer." Peach's label claims it's "sweet as a peach," but we thought it tasted just like licorice. Rainbow reminded us of berry drink mix. And Tube Rose had a flowery sweetness, more lavender than tuberose. Yuck!

Another much smaller industry in this part of the state is the bottling of Blenheim ginger ale. A classic South Carolina beverage, it has a hot chili-pepper and ginger flavor and the clean body of soda made with cane sugar (as opposed to the corn-based sweeteners found in big-time sodas). Blenheim also recently revived three vintage fruit flavors in lurid colors: Bee Gee Strawberry, Grape, and Orange. We can't get enough of them.

Blenheim is bottled in the shadow of South of the Border, a noisy, tacky Mexican-themed pit stop in the town of Hamer, right where South Carolina meets North Carolina. It's a complex of six restaurants, two pools, a miniature golf course, and fourteen gift shops stocked with things like bawdy hats, plastic dog doo, and bamboo back-scratchers. We bypassed the rest and headed straight to Pedro's Country Store, the only place within miles where you'll find ice-cold bottles of Blenheim.

For total immersion in a Southern-deluxe Victorian fantasy, we stayed at Latta's Abingdon Manor, a stately 1905 yellow brick mansion with an Oriental-carpeted porch. It's a hoot. We passed through twelve-foot-tall cypress doors into a hall so lofty it reminded us of Grand Central Station. The design similarities end there. The manor's bracingly air-conditioned anterooms and parlors are chock-full of mirrors and nineteenth-century knickknackery. Patty Griffey, co-owner and decorating genius, led us upstairs to the Red Room, a decadent chamber with crimson walls, brass fixtures, and other full-blooded flourishes. We detected her sassy humor at work: a Japanese geisha doll was propped on the bed, and reposing on the mantel was a dime-store bust of

Michelangelo's David looking as if he'd dipped into the champagne that Patty puts out for guests.

After a deeply restful night on a featherbed and a delicious (candlelit!) breakfast of goat cheese omelettes and fresh pineapple, we were on our way. But before we'd cleared tobacco country, Matt was pulled over for going 63 in a 45 mile per hour zone. The officer, puffing a half-lit Marlboro he evidently did not want to extinguish, gave us a friendly warning. Thank you, Philip Morris!

As you drive from the eastern part of the state to the center, tobacco and cotton fields yield to row upon row of low, lush shrubs with tiny purple flowers and hairy pods clustered beneath the leaves. Soybeans may not be the first commodity that comes to mind when you think of the South, but they're big business here, sold not only for food products but also for industrial oils. Mature soybean pods resemble pea pods (their cousins), though soy kernels, top-heavy with protein, taste richer, less sweet, and not so beanlike.

Salty boiled soybeans, a snack much like boiled peanuts, are an Asian staple, particularly in Japan, where they're called edamame. We're nearly as crazy about boiled soybeans as we are about boiled peanuts and believe there's great potential for them here. They're currently available only in Japanese restaurants and in Chinatown markets. Hoping to further the cause, we stopped in St. Matthews to meet Mary Jo Wannamaker, subpresident, as she calls herself, of her father-in-law's vast soybean and seed-crop empire. Lately the Wannamakers have had Japanese characters on their minds and rolling out of their fax machines. Among the first South Carolina farmers to recognize the "tofu potential" slumbering in their fields, they've tapped into Japan's huge market for fresh, edible soybeans. Mary Jo described the five varieties they grow, the most intriguing being the shotgun-pellet-size Natto and the large black soybean, which she said is used ceremonially. She agreed to supply us with her best soybeans for some kitchen experimentation and promotion. One mission accomplished.

The tidy hamlet of Boykin in neighboring Kershaw County is just a clutch of old whitewashed buildings in the middle of prime hunting forest and soybean fields. There's a church, a broom factory, a general store, a restaurant, and one of the state's last remaining gristmills. The setting is breathtaking: ibis and egrets soar above the 400-acre millpond. The baying of hounds echoes from the woods, and the millstream gurgles. The place has gravity, too: it's the site of the last Civil War battle fought in South Carolina, in 1865, when a few hundred Rebels tried to interrupt the plans of 2,000 federal troops, including the famous Massachusetts 54th Infantry, which ultimately prevailed that day.

As a tractor buzzed nearby, we clambered up the mill's three flights of rickety stairs to the attic. Darts of daylight shot through gaps in the wallboards to illuminate cast-iron gears, millstones, wooden chutes, and hoppers. We luxuriated in the chicken-feed aroma of corn flour, metal, and wood.

The Mill Pond Restaurant, converted from the original post office and other structures, is the main reason people make their way to Boykin. We started with wild boar tenderloin and robust, pebbly-textured yellow grits (ground next door). Stone-grinding is key, as it preserves the essential oils and fugitive flavors of fresh corn. Salsa and chips might be a cliché, but chef Greg Sheppard's spicy sweet potato chips and black bean salsa reinject life into the formula. Sheppard garnishes his salsa with a show-stopping Cajun inspiration you have to taste to believe—fried, pickled okra. Buttery grouper with a dollop of crabmeat on top was a superb entrée, but the biggest revelation of the evening was a frozen white chocolate terrine veined with pistachios and rum-soaked sun-dried cherries. Occasionally, they cook like this in the country!

Invoked breathlessly by waiters in the best Southern restaurants, Clemson Blue is South Carolina's most recognized locally produced cheese. Legend has it that Clemson Blue is aged in caves in the mountainous northwest corner of the state—and the legend is so pervasive that a restaurateur only ten minutes from the cheese-making site earnestly told us that the aging "cave" is an abandoned pre–Civil War train tunnel. We suspected she didn't have the story absolutely right, so here in Oconee County's dairy country, we sought out Stan Guinn and Jeanette Hanberry, who manage Clemson University's cheese production. They patiently led us through the many steps of the process, and the truth came out.

In 1940, a professor at Clemson, a land-grant agricultural college, experimented with blue cheese using milk from the university's 200 cows. He and his crew did, in fact, age the cheese in the fabled train tunnel for more than a decade, until the walls began to crumble. In 1958, the operation moved to a campus lab in the "Ag. Sales Center," where students line up for malts, milk shakes, and Clemson Blue (also available by mail order).

In the humid cheese-making room, a spick-and-span, tan-tiled bunker, we saw the two 300-gallon, stainless-steel vats where, on Tuesdays and Fridays, four workers set the curds. They then form the cheese in perforated stainless molds called hoops, dipping it in wax and setting it on wooden shelves in the "tunnels" (ha-ha!), the walk-in refrigerators the cheeses live in during the six-month aging process.

We bought a broad wedge and couldn't resist trying it, even at 10:30 in the morning. We broke off hunks and eagerly ate them. It's a deliciously youthful and creamy blue. With it we drank what we had on hand, a lemony, medicinal soda called Dr. Enuf, and we can't deny it—that was one fine breakfast. We had picked up the Dr. Enuf nearby, at Gandy's General Store. It's been bottled in the mountains of east Tennessee since 1949 and might be the only soda brazen enough to make nutritional claims, fortified as it is with vitamins B1 and B3 and potassium iodide, plus pearlescent mystery specks. Enuf was enough—we'd reached the limits of South Carolina and acceptable taste; it was time to head back east.

If you've never had a muscadine, you're missing out on half of life. This humble grape is not only delicious, it's a fruit to be proud of—a native American varietal that Thomas Jefferson once hoped would put the European competition to shame. It didn't quite turn out that way, and in fact, you have to search pretty hard to find muscadines outside the rural South. But because it was harvest season, which extends from August through October, we found them at nearly every farm stand and market we passed. In the coastal South, these grapes are often called scuppernongs, named for the popular strain that originated near North Carolina's Scuppernong River. Some South Carolinians also refer to them as bullets, perhaps because the soft pungent pellets make excellent ammunition for food fights. Whatever they're called, muscadines have an especially grapey flavor (wine snobs would say they're "foxy," meaning musky), with notes of gardenia and honeysuckle and a supersweet, almost bananalike finish. The green-gold leathery skin is not recommended eating. You hold the grape in your mouth and apply pressure until the juice and the slimy core pop out. After enjoying the initial waves of flavor, you perform a ballet of teeth and tongue to separate seeds from pulp. Be sure to squeeze the skin a second time to get the best part of the grape, the delicate nectar that clings to the inside.

Muscadines, like figs and pecans, are often microcultivated by backyard enthusiasts looking to turn their bounty into a little extra cash. Three Star Vineyard, in the horse country near Aiken, is one of the few large farms dedicated to the growing of muscadines (called scuppernongs here). Well before we could even see Three Star's fifty acres of fields, we smiled to each other as we caught the grapes' alluring honeysuckle aroma. The softly undulating vineyards were as manicured as the front-doorstep plots of the Sauternes châteaux.

Ken Hutchins, who runs the farm, greeted us cordially with his wife, Ann, though it was clear they had better things to do than give tours. Portable phone in hand, Ann was orchestrating a time-sensitive sorting operation in-

Scuppernongs, fresh picked, musty and sweet. Courtesy of Matt Lee.

volving twenty-or-so workers who transform skids of just-picked clusters into pretty, unblemished twenty-two-pound boxes. During harvest, work begins early in the vineyards and continues well into the night at the sorting barn. Wasps were orbiting the pails of culled grapes that get sold to drive-up customers, who turn them into a simple and occasionally superb sweet wine.

We can't imagine better-tasting grapes than Three Star's, and we should know—Ann gave us one of the twenty-two-pound boxes, which encouraged many spontaneous acts of generosity during our return trip, with enough left over for scuppernong daiquiris and sorbet.

Rural Highway 61, a leafy two-laner that parallels the old train route from Aiken to Charleston, is our preferred way back to the coast. Every fifteen miles or so you come upon a picturesque whistle-stop town with a train depot and post office and sometimes a small Piggly Wiggly grocery store. We also choose this road because it passes through Denmark, home to one of the state's finest farmer's markets. The honey sold here is harvested from an active hive encased above the cash register and connected by a hose to the clover fields behind the market. A friendly and knowledgeable gaggle of seniors shell the butter beans (also known as limas) as they chat. We stocked up big-time on purple-and-green-streaked "pink-eye" beans, slick green butter beans, and enough boiled peanuts for the two-hour drive home.

Our favorite thing to do after a long drive is to plant our toes in cool evening sand, so we headed forty miles south of Charleston to Edisto Island. We arrived just as the sun was setting over Edisto Beach, a quiet six-mile stretch popular with fossil hunters. Edisto remains largely uncommercial, though longtime residents wistfully invoke the time before the arrival of the BP gas station. There's only one place to eat on the beach, the Pavilion Restaurant & Coots Lounge, also known as Bobo's. Bobo (Robert Earl Lee on his birth certificate) is a combination outdoorsman and gastronome—a hunter who knows where to forage for wild chanterelle mushrooms and a chef who stages oyster roasts for 1,000. His restaurant, a comfy bungalow on stilts, serves the best, freshest bouillabaisse we've had in America. His seafood gumbo is full of fish and spice. And his buttery smoked Gouda grits would convert the stubbornest grits detractor.

A day after our return to Charleston, before Ted left for Iowa City, where he moonlights as a graduate student in fiction writing, we went out for one last meal. He has a fear of flying and worries that every preflight meal might be his last, so it was no surprise that on the drive to the airport he steered us to Martha Lou's Kitchen, a pastel-pink cinder-block hut on Morrison Drive, fifteen minutes south of Charleston International. It may not be grand, but we'd send kings and queens to Martha Lou's.

Immediately inside the screen door, you find yourself at a counter overlooking Martha Lou Gadsden herself. She works two venerable gas stoves at once, dropping freshly battered pork chops and fish fillets into the fryer and ladling peppery, creamy butter beans studded with ham hock onto plates. Everything savory at Martha Lou's bears the smoky, salty flavor of ham hock, so grab a large Styrofoam cup of iced tea from the old Coke fridge in back.

If you have a morning flight, you might try Martha Lou's traditional

Charleston breakfast of fried fish on a bed of grits. But give yourself plenty of time—you'll have to compete for booth space with the stevedores from the downtown port. And although all of Martha Lou's creations are available to go, resist the urge. The experience of eating her handiwork direct from the kitchen is one that, yes, even mail-order guys will admit, can't be packaged and shipped.

Dinner with Moth

BRETT ANDERSON

My first taste of Galatoire's came in the form of soufflé potatoes. I'd never encountered the oblong beauties before, and as I dipped each one carefully into a small dish of Creole béarnaise, our waiter brought out the rest of our appetizers—crab maison, shrimp remoulade, fried eggplant—each plate balanced expertly along his forearm.

It was early January, a Friday lunch, and I had lived in New Orleans for less than three weeks. I couldn't have hoped for a better introduction to the stately old restaurant. My dining companion, an old-line regular, was well-known by the staff, who treated us like senators.

My friend handled all of the ordering duties without ever looking at a menu. For our main course, he deferred to the waiter, who steered him to a veal chop and me to trout meunière, dishes rendered with the sort of faith and precision that Ella Fitzgerald brought to Cole Porter.

The brabant potatoes were nearly as delicious as their soufflé cousins (let's be honest: are any potatoes really as delicious as those crispy poufs?), and we washed it all back with iced Sazeracs and brandy milk punches. Cocktails at lunch!

I've since learned to love New Orleans, but I've rarely felt the intense, amused appreciation that I felt that day.

A week later, I hosted my first visitor. Gordy Aamoth—or Moth, my personal favorite of his many nicknames—was a high school buddy with whom I remained close through and after college, our friendship fueled by shared pasts, interests, and acquaintances, as well as by our close proximity to each other on the East Coast.

This was not someone with a strong interest in cutting-edge food; I'd seen him thrown off his game by a menu that didn't offer plain old steak. A banker by trade and, in some ways, by disposition, Moth nonetheless appreciated the implication of power that typically accompanies fine dining. He was also one of the most joyfully conversational people I've ever met. He flat-out loved to be, as he put it, "involved" — code for being close to the fun.

So while we didn't eat there when he visited in January, I told Moth about my Galatoire's lunch partly because it helped illustrate what little I knew about New Orleans at that point — a side of New Orleans I wanted to share — and partly because I knew he'd like the place. We stopped in for a drink, just to check it out, and made plans for his return trip this fall, a trip that was to be centered around a Louisiana State University football game and a soup-to-nuts Galatoire's expedition: a Friday lunch followed by no plans, just in case we decided to order another Sazerac or three and stick around for dinner.

Moth could accurately be described as a "sharp dresser," a phrase few people would use to describe me. He wanted me to buy a new suit for our meal. "Anderson!" he howled when I talked to him a few weeks back about trip logistics. "We need to do this right!"

From the beginning, my hope was that Moth and I would have an experience roughly akin to my first. He'd told me several times about a restaurant he particularly enjoyed in New York. It was not a famous place (I forget its name), but he enjoyed the fact that the staff knew him, that he could simply tell the waiters to bring out whatever looked good — just as my friend did at Galatoire's.

Most of all, of course, my intention was for the meal to be entertaining, and at first blush, I recognized the quality of entertainment that Galatoire's could provide us. One of the joys of riding into middle age with friends from the pimple years is that you see the kid in one another even after the visual evidence has faded. A restaurant critic in New Orleans? My source of pride was Moth's source of amusement, and that reality would be our centerpiece at Galatoire's.

Moth understood this when we stopped in to look at the classic room downstairs, with its heavy curtains, classic cuisine, and uniformed waiters. Moth had a taste for these things, but he also had a taste for the absurd. Our dinner would be both fulfilling and funny. The waiters would never know that beneath our thirty-something exteriors we were still just seventeen.

A lot ran through my head on September 11 as I watched both towers of the World Trade Center crumble on live television, knowing somehow in my heart that Moth was not, as he often was, away on business but in fact at work on the 104th floor of Tower 2. In those first few hours, I couldn't help but personalize the catastrophe to make it more digestible. I was specifically heartbroken that we'd never share a plate of those potatoes. I was angry, too, angry at the monsters who did this terrible thing.

When the date of my planned dinner with Moth arrived, I decided to go on to Galatoire's, hell-bent on eating the meal that the terrorists tried to take away. My girlfriend gamely stood in for Moth. I knew that creating something akin to my first experience would be hard, and it was.

But it was still an epic meal, and not just because it took a surprising amount of determination to stage it. Even when it's hitting just half of its cues, Galatoire's is a place where adults are given license to have corny fun, and we tried our best to get into that spirit. While poking forks into cool, firm, remoulade-coated shrimp, we enjoyed the fruits of a strange irony: For the first time since the tragedy occurred, we talked about something else. It took trying to wish Moth back into existence to forget that he was gone.

But the oblivion didn't last, thankfully. As I unfurled the inevitable Moth tales for my girlfriend, his memory gained flesh, which was the goal. I was not going to let terrorists keep me from dinner with my friend.

BRETT ANDERSON

SOUTHERN
FOODWAYS

The Southern Foodways
Symposium
An Overview from the Editors
of *Cornbread Nation*

The essays that follow are representative of what transpires at an annual gathering called the Southern Foodways Symposium. We first staged it in May of 1998, throwing open the doors of the Center for the Study of Southern Culture at the University of Mississippi in Oxford in hopes that someone would come. We were surprised: They came in droves. That first symposium sold out by early April. In 1999, we moved the symposium to the month of October. (The actual date depends on the University of Mississippi football schedule; home games soak up all available accommodations in Oxford, so we meet when the team is on the road.)

Nowadays, we like to think of the gathering as both an old-home week for Southern food folk and a forum for intellectual discourse. And, oh yes, we also eat very well. If you have not been able to attend one or more of the symposia—or if we sold out before you could snag one of the 100 or so spots— here's a taste of what you missed.

The 1998 gathering was a seat-of-the-pants affair, staged on a miser's budget and propelled to success by the great good will of an energetic band of attendees, speakers, and sponsors. We took as our topic "The Evolution of Southern Cuisine," and among the featured participants and topics covered were Norma Jean Darden, who presented a play based on her book *Spoonbread and Strawberry Wine*; John Egerton, who spoke on race, class, and food in the South; Barbara Ensrud, who delighted us with a "short cultural history" of Southern wine; and Betty Fussell, who read from her remarkable book on corn.

. We have chosen to include Jessica Harris's talk on the origins of soul food as emblematic of the weekend. Jessica explores how food functions as a marker of identity, both for born-and-bred Southerners and those who claim a family lineage of long remove.

For 1999, we chose the theme of creolization. Not solely Creole, as in Louisiana, but a lower-c creolization, as in an exploration of how, in the American South, myriad cultures and cuisines came to combine and complement. From a large roster of speakers we welcomed to Oxford in October of 1999, here are a few highlights: Leah Chase, "What It Means to Cook Creole in New Orleans"; Lolis Eric Elie, "Creole Feast: A Voyeur's Tour"; Damon Lee Fowler, "The Upright Anglo-Saxon Spine of Southern Cooking: The Pudding Factor, or, 'What Got Creolized'"; Vertamae Grosvenor, "Nyam, a Folk Opera"; and Ronni Lundy, "Shuck Beans, Coal Camp Spaghetti, and Oyster Fries: Roots and Routes of the Foods of the Mountain South."

We ate well that year—as we do every year. Featured foods included Ed Scott's sandy-brown fried catfish, chef Steve Zucker's modern interpretations of traditional Louisiana cooking, and burbling kettles of pilau, the prized stew of the South Carolina low country. But perhaps the best thing we tasted that long weekend was the sweet potato pies that Kathy Starr baked and handed out at the close of her talk. A transcript of Kathy's talk, drawing upon the text of her newly reissued book, *The Soul of Southern Cooking*, follows.

For 2000, we left the South behind, launching an examination of what happens when Southerners—and Southern foods—travel north, and west, and across the Atlantic. Though the symposia are programmed with the idea that academic inquiry forms the backbone of each gathering, we strive to not take ourselves too seriously—and with that in mind, we welcomed humorist and novelist Roy Blount Jr. as our keynote speaker. Other presenters included Ted Lee on the "secret life" of the peanut; geographer Richard Pillsbury, who examined the migration of Southern foods north and west; and William Rice, who gave a remembrance of Craig Claiborne.

As funny as Roy was, Peter McKee may well have stolen the show that year. The Washingtonian showed up in Oxford with his banjo in tow and his tongue planted firmly in cheek. A transcription of his presentation follows.

In 2001, we explored connections between the working of the land and the joys of the table with our theme "From Farm to Table." Prior to the symposium, we struck a deal with the University of North Carolina Press to publish excerpts from the symposium in this inaugural edition of *Cornbread Nation*. The roster for the symposium included Pete Daniel on the Southern farm; Glenn Roberts on growing and milling heirloom varieties of corn; Sam Bowers Hilliard on those Southern essentials hogmeat and hoecake; and Tom

Rankin on Crystal Springs, Mississippi, the American Tomatopolis. Three pieces drawn from the symposium—Lu Ann Jones on farm women and egg and butter money; Courtney Taylor on the sweet potato; and Karen Hess on okra—are presented here.

The essays that follow are as good a glimpse into the life and ethic of the symposium as we can construct. We hope you will find them illuminating and entertaining. And be on the lookout for the 2003 edition of *Cornbread Nation*. We plan to showcase presentations from the 2002 symposium, the theme of which is "Barbecue: Smoke, Sauce, and History."

Your Greens Ain't Like Mine—
Or Are They?

JESSICA B. HARRIS

There is much to be said about the distinctions among the cuisines of the South and even more to be said about the vast and (until recently) unheralded contributions of Southerners of African descent to the Southern kitchen. Your greens ain't like mine—or are they? The question is still very much open for discussion and debate. The whole notion of what is black and what is Southern is a thorny issue, to say the least—and all the more so when addressed by a black Northerner who is caffeine-sensitive enough not to be able to drink vast quantities of iced tea at all meals.

Over the years, I have learned just how Southern my Northern upbringing was, and I think that it is important to begin by making the point that the custodians of many of the old ways of African American foodways are also to be found in the ghettos of the North. My grandmother grew her own collard greens and peanuts in a small plot behind the projects, made her own lye soap on the stove in her apartment, and used Calumet Baking Powder and Alaga Syrup with the best of them. The only spanking I remember receiving as a child resulted from my not being able to come home from the neighborhood grocery with the proper kind of streak-of-lean for the greens. Heretical as it may be, my paternal grandmother made the South a state of mind and not a geographical compass point for me.

Up North, the South is recaptured in conversations, in codes, and in cuisine. I can remember living in Manhattan's Greenwich Village for twenty years and making pilgrimages on the A Train to purchase greens and okra in Harlem. As the years went by, a supermarket opened up north of 14th Street that sold greens, but the neighborhood was a Hispanic one, not a "mainstream" one. Many Southern staples were (and to a certain extent, still are) considered exotic by the same folk who carp and scream if fresh ginger, radish sprouts, and cilantro are not stocked by their favorite purveyor. I now live in

A cart full of collards. Courtesy of John T. Edge.

Brooklyn's Bedford Stuyvesant, and these items are readily available at my local greengrocers. I can find okra, ham hocks, mustards, collards, and even fresh black-eyed peas and raw peanuts at local stores—and all of that and more when I venture to one of the trucks that dot my 'hood and are full of sausages and hams and other Southern delicacies that have been brought for Up-South patrons by Down-South merchants. Is this solely a black experience? In the urban North, probably. The question is, what is it in the South? Are the foodways as separated as some claim?

Whose greens are whose? Consider if you will these words that I received in a letter from Jeanne Park, a white Southerner and former home economics teacher who read my book *The Welcome Table* and was kind enough to take pen in hand to write. She defines herself thusly: "I am proud of having grown up as a Bible-Belt Southerner, even though I am not proud of the bigotry toward African Americans that existed as I was growing up and still exists in some of my family members back down in Alabama even now. Everyone was not like that, as you well know, and all of us in the South had many shared parts of our lives—such as our cooking styles." Here, I think she hits on the crux of the matter—shared lives and shared cooking styles.

She continues, "Our recipes are similar in a broader sense than having a black cook, because we didn't. I didn't know how many foods came from Africa and I appreciate that. Life without black-eyed peas and okra (only fried) would not be so good." She also speaks of the sharing of recipes within her own family: "So much of life centers around the kitchen. One memory— the only biscuit cutter I remember was a Calumet Baking Powder can with both ends cut out. Now I have a kitchen full of gadgets, but I still cut biscuits, rolls, and cookies with a Calumet can. My sister and I scratched our fingernails upon each other's blackboards all our days at home. But one of my most tear-jerking memories was going into her kitchen and finding—yes, her own Calumet can!"

Where does black food (Dunbar food, to use Ishmael Reed's term, which I prefer to "soul food") stop and Southern food begin, or vice versa? The question is a difficult one, indeed one that is virtually unanswerable—for to answer it would be to attempt to decipher the complex intertwining of race relations in the region and indeed in the country. For example, if a child who has been raised on butter beans as prepared by the African American housekeeper (or Mammy) craves them as an adult and perhaps even prepares them for her own offspring and then contributes a recipe for them to a cookbook, is that recipe then African American or simply Southern (which in this case means white—oh Lord, I said the "w" word!)? Eugene D. Genovese, in *Roll Jordan*

Roll: The World the Slaves Made, argues for the culinary despotism of the slave cabin over the Big House in the antebellum South. Food historian Karen Hess reminds us in her afterword to *What Mrs. Fisher Knows about Old Southern Cooking* that "in the antebellum South, any house of pretension had skilled slaves in the kitchen. The white mistress may have taken an interest in the kitchen; traditionally she supervised the making of bread and desserts, as well as the preservation of various foods in the winter. But she never actually toiled in the kitchen. The excruciating labor and the 'stirrin' of the pots' were done by black women cooks."

The African influence is clear. It is evident in recipes like Martha Washington's one for gumbs, a West Indian dish, a recipe that takes its name from one of the Bantu words for okra, *quingombo.* Emily Wharton Sinkler of South Carolina's circa 1840s recipe for winter pea soup calls for black-eyed peas and a seasoning piece of smoked pork and also hints at confection by African or African-inspired hands. Certainly this is true for the plantocracy, but what of the rest of the population? The privations and upheavals of the uncivil Civil War and its aftermath account for some of the confusion as the culinary social order was turned topsy-turvy. This was one consequence, as described in a 1987 social history, *Southern Food:* "With no access to the expensive imported products they had once used freely, these white homemakers and the black women who cooked for them were thrown back on their own resources. They responded by practicing economy as impressively as they once had practiced extravagance—and this time, the black women were the teachers."

Simply put, and continuing with Genovese's metaphor, the sharecropper's cottage or the housekeeper's small apartment maintained its culinary dominance over the house on the hill, and the culinary legacy became even more confused. Today the notion of shared lives comes into play for all, and the question remains: Where does one tradition stop and the other start?

I'd like to suggest that rather than attempt to delineate individual cuisines, we look at the divergences in traditions. This can best be done by looking at three elements. First, there is the possibility of using cookbooks as texts. This only leads so far, as the African culinary contribution was one that was maintained via the oral tradition. While some of the late nineteenth-century and early twentieth-century cookbooks do pay homage to the culinary inspirations of the African American cooks, it is often done disparagingly, as in *The Kentucky Housewife* (1839), or with nostalgia for the good old days when Mammy was in the kitchen making all of those wonderful things, as in *The Picayune Creole Cook Book* (1900).

The other two methods are more complex, yet also yield a rich lode of information. They are an examination of the African culinary matrix that would have influenced the cooks who originated on that continent and an examination of similar cuisines in areas of this hemisphere where the common thread is not European colonial power but the history of enslavement—the idea being that if some of the same dishes turn up without there having been the prevailing colonial influence, the influence may well be that of the African continent.

The examination of the African culinary matrix is problematic, for with several notable exceptions (Louisiana and the Gullah regions of South Carolina and Georgia come most immediately to mind), the African origins of many of the enslaved peoples who populated the American South have not been studied. It is possible to trace New Orleans cala to certain parts of Liberia and perhaps Nigeria and to trace South Carolina's red rice and hoppin' John to particular districts of Senegal, but here there is much work to be done, and transformations that have taken place over the years must be taken into account.

More important to our current examination, though, are some of the cooking techniques that were and are extensively used on the African continent, for they are among those that influenced and still influence the cooking of African descendants not only in the United States but throughout the hemisphere. The late William Bascom researched the cooking of the Yoruba people of Nigeria and determined that they had six basic techniques: boiling in water (when pottery is sufficiently developed); steaming in leaves; frying in deep oil; toasting beside the fire; roasting in the fire; and baking in ashes. With little variation, these techniques can be seen in the cooking pots of the entire African continent and most certainly in those of the western segment—the point of origin for most of us of African descent in the Western Hemisphere.

From its beginnings as a trickle in the seventeenth century to its tidal wave proportions in the eighteenth to its ebb in the middle of the nineteenth century, the trans-Atlantic slave trade sent millions of Africans across the water to become, eventually, African Americans. All brought with them in their heads and their hands the foodways that would transform the tastes of the hemisphere. Here it is also possible to suggest that there are more than a few similarities in dishes of African origin throughout the hemisphere, notably the preparation of composed rice dishes; the creation of various types of fritters and croquettes; the use of smoked ingredients for seasoning; the use of okra as a thickener; the abundant use of leafy green vegetables; the abundant use (some would say abuse) of peppery hot sauces; and the use of nuts and seeds as thickeners. The matrix was fixed.

JESSICA B. HARRIS

These African culinary tendencies turn up throughout the South and indeed throughout the African Atlantic world and in many cases have become prized there as well. Think, if you will, of the hoppin' John of South Carolina, or the red beans and rice of southern Louisiana, or the riz au pois rouges of Haiti, or the hoppin' John of Bermuda, or the Moros y Cristianos of Cuba — or even of Brazil's feijoada (and that's only a very abbreviated list). In the matter of frying, a mention of fried chicken should suffice, but I'll yield here to Karen Hess again. In a discussion of the numerous croquettes that are found in *Mrs. Fisher*, she reminds us, "It is generally accepted that black women were adept at their confection and frying." Think then of the calas of New Orleans, the acaraje of Brazil, or the festival of Jamaica. The use of smoked ingredients as seasoning ranges from dried smoked shrimp, which are necessary to the preparation of many Bahian specialties, to smoked pork, which some folk in the United States have unsuccessfully attempted to replace with turkey wings.

Wherever okra points its green tip, Africa has been; 'nuff said. Think callaloo, gumbo, and soupikandia. Leafy greens turn up throughout the hemisphere in everything from Brazil's efo and couve to the collards, mustards, and more that are consumed daily right here. And as for hot sauces: Take a quick browse through any supermarket in the ghettos of Boston and New York or the open markets of Port au Prince, or from Bahia to Benin to the nearest black restaurant serving Dunbar food, and you'll find the chiles and hot sauces there. Whether it's called mojo picante or pimienta malagueta, Red Devil or Crystal, it's a silent witness to virtually all African-inspired meals of the hemisphere. (Here, I'm referring to the period B.C. — before chileheads. The proliferation of chile lovers has certainly confused this issue.) Finally, there's the use of nuts as thickeners; think of Brazil's xinxin de galinha and of Haiti's cuisine du Nord and you have your answer.

Another item could be added to this roster when referring to this hemisphere since it really is not seen on the other side of the Atlantic: the exaggerated use of sugar — refined sugar. Sugar has become a testimonial of wealth (perhaps as a result of its scarcity in the days of enslavement). African American sweets are therefore sweeter than those of the European American population. There is a whole discourse to be given on pralines, pinda cakes, peanut patties, and prasle de cacahuatl, but not here, except to say that the peanut pattie — like the fritter, like the use of leafy greens — is a hemisphere-wide phenomenon and more than likely an indicator of Africanity. Consider Brazil's pe de moleque and Curaçao's pinda, as well as New Orleans's praline, which was probably also prepared with coconut and colored with cochineal in its original form.

Certainly, the history of enslavement and the African hands that turned spoons in the pots of Big House kitchens are at the core of many of the tastes of the South. That the dishes seeped into the matrix of the South's culinary culture over the decades, if not centuries, is not surprising. Remember that while many Southern households did not have slaves in the antebellum period or even servants in the period after Emancipation, the proximity of life was such that traditions remained intertwined. Up until recent memory, this has continued, with generations of black housekeepers who raised white children, nursed the ill, and cared for the elderly of families not their own, more often than not accompanying those duties with lavish ministrations of love and of the African-inspired dishes and seasonings of their own homes. This was brought startlingly home to me as I traveled the country on a book tour for *The Welcome Table.* A large number of folk took me aside and revealed that the comfort foods of their childhood were not those prepared by their mothers and relatives but rather those African American dishes lovingly confected by their housekeepers. This food has triumphed over adversity and is a living testimonial to the role that African heritage has played in the building of the cuisine of the South and its heritage of hospitality. In short, your greens ain't like mine, but mine have nurtured us both for centuries.

The Soul of Southern Cooking

KATHY STARR

My love of cooking started early. I was learning from my Grandmama by the time I was five years old. That was in the late fifties. She had a café called the Fair Deal, located over on Blue Front, across the railroad track in Hollandale, Mississippi. Blue Front was a string of little cafés where everybody gathered on the weekend. It was the only place blacks had to go to get rid of the blues after a week of hard work in the cotton fields. Everybody lived for Saturday night to go to Blue Front and get a whole or half-order of buffalo fish or a bowl of chitlins. (People didn't like catfish then like they do now.) As soon as the fishermen came by with the big buffaloes, Uncle Ira would get out in the back and start cleaning them.

My grandmother, who everybody called "Miz Bob," would always start a Saturday night with 100 pounds of chitlins and 75 pounds of buffalo. Once the people started drinking, the hunger would come, and before eleven o'clock all of the fish and chitlins would be sold out. They would be eating those hamburgers and flatdogs—fried bologna sandwiches—too.

During that time, beer was legal. The hard stuff wasn't. But if you wanted a half-pint or a pint of whiskey or corn liquor, you could get it at the Fair Deal because Grandmama and the chief of police had an "understanding," which was as good as a license to sell. The chief had his way of coming by. He'd get his little tip, and then we'd put the liquor on the table. The Seabirds—what we called the Seeburg jukeboxes—would be jammin' all up and down Blue Front with Howlin' Wolf, Muddy Waters, and B. B. King. Sometimes they would be there in person, over at the Day and Night Café. The great blues singer Sam Chatmon came to the Fair Deal often. People danced, ate, drank, and partied 'til the break of day. There was always a fight on Saturday night. But the people always knew that no matter how drunk you got, you couldn't fight in Miz Bob's café. If you wanted to fight, you stepped outside and knucked it out.

My grandmother served dinner in the middle of the day. She considered it a disaster if dinner wasn't ready by twelve noon. A lot of her regular customers

211

were farm and oil mill workers. The section workers on the Y&MV Railroad (Yazoo and Mississippi Valley, later merged into the Illinois Central) were regular boarders. They paid her every two weeks when the railroad paid off. The girls at the pressing shop were regulars too.

Every morning about 5:00 A.M. my grandmother put the dinners on. I remember crossing the railroad tracks on cold November mornings. The wind would be howling, and pecans rattled down on the tin roofs of the shotgun houses. Sometimes you could hear the towboat whistling out on the Mississippi River, fourteen miles away. We'd pass the cottonseed oil mill. Whenever it was running, it always smelled like they were making ham sandwiches or cooking fried chicken. The compress was running too, day and night, pressing those bales of cotton. When I'd get over to the Fair Deal, I'd crawl up on top of the drink box under the counter and go to sleep to the steady thumping and hissing of the compress. And I'd nap until the good smells and sounds woke me up—big pots of greens and vegetable soup simmering on the stove and Grandma stirring up the cornbread.

Grandma got her love of cooking from her mother, my great-grandmother, Frances Bolden Fleming. Everyone knew her as Aunt Frances. In the 1890s, my great-grandfather, David Fleming, and Aunt Frances sharecropped on the Friley place, a little way down the railroad track from Hollandale. They lived in a big, tall house set up on pillars, with a dogtrot through the middle of the house. The house was so high off the ground that a cow could walk under it. And that's where they kept the farm implements, away from the weather. Houses were built up high back in that time so if there were floods—which there often were—the houses wouldn't go under water.

My great-grandparents had been born in slavery. They were babies during the Civil War and grew up during Reconstruction. After the war, they mainly made their living from sharecropping. Sharecropping provided them with the bare necessities: a house and some land to raise a cotton crop. In return, the landowner received a share, usually half the value of the crop. The sharecropper got the other half minus bills he had run up over the year. We called that "farming on halves." My great-grandfather, like most black farmers, began the year with high hopes, only to find out at the end of the year that he was faced with just breaking even because the rest of his money was tied up in farming or living expenses. If the crop was food, he might make a little money, but you couldn't eat cotton.

Most years, my great-grandfather ran a molasses mill where he made molasses on halves. Farmers from miles around would bring their sugarcane and sorghum to his mill and then pay him with half of the yield. My great-grandfather had two mules, Meg and Henry. Meg was the buggy mule, and Henry turned the pole that crushed the sugarcane. My great-grandfather would sell some of his molasses and keep some for his family.

During that time, Aunt Frances made lye hominy. She would put it into jars. It was very popular, and she had regular customers, both black and white. Even though times were hard, Aunt Frances never stopped putting on the great meals. She spent days canning and preserving vegetables from the garden and preparing for the winter months. Money was so tight for black families that they had to learn different ways of saving.

She threaded items like okra and red peppers on strings, allowing them to dry over the fall. During planting time of the next year, she removed the seeds for planting. She also saved the eyes of sweet and white potatoes, cutting them away and replanting them for a new crop. She piled up the sweet potatoes and covered them with grass or hay. This pile was called "sweet potato pump," and it lasted from one year to the next.

There were thirteen children in the Fleming family, and everybody worked. My Grandmama was the youngest and the pet, so when everybody went to the field, she stayed home and helped her mother cook. She would watch Aunt Frances make the lye hominy. Her job was to stay outdoors and stir it with the long wooden paddles. She also helped prepare vegetables, sometimes standing on a chair to stir the big pot of soup on the old woodstove.

Her father's best friend was Bob Sanders. She was crazy about Mr. Sanders, and when he would sit and talk with her father, she would climb onto his lap and play with his hair. He had this beautiful curl that hung over his forehead, so everybody started calling her Bob, and that's how she became Miz Bob.

The older girls in the family had charge of sweeping the front yard clean with homemade brooms. After frost, they would gather the "sage grass" that grew on the ditch banks and the edges of pastures. They would tie the grass around a stick and bind it with rags. Sometimes, they would just bind the grass together with rags and make a floppy broom that they would push around. Everybody took pride in keeping their yard swept clean. Some people say it was an old African custom. Others think it was to keep out snakes, but Grandmama said it was just because the children played so hard, you couldn't grow grass. The children had to play in the yard. Their mamas wouldn't let them play in the house and get underfoot. And when it was really cold and they had to stay inside, they had to sit still and be quiet.

Another one of Grandmama's childhood jobs was to polish the silver every Friday. Someone had given Aunt Frances some silver, and if the preacher from Bethel Church was coming, it was used for Sunday dinner. My grandmother polished the silver with a brick. She would rub an old brick with a rag, until some brick dust came off. Then she polished the silver with it.

When my grandmother was still young, she went up to Memphis to live with an older brother and go to school. She got a third-grade teaching certificate from LeMoyne-Owen Normal Institute and came home to teach in a little one-room school at Percy, out from Hollandale. She was nineteen. After school, she would ride back in the buggy with the principal, Bridget Davis.

That was when she married my grandfather, Ed Hunter, a blacksmith. He was very talented in his trade. He decided that since the majority of his work time was spent sharpening the blades of hoes, he would try to develop a device that would allow the farm worker to pull the cocoa grass from the cotton more easily. Many a farmer had failed because he could not stay ahead of the cocoa grass. So my grandfather developed the cocoa plow. During that time, blacks knew very little about patenting a product, and Grandpapa's invention was lost to another person.

In 1926, my grandmother became one of the first black postmistresses in Mississippi. It was during the Republican administration of Calvin Coolidge. She ran the post office at Mt. Helena. My grandmother well remembers the famous 1927 flood. Here's what she told me:

"The community around Mt. Helena had been well informed about the flood coming. The government didn't wait until the levee broke to tell people. My husband and I and all our friends spent many evenings moving furniture and house items onto scaffolds we built high up in our houses. The floodwaters came by night one evening in April 1927, and, thanks to God, the Indian Mound where my girlfriend Henrietta worked as a cook was no more than an eighth of a mile from our house. So we fled to the Indian Mound the night the flood came.

"Henrietta cooked for Mr. George Harris and his family, who lived on top of the mound. Although we carried as much food as we could with us, Henrietta cooked for our family just like hers. Everybody couldn't get on the mound, so some families took boats to higher ground and the government provided boats for others. I always thought that the water no doubt, as much as it was, came from someplace else. The flood killed all the crops and gardens.

"It wasn't long before the Red Cross and the government workers were bringing food supplements to us, like canned salmon, canned peaches, vegetables, and Pet milk. Some people ate better when the water was up than when it was down. I was still the postmistress at Mt. Helena at the time. The mail would come up from Rolling Fork by boat, to the foot of the mound. We had a boat tied there, too, which I used to carry the mail out to nearby places."

My grandmother's success in the professional world was rare for those times. But she decided to turn to cooking anyway, and in 1932, she went into the café business. She had the Fair Deal Café and later Miz Bob's Café. By the 1960s, Mt. Helena and its post office and the little cafés were up against hard times. Fast foods were becoming popular, and people were too busy to find the time to eat and visit in the cafés. Grandmama decided it was time to quit the café business. Gradually, the places on Blue Front closed, and now it is mostly a block of vacant buildings.

But even after Grandmama closed the café, she still loved to cook. One year, when the cottonseed delinting plant was having an extra busy season, they asked her if she would cook dinner for some of the workers. She said yes. So seven of the mill workers came up to the house and ate dinner every day for several months. Grandmama enjoyed preparing and serving food so much, she encouraged me to go into the catering business. So now I am carrying on the family tradition of cooking and serving good meals. I thank my Grandmama for showing me the way.

It's the Cue
The Life-Altering Impact of Southern Food
on One Unsuspecting Yankee

PETER McKEE

I can't believe I'm here. I keep asking myself what my friends are asking me, which is "Why do they want you there?," and I still have not been able to answer the question. I would say that I am stunned, confused, and absolutely thrilled to be invited. People have talked about their credentials. I have absolutely no credentials professionally for being here. People have talked about "raising issues" here. Before I walked in the door, I didn't know there *were* issues. If I had known, I would not have handed out a clearly mutant recipe for biscuits. I was crossing the Biscuit Line without knowing it.

Since I was coming to a food conference, I figured I needed recipes. There has been one recipe mentioned so far. I sent in a booklet of my recipes and others from this barbecue thing I do. I have also learned that I have crossed over the Lard Line. I may be the only person in Seattle who admits to using lard, but now I learn it's "mutant" lard because I don't render my own lard as the Lee Brothers do. So again, I'm failing here—but I do use it.

After yesterday's session, I have come to realize there has *never* been an edible biscuit cooked above the Mason-Dixon Line, so last night I immediately threw away all of my clothes I packed for this trip so I could fill my suitcase with self-rising flour. Now I can begin to make real biscuits. I am also a devoted carnivore and have made myself annoying to some healthier people in Seattle because of that. What I can tell you is that grease is something I enjoy on occasion. I come from a town that is pre–Krispy Kreme. I'm told it's coming to Seattle. I'm the only one who is interested that it is coming to Seattle.

I have been trying to figure out how to describe to you what it is like for me to be here. I have bad analogies, but this one sticks in my mind. Imagine that in your hometown, say, in Oxford, Mississippi, you were a fan of diving. As a youth, you learned to dive, maybe a back dive, and you like the Olympics. So

Peter McKee wields a mean knife. Courtesy of Tim Matsui.

you did a back dive, and, for fun, you'd have people who like to dive or watch diving come to your house and have a big pool party. You'd do your back dive, and that was fun, and other people would do cannonballs—more fun.

So you start to have a yearly event that you call the Mississippi Olympic Tribute. And you have these events for twenty years. Then one day you get a call from the International Subcommittee for the Study of Recreational Hydraulics. Now you've never heard of these folks, and you are wondering what that is all about. They ask you to come to Grenoble, Switzerland, to speak. You say, "Man, I love the Olympics, you bet I'm coming—but do you really want me to be there doing my back dive?" For me, being here in Oxford is like going to Grenoble!

So what I can say is, thank you *very* much for inviting me. If you are silly enough to invite me, I am certainly silly enough to come.

You've got to understand that I come from Seattle, Washington, a city that is not known for barbecue. What it is famous for is drive-thru espresso stands. That's what we've contributed to the culinary world. Seattle has Microsoft, and this slide I am showing you of a recent story in our newspaper shows a

Microsoft employee who networked his barbecue grill to his computer, which allows him to monitor all aspects of cooking! Welcome to the Northwest. Also, the winning recipe for barbecue from *Sunset Magazine* in 2000 went to a Seattleite for his "traditional" barbecue sauce: a blackberry, ginger, and hot pepper sauce. So this is where I'm coming from.

I was born and raised in a rather affluent white suburb in the San Francisco Bay area by two New York City–raised parents, neither of whom could cook much. I graduated from Brown University in Providence, Rhode Island. We have no Southern relatives. My entire Southern exposure up to age twenty-one was probably reports in the newspaper about the civil rights movement and a growing love for folk music, first through Pete Seeger. Thanks to him, I became a self-taught banjo player.

In 1974, I enlisted in VISTA — Volunteers in Service to America. I had by that time some exposure to Southern music and thought I wanted to go to Appalachia, take my banjo, and "do it." Instead, VISTA sent me to Atlanta for training, and six weeks later I was told I was being sent to Macon, Georgia. I had no clue where Macon was — I had to look at a map. When I learned that it was not in Appalachia, I was not pleased, but I went down to Macon, and it was in Macon that I had my first soul food at a place called the H&H. I had my first black-eyed peas at the H&H. I had my first Southern-style family restaurant meal at a place in Savannah, I think it was called Mrs. Wilkes's Boarding House. It was fabulous.

The first real fried chicken I had was at a place near a public-housing project in Eatonton, Georgia. I went into this place because it looked like it had good food. I was clearly the only Yankee there and, the best I could tell, the only white person. They had great fried chicken, so good that I stood up and asked them, "Could you tell me how you cook your fried chicken?" That was not a question they had been asked frequently by people like me.

One day I was interviewing a woman in Eatonton about the amount of rent she was paying in the public-housing projects, and she said there was a woman down the street there in the project who wanted to see me. I went over and knocked on the door, and she opened the door and said, "Why you are just a boy!" And I was. She told me to come on in, and we talked, and she had a lot of plants in her house. She told me that I needed a wife and that I needed some plants. She gave me some plants and mentioned, by the way, that her daughter wrote some books. She pointed to the books, and I noticed they were published by places like Random House, and I thought, "Whoa, that's impressive," but I didn't at the time know enough to realize that I was meeting with Minnie Lou Walker, Alice Walker's mother.

In traveling up and down U.S. Highway 23 to Eatonton, I saw the Jackson Fresh Air Barbecue. I like eating at places that sort of look out of the way and kind of exotic, so one day I pulled into the Fresh Air Barbecue. It has been there, as I understand it, since 1929. The Fresh Air Barbecue is still there today. They actually have expanded, I'm told. It originally was an open-air place, and at some point during the 1950s or 60s the health department told them they were going to close it unless changes were made, so the open-air seating is now covered. Their menu is very limited now. They cook their barbecue over a wood fire—smoke it for eighteen hours. It's pork. The legendary Toots Caston had owned it since 1949 and apparently came daily until he died just three or four years ago. Fresh Air became my definition of barbecue, and I am convinced that the best ambassador for Southern cuisine has got to be barbecue.

I'm here to tell you that, for us Yankees, grits ain't gonna make it as a culinary ambassador from the South. But that's OK. Why do you want them to make it? Just enjoy them here. Just like bagels aren't making it in some places. But barbecue, now that's different. Barbecue, as it has been defined by the Fresh Air, is not simply a food; it is a spirit, an atmosphere, a way of life. It is pork smoked eighteen hours until it falls to pieces, slapped on a bun with a vinegar/pepper sauce and a side of lukewarm Brunswick stew. It is also the two pieces of Wonder bread wrapped in paper, whether you want it or not, with a Coke. That's, for me, barbecue.

I also have a collection of what are called community cookbooks. And in 1986, I actually put together a family cookbook. I sent requests to all my family all around the country, none in the South. And I said to them, "Can you please send me one recipe that is important to your particular family?," and everyone did. They revealed that the McKees eat only two vegetables: frozen peas and frozen beans. They eat a lot of meat. They eat a lot of rice and potatoes. And they love desserts.

For me, cooking barbecue requires an event. Or at least large volume makes it better, so I decided that since I didn't have an event, I would invent one. I began in 1981 by hosting the event I called "The Jackson Fresh Air Barbecue/ Weber International Cook-off and Feed"—a slick ploy for corporate sponsorship that failed. I sent a letter to Weber looking for endorsements and got nothing. The Cook-off started out with two trophies that I assembled from scraps I found at the Salvation Army, although I think I actually bought the pig that sits on top of the main Jackson Trophy.

Since 1981, the basic rules for the treasured Jackson Trophy/main dish category require that you cook your main dish entry on-site in an enclosed barbecue. You can come anytime. Three days in advance? That's fine. Side orders and desserts may be cooked off-site. But every person who attends must bring a recipe and an entry. And the accounting firm of Tush and Tush certifies the results.

One other thing to know: I also thought—back in 1981—that calling it the "First Annual" sounded boring, so we started with the "Seventh Annual." By the time we got to seven, then we continued on. We will have the twentieth annual next year.

Now we have four trophies. There is the treasured Jackson Trophy. There is also the Side Order Cup. Originally, when we had only two trophies, the people who entered desserts were kicking butt over the salads. I mean, gee, that's a tough one: "Mmm, chocolate cake or salad?" So they insisted that there be a separate Dessert Trophy, and we got that. Then my wife wanted hot dogs. Hot dogs? Well, she won the Jackson Trophy with hot dogs. So the Rules Committee met—that's me—and we decided that there needed to be a Kid's Choice Trophy to cancel out the bribery of children with hot dogs and cheese whiz. Now, the rules require that if you are under the age of fourteen and you don't bring an item, you can only vote for a kid's item, and that's across all the other areas.

The scariest thing was that at one point, the owner of the Fresh Air called me and said that he would like to come, and I said, "Oh my god. He's seen all this stuff I've sent him, and he thinks that all of Seattle is coming. What am I going to do when he finds out that it is just a very large backyard barbecue?" But he never came, and I breathed a sigh of relief.

At last year's event, my sixteen-year-old daughter was going to go for it. Just straight out: five pounds of bacon. That was going to be her entry. And I thought, yes, I would love to eat five pounds of bacon. And I said fine. You are sixteen. But she wondered how you cook five pounds of bacon on a Weber. So we designed the "Baconator," which allowed her to cook without flare-ups. That was her entry. She loaded up the "Baconator," which is an angled rooflike pan made out of stainless steel. It let the fat drip down the sides and collect in some holes, down to some cans, which caught the grease. Unfortunately, the cans themselves caught on fire and flamed out the grill. But it was good bacon.

At our annual Cook-off, the five o'clock feed bell rings. There are maybe twenty or thirty dishes. You've got to remember what you are eating because you're going to vote later. And then you sit down to eating. If it tastes good, eat it. Now, to be honest, I'm not sure how much of it is real Southern cooking. Few if any participants have ever been to the South. But I think if anything is Southern about our event, it is the spirit. And I think that that is what these kinds of things should be. Now I won't go into my story about the most widely distributed Southern food—which is Coke—and why I would drive 300 miles one way down to Oregon to get what we call Baby Cokes. That is a whole different story.

Moon Pies might just be the next most widely distributed Southern food. My folk/bluegrass band in Seattle plays a song called "Moon Pie," which I wrote. [McKee tosses Moon Pies into the audience.] Now, what I need you to do is look on the back of your Moon Pie packages and tell me, is there any vitamin C in a Moon Pie? How about vitamin A? Don't you feel foolish just reading that nutrition label? I mean what are they putting in Moon Pies? When I went back to Macon and Savannah in 1994, I was driving past Statesboro on a back road, and I thought, well, I'm gonna have another Southern food experience. I thought I would have something in Statesboro, but all I saw were car dealerships. When I was about five miles out of town, headed to Savannah, I pulled off to stop at a small country store. The store had nothing. Well, nothing edible. And so I said, well, I should get a Moon Pie. And I got a Moon Pie. As I began eating it as I was driving, I thought, "Putting food disclosures on Moon Pies is odd." So I wrote this song [McKee sings, while playing his banjo]:

> There are certain foods I sometimes eat of which I am not proud,
> I eat 'em once or twice a year, alone, not in a crowd.
> When I bite into my sins, I just don't give a damn
> If Moon Pies aren't nutritious or there's too much salt in Spam.
>
> *Chorus*
> Moon Pies don't need labels despite the FDA,
> 'Cause when you scarf a Moon Pie, all reason fades away.
> No one checks the fiber count or sugars when they snack,
> No one reads the label on a Moon Pie—that's a fact.
>
> *Chorus*
>
> Well I am all for healthy hearts, eat broccoli by the head,
> And I've even checked my sodium, and I've cut way back on lead.
> But in my times of weakness, when those pork rinds must be had,
> Don't need to count those grams of fat to know I'm sinning bad.
>
> *Chorus*
>
> Now if a box of Twinkies is the breakfast that you crave,
> Then you're the kind of person that no label's gonna save.
> Don't give a damn if Twinkies got no vitamin A or C,
> 'Cause they got that creamy filling that is good for you and me.

Chorus

Twinkies don't need labels despite the FDA,
'Cause when you scarf a Twinkie, all reason fades away.
No one checks the fiber count or sugars when they snack,
No one reads the label on a Twinkie—that's a fact.
And no one reads the label on a pork rind—that's a fact!
And no one reads the label on a Moon Pie—that's a fact!

PETER MCKEE

Taking What She Had and Turning It into Money
The Female Farm Economy

LU ANN JONES

Lurline Stokes Murray remembered the exact moment her mother decided to produce for the market. Born in 1915 on a tobacco farm in Florence County, South Carolina, Lurline had no arches in her feet. Her father "finally scraped up enough money" to purchase special shoes with metal supports, but the metal quickly wore holes in her socks. "Mama decided then, honey, that she had to do something," Murray recalled. "Mama said she decided that she'd get anything she could sell, and that's when she started to taking what she had and turning it into money." Butter beans and peas, eggs and butter, blackberries gathered from the woods—all could be sold in the town of Florence in the 1920s to buy socks for a little girl.

Lurline's mother, Julia Benton Stokes, already had a reputation among neighbors for making good butter and buttermilk and for reserving a little extra to trade. Black neighbors, in particular, patronized her. They started "bringing their little bucket [for the buttermilk]," Murray recalled, "and in it would maybe be a half a dozen eggs or what you reckon? Octagon soap wrappers. They would come during lunchtime, when we were at the house for our dinner. They'd send the children." Julia Stokes, in turn, redeemed the soap wrappers at a Florence furniture store for dishes and "the nicest pots," some of which her daughter still used fifty years later.

When she decided to sell more widely, Julia Stokes quickly discovered a ready market for all kinds of produce. A neighbor who sold vegetables at a curb market in Columbia, South Carolina, turned to her for help one week when he found himself short of turnip greens. "So Mr. Wallace Jones came out there one day," Murray explained, "and he asked Mama, he said, 'Miz Julia, how 'bout selling me some of them turnip greens? I got orders.' And them was the sorriest things. Mama said, 'You mean there's anything out there?' He said,

'Yeah. Just cut the greens off and let 'em grow back out and there'll be another cutting in a few weeks.' So one thing [led] to another."

Just as food has shaped Southern cultures, so has it played a central role in the female economy of the rural South. When compared to descriptions of cultivating and selling the region's major cash crops, women's trade appears ephemeral, fluid, and elusive. The value of women's trade might even appear inconsequential compared to the proceeds of tobacco and cotton. Local markets and individual sellers and buyers often determined prices, and these decentralized transactions that often occurred in domestic spaces left fragmentary paper trails for us to follow.

But it is important to examine what happened when "one thing led to another" and to understand the nature and meaning of the female farm economy. How did farm women turn food into commodities? What marketing strategies did they pursue? What did women do with the cash and credit they earned? What difference did women's trade make to farm families and to the women themselves?

To answer these questions, I have turned to memoirs of rural life, farm periodicals such as the *Progressive Farmer*, store ledgers, and reports of home demonstration agents who worked for the federal Agricultural Extension Service. I also pursued answers while conducting interviews for "An Oral History of Southern Agriculture," a project sponsored by the Smithsonian Institution's National Museum of American History between 1986 and 1991. Conversations with older men and women like Lurline Murray revealed the intricacies of the "butter and egg trade," a hidden portion of the South's farm economy that women controlled.

In the early twentieth century, Southern farm women's production for market grew out of their production for home use. Rural families tried to meet as many of their own dietary needs as possible. Women raised and processed much of what their families ate and practiced what was known as a "live-at-home" philosophy.

The farmers I interviewed often used a common phrase to express this orientation toward subsistence. As people remembered the lean years of the 1920s and 1930s, a standard of well-being that they cited time and again was that their families never missed a meal. A. C. Griffin's experience was typical. Born in 1908, he grew up in a white family that raised cotton on an eighty-acre farm in northeastern North Carolina. Although cash was scarce throughout his childhood and early adult life, he recalled, "We didn't go hungry." As Griffin marveled at his father's ability to provide even that measure of security for

Ivy Ann Cronin on her farm in McDade, Texas. Courtesy of David Wharton.

twelve children, his wife Grace reminded him that his mother "was responsible for a lot of it. She *was* a hardworking woman." "She was a hardworking woman," Griffin agreed, "a very hardworking woman."

Not far away in Edgecombe County, North Carolina, Bessie Smith Pender was born in 1919. Her African American family raised cotton and peanuts on rented land, sharing 40 percent of the profits with the owner until they saved enough money to buy a farm of their own. "They were tough days," she remembered, but "we were happy, because we had a-plenty to eat, growed plenty of food in the garden. And raised plenty of hogs."

Lurline Murray recalled her father's admonition: "'Make something to eat if you don't have nothing else, because a hungry man will steal.'" As a consequence, Murray's mother raised a good garden and kept chickens and cows, and so did Lurline when she had a home of her own. "In all these years," she boasted, "this woman has never been hungry." But she added, "There's many, many years I didn't know what a piece of money was."

Food could satisfy hunger *and* generate income. Through their marketing ingenuity, women turned a variety of goods into commodities for trade. Poorer women, in particular, gathered and sold what nature offered freely, picking and selling berries that grew wild in the woods. John Dillard's parents were white sharecroppers near the south Georgia town of Tifton when he was born in 1920. His mother foraged for berries in snake-infested thickets to ward off want. "In the summertime," he recalled, "she'd get out and pick black-berries and huckleberries and haul them up here to town and sell 'em. She would get 5 cent a quart for blackberries and 10 cent a quart for huckleberries. A lot of times she'd have a number 2 washtub full. She'd just set 'em in the buggy and come up here around the edge of town and sell 'em. You'd be sur-prised how people'd buy that stuff."

For most farm women, poultry and dairy products formed the backbone of their trade. A flock of chickens in the yard and a good milk cow or two could provide a surplus for market as well as food for the family table. Because milk cows required pasture and hay, they were more often found on the farms of landowners. But flocks of fifty or fewer chickens scratched and roosted everywhere.

Raising chickens on a small scale required little capital, and their care could fit easily into a farm woman's round of duties. Eggs and live chickens served as a ready medium of exchange; in fact, some women kept poultry with an eye toward trade as much as toward the dinner table. Zetta Barker Hamby grew up on a fifty-five-acre farm in northwestern North Carolina, and in her mem-oir of life in Grassy Creek, she described how her mother balanced household production for consumption with production for exchange. "Every family tried to have chickens for eggs and to eat but mostly to sell," Hamby explained. "It was reassuring to have eggs and chickens to barter at the local store for sud-den, urgent needs." Young fryers that would fetch a good price were judged too valuable for their growers to eat; instead, when Hamby's family wanted to enjoy chicken, they killed old hens that had quit laying and boiled the tough meat to tenderize it before dredging it in flour and frying it.

The products of women's labor entered the channels of commerce in a number of ways, ranging from casual exchanges to formal, state-sponsored markets. Modest transactions occurred so routinely that they might be taken for granted. In eastern North Carolina, women traded eggs with men who peddled fish caught in the area's rivers. At the home of Roy Taylor, son of white tobacco tenant farmers, the "fish man's" arrival on Saturdays signaled that his mother's stockpile of eggs would be raided. "Go see if your Mammy has any extra eggs," Taylor's father would instruct him. "If she's got three dozen or so eggs, the dollar added to the egg money will be enough to git the speckled trout." Nellie Stancil Langley's eastern North Carolina family also patronized a "fish man" who accepted eggs in exchange for perch and spots as well as the Coca-Colas that he kept iced down.

Storekeepers in country and town alike took eggs and live chickens in trade. Nellie Langley carried several dozen eggs to the store, where the family ran an account and paid "on our bill, so we could get us at least a piece of cheese to eat. It was Christmas if we could get a piece of cheese; we thought that was something." In anticipation of swapping chickens for supplies at the store, Zetta Hamby's mother confined the birds to a coop and fed them generously for a few days so they would gain weight and fetch a good price.

Although the women might not have known it, they formed the first link in a supply chain that connected home producers, country stores, and wholesale markets. Rural storekeepers connected scattered small producers to wholesale merchants located in towns and cities. An egg trade was at the heart of the general store that John Ward owned and operated in western North Carolina. The ledger that the Watauga County merchant kept in 1914 documents daily transactions with customers and demonstrates that "the economic life of the community surrounding the general store was one based on eggs more so than cash." Customers covered most of their bills with eggs, and occasionally corn, and paid the difference in cash. No doubt, such trade patterns were common throughout the South.

Nestled on the border between North Carolina and Virginia, the country store where Zetta Hamby's family traded was the first stop on a long trip between the producers of poultry and dairy products and their consumers. For example, the butter that Grassy Creek women churned and traded at the store—where it was held in wood barrels—might wind up as far away as Baltimore. Hamby speculated that the Baltimore dealers sold the Grassy Creek butter to a creamery, where it was reworked and packaged for retail sale, eventually appearing on the city's dining room tables.

Another marketing outlet were itinerant merchants known as hucksters who traveled the South, paying cash for poultry and dairy products to the farm women who greeted them in their backyards. In northeastern North Carolina, G. Emory Rountree earned much of his living between 1932 and 1960 working as a huckster. He visited sellers each week and bought eggs, live chickens, and rabbits, which he then sold in the Tidewater Virginia area some forty miles away. Although other buyers established routes in the vicinity,

Rountree considered himself "one of the big hucksters" because he drove a larger-capacity truck, covered a wider area, and operated several days a week. In addition to buying from individual customers, Rountree purchased eggs that storekeepers had accumulated when customers brought them in for swapping.

The eggs and chickens that farm women in Gates County produced wound up for sale at a variety of outlets. Rountree sold some to retail customers at the city market in Portsmouth, Virginia; he sold some directly to independent grocers in the Tidewater area; and he sold some to wholesale dealers in Norfolk. To take advantage of the highest prices, Rountree housed crates of eggs at rented cold-storage facilities in Norfolk for several months at a time.

Women also controlled their own retail operations, thus sidestepping intermediaries. Prime examples of women who used this marketing strategy were Julia Benton Stokes and Lurline Stokes Murray, who developed a mother-daughter partnership that spanned three decades and catered to customers in Florence, South Carolina. Beginning in 1925, at the age of ten, Lurline accompanied her mother into town twice a week to dispose of buttermilk, eggs, and seasonal fruits and vegetables. These sales remained a vital part of the family's income even after Lurline and her husband bought a 390-acre farm in 1938. Lurline and a tenant tended the land while J. W. Murray worked as a machinist for the Southern Railway. By the 1940s, Lurline and her mother supplied twenty-five regular clients and restaurants with eggs and dressed chickens. Customers reserved standing orders, and if their needs changed, they would advise Murray to adjust the quantity to be delivered the next week. Stokes and Murray sold to a wide spectrum of patrons that ranged from doctors, lawyers, bank presidents, and preachers to J. W. Murray's blue-collar coworkers at the railroad roundhouse. Customers found them by word-of-mouth recommendations. "I have never asked nobody to buy something," Murray declared. "If you've got something and people know what you've got, it'll sell itself. I've sold to some of the richest and the poorest."

Another mode of selling was state-sponsored cooperative markets. During the 1920s, home demonstration agents who worked for the Agricultural Extension Service organized curb markets in county seats across the South. Responding to the downturn in the agricultural economy, women's markets expanded at the same time that prices for cotton and tobacco began to decline. In the late 1920s and early 1930s, the regional network of home demonstration markets grew. Women in Alabama, South Carolina, Virginia, and North Carolina praised these markets for helping them support their families as crop prices went into a tailspin. In North Carolina, a handful of markets in 1922 mushroomed into thirty-six by the mid-1930s, and other Southern states followed a similar pattern. By 1938, some 1,700 Tarheel women sold $309,000 worth of goods at organized markets. All the while, home demonstration clubwomen reported that they earned thousands more dollars from sales to individuals, schools, and hotels.

Marketing women learned that they themselves were part of the promotional package. Personality, self-presentation, and "salesmanship" mattered nearly as much as the quality of the food for sale. "Wear a smile," the Beaufort County, North Carolina, agent advised, and "have a pleasant word for your customers." In 1931, the agent in Carteret County, North Carolina, praised women who had "learned very quickly to gauge the customer to a nicety and be neither too insistent nor too listless in addressing her."

Home demonstration markets practiced racial segregation. The bylaws that governed the market in at least one North Carolina county stated explicitly that only whites could sell under its auspices, and other markets followed the color line. Nonetheless, black home agents in North Carolina acted as intermediaries between producers and buyers, encouraged clubwomen to participate in city markets open to sellers of both races, and occasionally organized small curb markets of their own. When black clubwomen in Columbus County decided in 1930 to coordinate their sales, agent Sarah J. Williams gathered all they had to offer, parked on the street in the county seat of Whiteville, and turned her own car into a curb market. In 1932, a club member in Alamance County worried because "she could not call on her husband for the family necessities" after crops failed the previous year; in response, the agent advised her to sell her garden and poultry products in a nearby town. Added to cash earned for prize-winning exhibits entered at a county fair, the club member reported contributing $128 to the family budget.

The income-earning strategies that Tom Cunningham's mother pursued in the 1920s and 1930s combined sales at home demonstration curb markets in South Carolina with sales to individual customers. Tom's mother sold first at the curb market in Greenville and later in Darlington after the family moved in 1929 in search of better land. At the market, Cunningham's mother sold milk, butter, and eggs year-round and offered other goods as the seasons changed. She also maintained a route of customers in Darlington. The family had a telephone, and townsfolk called the farm to put in their orders. On their morning trips to school, Tom and his siblings delivered milk, eggs, and butter to town doorsteps. "My mother," Cunningham recalled, "knew exactly who got milk what day and how much."

Many women, whether white or black, enjoyed marketing in a lively public venue where they mingled with friends and strangers, managed the transactions, and turned their private work into social labor. Sellers engaged in good-natured rivalries, and women who baked mouthwatering cakes, preserved clear jellies and crisp pickles, or turned out well-molded butter reveled in the reputations that their products and their skills earned them. Many women who evaluated the merits of various selling options believed they made more money at the curb market than anywhere else. In addition, farm wives and mothers who could boast market earnings might influence how the family allocated its labor, and husbands and children who helped them set up and sell also witnessed the value of their work firsthand.

Even small sums of cash stretched a long way in the 1920s and 1930s. A half-century later, Lurline Murray could remember precisely how she spent the dollar that she earned as a teenager by picking twenty quarts of blackberries for the wife of a Florence, South Carolina, bank president. "You could buy rice, three pounds for a dime," she began. "You could buy sugar, five pounds for 19 cents. Salmon was two cans for a quarter back in them days, if you could get your hand on any money. You could get a pound of coffee for 15 cents, two pounds for a quarter. I bought a little box of macaroni. I bought a little piece of cheese. When I got it added up, it was 89 cents. I had my tithe and 1 cent over."

Murray also recalled that during the winter, when the fewer eggs that hens laid brought higher prices, "you didn't eat the eggs for breakfast. You know, they wasn't that plentiful. Eggs was a treat when you had eggs to eat. And there was times when hens would lay more eggs, and prices were real cheap, and we'd eat the eggs. I mean, they'd make enough to get the soap, and coffee, and sugar, and stuff like that. . . . But the eggs was a precious commodity because as long as the old hen laid you could kinda count on falling back on that to get some things."

During the bleakest years of the Great Depression, the income that farm women generated made a crucial difference for many families. In hindsight, Tom Cunningham could not estimate what proportion of the family economy his mother's earnings represented because he was a child during the heyday of her sales to private and curb market customers in Darlington. He did know, however, that his mother "helped to keep body and soul together back during those depression years, when there just wasn't any money. I know that she worked at it diligently and that my father worked at the farm and between the two of them, they kept the bills paid and we were fed well; we had adequate clothing, even though sometimes we had patches on our elbows and knees.

But we fared well. We got along real good. And I know it took both of them to do it." The Cunningham family was not alone.

In oral history narratives, older Southerners often remember the ways in which women's earnings were spent with a loving precision unmatched in stories about men's earnings. The income that women generated sometimes provided the few small luxuries that rural children enjoyed. In the early 1920s, when it came time for Jessie Felknor to graduate from high school in east Tennessee, her mother's chickens paid for her class ring. "I asked Daddy for the money," she recalled. "He said, 'Sis, I don't have any.' So mother sold eight old hens; no, she sold sixteen. We'd catch 'em and tie strings around their feet and we'd tie 'em in bunches. And we'd tie four of those hens together. We took enough hens to the store that I paid for my class ring, 'cause Daddy didn't have any money."

In eastern North Carolina, Roy Taylor paid his way into movies and drank fountain Cokes during the 1930s with money that his mother gave him from her egg earnings. In the early 1930s, Ruby Byers's mother gave her daughter eggs to swap for the fixings for sandwiches that she and her siblings ate on an end-of-school field trip. "In order for Mama to have something for us to take on that picnic," Byers remembered, "she had to gather up the eggs and send us to the store to get something to make us a sandwich out of. They paid you, say, 15 cents a dozen, and this particular time we got crackers and peanut butter, and my aunt made us some cupcakes and put chocolate on 'em and, boy, I mean we had a treat!"

Although practices varied, many women controlled the money they earned. In east Tennessee, for example, Della Sarten sold dairy and poultry products, and the income guaranteed her a measure of autonomy after she married in 1927. Will and Della Sarten grew grain and raised cattle, and she separated cream and churned butter from the milk that half a dozen cows produced and kept plenty of good laying hens. Hucksters, commercial creameries, town merchants, and neighbors bought from her. "That's exactly how I made my living," Sarten declared. "I'm not a stretcher, but I bet I've sold 2,000 pounds of butter." She used the money to purchase groceries, children's clothes, and household amenities and to contribute to the general farm operation. Accustomed to having money of her own before marriage, Sarten controlled a separate bank account all of her adult life. "I never did have to beg for no money," Sarten said. "I'm not a-bragging, but I never did have to. . . . I know a lot of husbands wouldn't even let their wives have a dime. Well, you know the difference in people. That's one good thing that I've had a say-so over my milk and butter and eggs ever since I kept house."

The proceeds from women's trade could guard against profligate husbands. Early in her selling career, Julia Stokes deposited a portion of the money that she earned in a savings account at the urging of Lurline Murray, who feared that her father would leave them poor and dependent. "My daddy drank," Lurline confided. "And every time he thought Mama had a little bit of money, he'd make her mad. You know how he made her mad? Tell her she give it to her people. And she'd get mad and say, 'Here. Take it.' It went on thataway and went on thataway. I said to Mama one day, 'Mama, I'm gonna tell you something. If you don't start taking a little something and putting it somewhere . . . there ain't gonna be nothing to bury us with.' I said, 'If you don't, I'm gonna start taking something and I'm gonna put a little bit somewhere.' So, Mama started [setting aside some money]." In the years that followed, Julia Benton Stokes provided her own "nest egg."

Women's trade might even provide a way for them to achieve control over their reproduction. In the 1940s, Watauga County, North Carolina, residents participated in a pilot project that tested the efficacy of various birth control techniques. When rumors circulated that the public health nurse planned to stop distributing free condoms, one woman "told her husband that she would simply catch a hen and take it to the store and sell it in order to get money to buy some Trojans." While many of the Watauga mothers did not have the 50 cents needed to purchase a package of three prophylactics, the nurse noted, she was heartened that "some will be willing to sacrifice their chickens and eggs in order to stop babies from coming." Swapping a setting of eggs for reproductive freedom was enterprising, indeed.

In addition to the cash and credit that women earned, the relationships that they developed with customers accrued value for them and their families. By the 1940s, Julia Stokes and Lurline Murray generated about $50 a month from their route of long-term customers. They also made "an avalanche of friends." Town women to whom they sold gave Lurline booties and baby clothes for her two boys, items that she had no time to make because she was busy working on the farm. Contacts made among professional people in town paid off in services rendered for reduced prices or other forms of help. When the family needed an electric motor but found it difficult to obtain, Lurline Murray consulted a furniture store owner who bought her buttermilk and eggs, and he located the equipment they desired. When the Murrays wanted to refinance their farm mortgage, they consulted a banker to whom she sold produce. Her mother's doctor, another longtime customer, refused to accept payments for Julia Stokes's care. "So often when I'd take Mama in there, Dr. Meade would say, 'No charge, Lurline. No charge.'" When she protested his generosity, he retorted, "'Now you just let me run my office.'" Lurline Murray concluded, "There ain't many people in the town of Florence that I didn't know."

Women used their earnings to meet immediate, day-to-day needs of farms and families, and they also invested their income in their children's futures. The "butter and egg trade" underwrote education and supported occupational mobility for the next generation. Evidence of this phenomenon spans decades and transcends race.

Consider the example of Mary Pauline Fitzgerald of Orange County, North Carolina. In 1880, Mary Pauline's mother and father, like many African American parents, desperately wanted their oldest daughter to get an education. At the age of ten, Mary Pauline enrolled at St. Augustine's School, a high school for blacks in Raleigh. By this time, the girl's father was nearly blind and unable to do much work, so it was left to her and her mother to finance her education. Mary Pauline helped pay her own way by working at the school, and her mother subsidized her daughter's tuition by sending butter, eggs, and chickens to St. Augustine's to defray expenses. After graduation, Mary Pauline Fitzgerald went on to become a revered teacher, thanks, in part, to the "butter and egg trade."

Consider the mothers and children on South Carolina's St. Helena Island. White Northern teachers at the Penn School noticed that poor African American mothers looked forward to rummaging through barrels of clothing donated by Northern philanthropists. In particular, the women wanted shoes for their children to wear to school in the winter. "It is a sobering thing to have a dress or a pair of shoes stand between you and an education," observed one teacher. Mothers surmounted that obstacle when they offered sweet potatoes, chickens, and eggs in exchange for simple items that would keep their children "on the road to education."

Finally, consider a story told to me in December of 1986 by Nellie Stancil Langley, the first person I interviewed for "An Oral History of Southern Agriculture." As a child, Langley had swapped eggs for the catch peddled by fish men or for a piece of cheese at a country store. By the 1950s, she and her husband had two children to support on their tobacco farm in Wilson County, North Carolina. Langley pulled her weight in the tobacco field and then raised a garden and preserved as much food as possible. "If we didn't raise our food we didn't have anything to eat," she said. "I'd just raise and can and raise and can and raise and can." One day, the county's home demonstration agent visited the farm and urged Langley to sell vegetables at the curb market. For eight years, every Tuesday and Friday, she loaded the family's "old pickup truck" and headed to the market in Wilson. Besides selling eggs, dressed chickens, cured pork, and vegetables, Langley added value to her products by making chicken salad, soup, cakes, and pies. Some weeks, she would sell as much as $100 worth of food; some years, she won recognition as the market's biggest seller. What did she do with the money? "That's the way I sent my son through college," Langley said. "He just happened to come home one day and said, 'Mama, I want to go to college.' I said, 'You can't go to college. We don't have the money.' He said, 'Well, I'm not going to work like you have. I'm going to college.' By that time, I had started going up to the curb market. So when you want to do something, you can do it. The first money I ever had, really had in my hand, was going to the curb market." That money sent her son Jack to East Carolina College and on to a successful career as a certified public accountant.

I now teach at Jack Langley's alma mater. And some days as I walk across campus, I wonder how many young men and women from eastern North Carolina—and places like it throughout the South—owe their educations to marketing mothers who took what they had and turned it into money.

My Love Affair
with the Sweet Potato

. . . .

COURTNEY TAYLOR

I come from an agrarian family in Adams County, Mississippi—a long line of cattle farmers. In the West, they're called ranchers; in Natchez, they're called cattle farmers. Most of the land came into my mother's father's family before Mississippi became a state, and they've been farming it ever since, enjoying and surviving the peaks and valleys of wealth and poverty, but always admiring and caring for the land. And it gave back even if profits were not always part of the equation.

There's an old story my great-uncle used to tell about a guy selling hammers on the street corner for 10 cents. A fellow walked up and said, "That's a good price you got on hammers." He said, "Yeah, I buy 'em for a quarter and sell them for a dime." The other guy said, "Man, you can't make any money like that." And the hammer guy said, "Yeah, but it beats farming."

Anyway, the land always gave a little back to the landowners and provided for their extended family and the extended family of those who worked on the farm and in the house. If nothing else, we always had a cow in the freezer. It provided as well for the people my great-grandmother adopted because they needed a roof and plate of food or maybe a college education. Any number of these relatives and friends showed up with regularity at the dinner table, particularly during the holidays.

One such gathering took place at my Great-Aunt Hattie's house (we called her Sister). Let me add that like many families that are based along the river, we like to take an occasional drink. Sister liked it more than occasionally. While she drank more than most of us, she was very creative and smart. It is my opinion that she was bored with the rest of us and drank to entertain herself. She was a marvelous cook. She turned out elaborate and sophisticated cakes and desserts. It was at her table that I first tasted sweet potatoes. They were whipped up with butter, eggs, and brown sugar, topped with pecans and

235

nutmeg—and laced with a good bit of bourbon. Thus began my love affair with the sweet potato—and Old Charter.

Sweet potatoes were usually given the same baroque treatment in my mother's kitchen. Just about anything will taste pretty good with butter, sugar, and bourbon—except maybe pig lips.

To uncover the true pleasures of the sweet potato, we have to wade our way through its confusing history and linguistic briar patch. Grown for centuries by the Incas of Peru and the Mayas of Central America, the sweet potato was called *cassiri* and was described in the records of Columbus's fourth voyage as tasting not unlike chestnuts. Later in 1540, De Soto found sweet potatoes in Native American gardens in what is now Louisiana. Haitians called them *batatas*. One Portuguese navigator wrote: "The root which is called by the Indians of Hispaniola *batata* is named *igname* at St. Thomas (off the coast of Africa) and is one of the most essential articles of their food."

Not only did the Spanish explorers bring the sweet potato back to Spain; it is also believed that they took the sweet potato to the Philippines and the East Indies, after which Portuguese voyagers carried it to India and China. Being a tropical plant, sweet potatoes took happily to the warm growing conditions of Spain, and the Spanish relished them. Soon they were exporting them to England, where spiced sweet potato pies were included in the vast and rich table of Henry VIII. And *batata* eventually became *potato*. The sweet potato gained popularity during the Renaissance, perhaps because of the sweet tooth of the elite, so many of their dishes, even the meat dishes, were embellished with fruit and spices. In Shakespeare's day, for instance, they were sold in crystallized slices as an aphrodisiac. In the *Merry Wives of Windsor*, at his long-awaited meeting with Mistress Ford, Falstaff exclaims, "Let the sky rain potatoes; let it Thunder the tune of Green Sleeves, hailing kissing-comfits and snow enringoes." (Enringoes, or candied sea holly, was another aphrodisiac of the time.)

Just how and why the sweet potato was given such attributes is a mystery. Perhaps it says something about the Incan or Mayan virility—or maybe the Spanish exporters were quite clever in their marketing. That might even get some fool to eat pig lips.

The French, never to be outdone in the kitchen or the boudoir, planted them at the request of Louis XV. Thirty years later, the Empress Josephine, who was a Creole from Martinique, introduced them into the gardens of Malsmaison. Soon the smell of sweet potatoes was wafting through the salons of Paris, where courtiers served them at intimate dinners to stimulate the ardor of their lovers.

Such an important indulgence couldn't have been left behind, and it is thought, perhaps, that sweet potatoes not only crept up from Central America but also were introduced to the Southern colonies by lusty Europeans.

To further confuse things, I'd like to point out that sweet potatoes are not even potatoes. While potatoes are members of the nightshade family (a poisonous plant, much maligned in Europe until the eighteenth century), sweet potatoes are in the morning glory clan. The potato is a tuber; the sweet potato is a root. And true yams are something altogether different.

Yams are indigenous to West Africa and are considered sacred plants there. They don't grow from seeds. Rather, new yams sprout from old yams, evoking life's cycle of birth and death. *Nyam* is a form of the West African verb "to eat."

When African slaves were brought to toil in the American fields and kitchens, they found none of their beloved yams but substituted sweet potatoes. So a yam by another name would taste as sweet. Since the yam had been such an important food to Africans, it was extremely popular in the early American kitchen. Thus began, in the American cookery, the confusing vernacular of the sweet potato/yam.

To further perplex the American public, while a true yam is not as sweet as a real sweet potato, the sweetest variety of sweet potato is called a Louisiana yam. In the 1930s, horticulturists at LSU developed a sweet potato that was high in nutrition and sugars and without the fibrous stringiness of other sweet potatoes. It had the distinct advantage of staying moist when baked. So to differentiate their new variety, they began marketing it as a yam, forever intermingling the terms and bewildering the consumer. But most shoppers can ignore all of this since true African yams are hard to find, and mostly what you see in the grocery store or farmer's market will be the Beauregard sweet potato or Louisiana yam (also called, in the Cajun vernacular, *bon bon du close*— candy from the field).

Before yams or sweet potatoes make it from the farm to your table, they must be cured. Their inherent moistness makes them prone to rot, so to avoid spoilage, farmers once cured them in huts where they were stacked to be dried for several days by the smoke and heat from a wood fire. Or they were laid out to dry in the wind and sun, then placed in barrels or buried and covered with hay to be stored and dried out. Today, this process takes place in giant industrial kilns, where potatoes are held for five days in relatively high humidity. As they cure, the white sap is dried out, somewhat ironically producing a creamier flesh. Also, the long, low heating converts some of the starch to sugar, so they are sweeter.

Sweet potatoes are normally harvested in October and cured so that they

Sweet potato cellar. Photograph by Marion Post Wolcott. Courtesy of Library of Congress.

are at their best at Thanksgiving. When shopping for sweet potatoes, look for those that are heavy for their size, very hard, and without soft spots. Smooth skin is not necessarily a sign of quality. When you get them home, do not refrigerate them, but put them in a well-ventilated spot. They'll keep for about a week.

Finally, we are in the kitchen with the sweet potato, which is where my true love affair with it begins. A Southern purist will tell you that there is no better cold-weather lunch than a baked sweet potato. Just scrub it, pop it in a 450 degree oven for about an hour, split it, put a dollop of butter on top, salt and pepper if you like, and eat it while it's still steaming. A cold glass of milk goes well with it. Any good Southern cook can tell you a hundred different ways to enjoy this most versatile vegetable.

One of my favorites is what I like to call sweet potato aioli. Roast sweet potatoes and whole heads of garlic at the same time. Then place the pulp of both in a food processor, add enough melted butter or olive oil to make the mixture creamy, and serve it warm or cold with good pumpernickel bread. A healthier version is to puree the sweet potato with a very ripe peach, then add salt and cayenne to taste. The creamy texture of the peach adds just the right moisture to the sweet potato puree. Served hot, both of these spreads make a great mound of mashed sweet potatoes.

Then there's sweet potato chips, sliced about as thick as a quarter and deep-fried in batches, then drained and seasoned with cayenne, a little sugar, and salt. They're addictive, especially with mango salsa. I've also made bite-size pecan pastry tartlets with sweet potato puree inside. These are particularly good with scotch.

The list goes on and on: soups, salads, grilled versions, biscuits, and of course desserts. You dream it up, and there's probably a good way to do it. With sweet potatoes, you can hardly fail. I could go on for a couple of days about how to cook sweet potatoes, but in the interest of time, I'll stop and tell you another reason why I love them: They are good for you.

When God and LSU made the sweet potato that we eat today, they made it just about nutritionally perfect. It's a good source of fiber, fat- and cholesterol-free, low in sodium, and easy to cook. It's a treasure trove of vitamin A and beta carotene, too; it would take twenty-three cups of broccoli to provide as much beta carotene as one cup of sweet potatoes. Sweet potatoes also contain significant amounts of vitamins C and E, protein, carbohydrates, iron, and calcium.

Now that we've covered the sweet potato as a food, I'd like to put in my 2 cents about the term *sweet potato*. I prefer it to the word *yam*. And I don't mean the beautiful West African word, which is not pronounced with an American accent or even the south Louisiana accent. I don't blame them for holding onto that sound. But to me, *sweet potato* (and it is pronounced as one word, not two) has a natural music, a beautiful sound and rhythm that *yam* just doesn't have. Have you ever heard of a yam queen? I have known personally a dachshund named Sweet Potato, and his name was his best attribute. Have you ever heard of a dog named Yam?

Okra in the African
Diaspora of Our South

· ·

KAREN HESS

According to Harvey A. Levenstein in *Revolution at the Table: The Transfor-mation of the American Diet*: "Even before independence, waves of immi-grants from Europe and Africa washed onto America's shores, but left few traces of their cuisines on the American table." Those "waves of immigrants from . . . Africa" were peoples torn from their motherland, brought here in shackles under unspeakable conditions to be sold on the auction block as chattel. It was slavery, not immigration. The passage gives us some measure of the overweening Anglocentric attitude all too common among white aca-demic historians. For Levenstein to add that they "left few traces of their cuisines on the American table" gives us some measure of his abysmal igno-rance of historical American cookery and subsistence farming. He vaunts his eschewal of historical receipts as "proscriptive literature," whatever he means by that, preferring to make use of "production and, where available, con-sumption statistics." Now this sounds very scholarly indeed, but such statistics are only as good as the data that go into them. Agriculture is trade, and trade reports, so dear to the hearts of academic historians, are by their very nature idiosyncratic and incomplete. They are compiled by bean counters; what I want to know is how those beans were cooked. Or okra, as the case may be.

In this regard, I cite *Consumption of Fresh Produce in the Metropolitan United States* by Professors Barbara G. Shortridge and James R. Shortridge, an analysis of USDA marketing data for the year 1985, which showed that not a pod of okra was sold in New Orleans that year. Even the Shortridges were a bit taken aback by that. Well, yes.

I like to shock my audiences by saying that I was a grown woman before I ever ate a *documented* carrot. Or a *documented* egg. Or a *documented* rasher of bacon. Or drank a *documented* glass of milk. For myself, I exaggerate a little, but only a little; for my mother out there on the Nebraska prairie, not in the least. Who on earth would have counted it all? Agricultural trade figures tell us little about what people actually eat; in some cases, indeed, they can be wildly misleading. Witness the people of Tellicherry, who cultivate prized black pepper but cannot afford it because it is an expensive cash crop; they use capsicum peppers, which grow outside their door and cost nothing. Just so, in *African Americans at Mars Bluff, South Carolina,* Amelia Wallace Vernon tells of African Americans not ever having seen black pepper (this in the 1920s, if memory serves); they likewise had always grown capsicum outside their door. Undocumented. It drives the cliometricians wild. But until they learn to factor in subsistence farming, they shall continue to make the same egregious errors over and again.

For comic relief, I proffer this gem from Levenstein's work: "Asparagus . . . was practically unknown in the United States until the 1920s," citing handouts in the *American Restaurant Magazine,* part of "a substantial promotional campaign" paid for by "the Asparagus Section of the Canners League of California." The 1620s would be more like it, but he preferred to take the word of paid hacks over that of manuals kept by housewives and gardeners down through the centuries. This from a professor of history. I suspect that I am preaching to the convinced, but it needs to be said. Again and again. I am the daughter of a Danish Lutheran pastor; I cite chapter and verse to the consternation of all.

Given the overwhelming presence of English settlers, the *warp* of cookery in the colonies was English. I myself have written about it. But from the very beginning, there were other peoples on the scene contributing brilliant streaks and splashes of color to the tapestry that was American cookery. I speak not only of Native Americans, to whom we owe an incalculable debt in terms of produce, but also of scattered enclaves of French Huguenots and others— above all, enslaved Africans, whose presence in the Southern colonies was primordial in the evolution of their cookery. In Virginia, for example, slavery dates back to 1619. From then on, black hands "stirred the pots" and worked the fields for the gentry. And what was true in Virginia was even more so in South Carolina, where both African and French influences were infinitely more profound. Not to mention New Orleans down the river, which, to be sure, was not an English colony, but there were influences, by way of the slave trade if nothing else.

I say that the warp of colonial cookery was English, but in the Southern colonies, a funny thing happened on the way to the hearth. In households of any importance whatsoever, African women slaves did nearly all the cooking. It's as simple as that. The mistress of the Big House has been described as standing at the kitchen door reading aloud receipts from English cookbooks or family manuscripts for the instruction of the African cook. Well, yes. But in a remarkable phenomenon known to the Chinese as *wok signature* or *wok presence*, a dish, the *same* dish, is going to differ somewhat among cooks, even professional cooks working side by side in the same kitchen, working with the same produce and the same receipts. Individual palates vary, individual noses vary sensing the temperature of the fat, even the size of the hand varies. When cultural boundaries are crossed, the effect is far more dramatic. Different hands. Different aromas. Different memories. And inevitably, different products and different dishes insinuate themselves. When speaking of this phenomenon in the African diaspora, sociologists use the awkward term *creolization*; I call it magic.

Let us take a look at the Southern table. I could carry on for hours on end about how the Africans brought their skills of cultivating and cooking rice to the Americas, thereby transforming the cuisine not only of South Carolina but also of the entire African diaspora in these United States. Instead, I wrote a book about it, *The Carolina Rice Kitchen: The African Connection*, including sections on those most African of pulse, black-eyed peas, cow peas, whatever, always served with rice in the manner of the peoples of primeval rice lands the world over, including Africa, a custom that spread over the entire African diaspora. In the Americas alone, I could list a score of such dishes, most often using beans or peas from Africa but making do with whatever pulse was available, as in Cuba with Moros y Cristianos, calling for black beans of the New World. Suffice it to further mention only specifically American versions, leading off with hoppin' John of South Carolina, the very name of which means beans and rice, and red beans and rice of New Orleans, of which Louis Armstrong wrote so fondly, "Red Beans and Ricely, yours . . . "; both dishes call for African pulse.

The synergistic combination of beans and rice constitutes good nutrition, especially if eked out with greens, all at very low cost. All of that I discussed in *The Carolina Rice Kitchen: The African Connection*. And there is guinea fowl, that bird whose very name bespeaks its origin in West Africa. And while we're about it, eggplant, while not strictly indigenous to Africa, had been cultivated in West Africa for so long that it had become naturalized; early Virginia writers called it guinea squash, a name that persisted in Southern cookbooks pretty much through the nineteenth century. And while it does not cut a big figure in cookery, well, aside from watermelon rind pickles, what would summer be without the refreshing watermelon, a gift from Central Africa? There are many other products that came here from Africa, or by way of Africa and the slave trade, some so early and so circuitously that their places of origin were long erroneously identified, even by botanists—most famously, the peanut (*Arachis hypogaea*), which had spread from Peru to Brazil by the time of the Voyages of Discovery, and thence to Africa in the first years of the slave trade, quickly becoming established as a staple there. And, of course, there is sesame or *benne*, to use its African name. While it is generally thought to have been of Indian origin, as indicated by its scientific name, *Sesamum indicum*, it had been cultivated in Africa "from time immemorial," as Sturtevant puts it. Jefferson spent a great deal of time and effort trying to cultivate it, primarily for its use as oil, but gave it up; for one thing, the Virginia climate was not as propitious as that of South Carolina and Georgia, where it flourished mightily and was already becoming an integral part of the cuisine of the gentry, as well as a staple among the African slaves. I might note that while sesame had long since been spread by the Arabs into certain parts of Europe—Sicily, for example—it was specifically described by American writers of the day, including Jefferson, as having been brought to America from Africa "by Negroes," as they put it.

The scientific name for okra, *Hibiscus esculentus*, effectively means "palatable mallow." It is perhaps the most African of all the products brought to the American table. In a work entitled *The Heart of Africa: Three Years' Travels and Adventures in the Unexplored Regions of Central Africa from 1868 to 1871*, Dr. Georg Schweinfurth reports that not only was okra a favorite food in Nubia but he also found it growing "perfectly wild on the White Nile," that is, indicating a point of origin as distinguished from being mere *escapees* or growing in great profusion and so accepted by botanists. It had long since swept across the Middle East, coming to India so early that it is very nearly regarded there as being indigenous. And to be sure, the Moors of North Africa brought it to Spain. It is nevertheless African, so African that okra stews came to be the signature dish of the African diaspora, even retaining their African names. It is largely a question of demographics. Enslaved Africans planted okra wherever it would thrive and wherever they were permitted to cultivate a plot of ground for their own use, a practice called subsistence farming, an all-but-undocumented source of food the world over, something that historians largely ignore, preferring the oh-so-comforting figures of commercial agriculture and trade.

To this day, the historical extent and importance of slavery in any given area in the Americas may very nearly be gauged by the extent and importance of okra, particularly by the degree of acceptance among whites. Thomas A. C. Firminger wryly noted in *A Manual of Gardening for Bengal and Upper India* that "though of an agreeable flavor, the pods, on account of their slimy nature, are not generally in favor with Europeans." And Peter Kalm in his *Travels in North America* (1770) described okra in some detail: "The Hibiscus esculentus, or okra, is a plant which grows wild in the West Indies, but is planted in the gardens here. The fruit, which is a long pod, is cut while it is green and boiled in soups, which thereby become as thick as porridge. This dish is reckoned a dainty by some people and especially by the negroes."

In all instances, we must assume that the cultivation of okra had long preceded documented observation by European writers. In 1782, Thomas Jefferson records the cultivation of okra in *Notes on the State of Virginia*; he does not say who was cultivating it. But in 1806, Bernard McMahon, Jefferson's seedsman, listed it in *The American Gardener's Calendar*, offering instructions on its cultivation, and this was the surest sign that creolization of okra had effectively been accomplished. Slaves did not buy seeds on mail order, nor did they have need of instructions on its cultivation. While the slaves at Monticello must have been cultivating okra from the beginning, Jefferson's *Garden Book* does not record cultivation by him until 1809; thereafter, it was planted regularly, with nineteen recorded entries. Further, there are receipts in the Jefferson family culinary manuscripts, one attributed to "Mrs Martha Randolph," his daughter. We shall return to those manuscripts.

Okra, the word, comes from *nkru-ma*, its name in the Twi language of Ghana, this according to our own Dr. Jessica B. Harris. Another popular name, *gumbo*, derives from Angolan *kingombo*, the *ki-* being the usual Bantu prefix and *-ngombo* the "real word," this according to the *Oxford English Dictionary*. In *Ethno-Botany of the Black Americans* (1979), William Ed Grim gives *gui bo* and *guimgombé*. (I highly recommend his work; greater use of it would reduce the fanciful and erroneous attributions of various products as having originated in Africa.)

Okra is the usual term in most of the South, but in New Orleans, it is *gumbo*, which applies to both plant and stew alike. One must suppose that this difference is due to the different lands in Africa from which the slaves originally came. As I noted in *The Carolina Rice Kitchen*, the term *gumbo* or *gombo* also refers to the patois of the Francophone Africans of the diaspora in Louisiana and the French West Indies. Just to complicate things a bit further, in that particular context, it could also derive from Kongo *nkombo*, referring to a runaway slave.

The earliest published receipts for okra that I have found are given by Mrs. Mary Randolph in *The Virginia House-wife* (1824), seventy-six years after documented use in our country as observed by Kalm, showing once again the lag of print behind recorded practice, let alone actual practice. (I emphasize the

Okra, along the River Road, St. Charles Parish, Louisiana. Courtesy of David Wharton.

date of 1824; there are a lot of misbegotten 1860 facsimile editions of Mrs. Randolph's book parading around out there, skewing culinary history by thirty-six years.) She gives three receipts in all, one of which is "Gumbs—A West India Dish," which calls for cooking whole pods of okra "in a little water" and serving them with melted butter. It has become my favorite way of cooking okra; I feel that tomatoes overpower their delicate flavor, which rarely gets a chance to shine on its own. I neither top nor tail them, using the bit of stem as a handle in eating. They're messy but lovely. I probably cook them rather more briefly than Mrs. Randolph did, and I use good Tuscan olive oil rather than butter because they are so delicious cold; the flavor deepens and intensifies a bit in the marinating. I regard it as simply a variant on Mrs. Randolph's receipt; I even gave it to Damon Fowler as such for inclusion in his book on cooking Southern vegetables. The West Indies were an important way station in the slave trade, which means that she may have gotten the name directly from one of her slaves; dressing with butter, however, was Virginian. Her receipt for "Ocra and Tomatoes" calls for simply stewing sliced okra with tomatoes, "a lump of butter," and an onion chopped fine.

We now come to her receipt for "Ochra Soup," which begins, "Get two double handsful of young ochra," going on to give a perfectly classic Virginia-style version, complete with the characterizing *cymlings*, the Virginia name for pattypan squash, as well as lima beans, a fowl or a knuckle of veal, "a bit of bacon," and six tomatoes, all to be cooked in "an earthen pipkin, or very nice iron pot." It is further thickened with the archetypical butter-kneaded-with-flour liaison of Virginia practice. The receipt ends: "Have rice boiled to eat with it." So she knew that rice was the obligatory accompaniment to an okra stew/soup, call it what you will, a telltale sign of its African origin. Very similar versions appear in the culinary manuscripts kept by members of the Jefferson family, all complete with cymlings. It would be folly to speculate whether this basic receipt came from the black cooks at Monticello and was passed to Mary Randolph or whether the similarities are simply those of a thoroughly creolized dish in slightly different versions. As I say in my work on the Jefferson family manuscripts, "No white hand ever stirred the pots at Monticello"; but Mary Randolph also was enormously influenced by black cooks, to be sure. I raise the question only because an extraordinary number of her receipts can be traced with certainty to Etienne LeMaire, Jefferson's maître d'hôtel at the President's House—so much so, that I have come to describe her as having very nearly been the amanuensis of the cuisine at Monticello, particularly with regard to its French aspects.

In the Jefferson family manuscripts—I should say extant manuscripts because so much has been lost—there are eight entries concerning okra; in addition, there is a receipt for "Gumbo," attributed by Virginia Trist to "Mrs Rosella Trist" but clearly one from New Orleans, complete with French phrases—*chaudière*, etc.—which calls for sassafras leaves rather than okra. The earliest in date of all I believe to be one simply entitled "Soup," the very first receipt in a fragmentary manuscript headed "Chap[ter] VI," indicating that it was part of a fairly elaborate full-scale manuscript cookbook. The manuscript has long been attributed to Martha Jefferson Randolph, Jefferson's daughter and the mother of Virginia Trist. I have only recently learned that it has been misattributed. The hand and internal evidence do indicate, however, that it is from the same period—let's say roughly the second decade of the nineteenth century—and from an intimate of Monticello; it may well have been copied from the manuscript we know to have been kept by Martha Jefferson Randolph. It is an archetypical Virginia receipt, calling for okra, cymlings, lima beans, onions, tomatoes, "some slices of lean bacon," parsley, and thyme, all in addition to a chicken; the only slight variant is calling for Irish potatoes as well, but this was not unusual. It is to be cooked "in an earthen pot," a frequent instruction, and even calls for thickening "the soup with flour & butter," meaning kneaded butter, the traditional liaison of Virginia—perhaps deriving from *beurre manié*, of classical French cuisine—but not common elsewhere in early American cookery. It does not mention the accompaniment of rice; it may not have been considered necessary to specify that. I find it telling that a receipt for okra—entitled simply "Soup," what's more—is the very first entry in the chapter on soups. This in a manuscript of a Virginia family associated with aristocratic Monticello. In short, okra had come to be completely accepted by the Virginia gentry by the early nineteenth century.

There is also a receipt for "Okra Soup," recorded by Virginia Jefferson Randolph Trist in the mid-nineteenth century, very formally attributed to her mother, "Mrs Martha Randolph, Monticello," that is, Jefferson's daughter; it was probably copied from a much-earlier manuscript, now lost. It is remarkably similar to that given by Mary Randolph: it calls for the same "two double handfuls of okra . . . , one handful of lima beans, [cym]lines, a piece of fresh meat or a fowl . . . , 5 tomatoes cut in pieces. When almost done put in a lump of butter rolled in flour. . . . Season with salt and pepper. Don't make it too thick. Put it on early & only let it simmer." Entire phrases are verbatim; she does, however, omit a number of important points, including the obligatory accompaniment of boiled rice, but includes the classic kneaded butter of Virginia cookery.

In terms of provenance, the most tantalizing receipt of all is one for "Okra Soup" attributed by Virginia Randolph Trist to the "University of Va." It appears in her hand on scribal pages 10 and 11 of her chapter on soups:

Take the okra so young as to be crisp, about two or three inches long—they may be used as long as they are tender, which may be judged by their brittleness; if good, they snap; if they bend, they are too old. A peck of pods sliced like cucumbers for eating, ½ inch thick; add 1–3 tomatoes, more or less, according to your taste, a shin of beef with 2½ gal. water. You may, if you choose add young corn and lima beans. A digester is best for boiling or an earthen pot; iron turns it black. It should boil five hours, during which time it is kept briskly boiling. It will be reduced to one half: When done the meat will be boiled to rags and quit the bone. The whole should be one homogeneous mass, in which none of the ingredients should be distinct. The consistency should be that of thick porridge; the color green, mixed with yellow or red from the tomatoes.

Note the admirably perceptive directions for choosing okra. While the receipt is perfectly clear in terms of procedure, there are certain elliptical aspects so characteristic of period receipts. There is no mention whatsoever of seasoning, nor of the obligatory accompaniment of rice. Further, the directions to keep the soup "briskly boiling" are counterindicated. As always, Mary Randolph knew better, counseling that "it must be kept steadily simmering, but not boiling." Another interesting aspect is that while I believe it to be a Virginia receipt, it calls for neither cymlings nor kneaded butter—indeed, no additional liaison whatsoever.

But that is not the point, at least not the most interesting one. The University of Virginia was chartered in 1819. Jefferson was a founder, designed the campus, and served as its first rector. The receipt could well have entered Jefferson family annals at that time; I rather believe that it did—he had a way of cadging receipts from one and all in his entourage. However, in the 1845 edition of *The Southern Gardener and Receipt Book* by P[hineas] Thornton of Camden, South Carolina (pages 141–43), I find a receipt virtually identical to the above, so nearly identical that they have to have come from a common source. That is, Thornton's receipt is far lengthier, but entire sentences, including some of the most charming ones concerning the brittleness of the okra pods and the meat being done "to rags," are verbatim; they both call for cooking the soup in "a digester" or "an earthen pot," for instance. (The digester was a prototype pressure cooker, well enough known in the United States to rate inclusion in Webster's dictionary of 1806.) Thornton uses rather more archaic phrases, which I believe to have been the original ones, whatever the source was: In determining brittleness, he says that, if good, the pods "will snap *asunder*," which bespeaks an earlier day. Now Jefferson used the term *asunder* any number of times; Martha Jefferson Randolph used it in directions for cutting up chicken in a receipt attributed to her, suggesting that the receipt could have come by way of Jefferson himself or his daughter and that Virginia Trist, in copying the receipt either from her mother's manuscript or from one of Jefferson's innumerable slips of paper, simply chose to ignore some of the more discursive passages and to modernize the language a bit here and there, a practice to which she was lamentably prone. To be sure, other writers of the nineteenth century also used the term, already a bit archaic, practically biblical. I do not believe that Virginia Trist got it from Thornton's work; while her manuscript dates from roughly the 1850s and 60s, she was exceptionally meticulous about attributing published receipts, and she firmly attributed this receipt to the University of Virginia. Thornton did not attribute his receipt, but published writers seldom do. The Jeffersons had strong ties of long standing with the University of Virginia; not so Thornton. So its provenance remains a mystery.

There are two all-but-identical receipts in the Jefferson family manuscripts for the New Orleans version of okra soup, both attributed to "Mrs G. W. Randolph" (surely Mrs. George Wyth Randolph): One, entitled "Gumba," was transcribed by Septemia Randolph Meikleham and dated 1857; the other, entitled "Gumbo," was transcribed by Virginia Randolph Trist, this time with an interesting caboose section: "Gumbo may be made with sassafras leaves dried & powdered instead of okra but the sassafras leaves must not be put in until the soup is done & poured into the tureen then add two tablespoons of sassafras." This precautionary note is perceptive; if boiled, the mixture turns ropy, hence the Creole name of filé. This addendum I believe was tacked on by Trist, borrowing from the New Orleans receipt attributed to "Mrs Rosella Trist," referred to earlier.

These receipts for gumbo bring up the two main divisions in okra stews in this country. In 1847, Miss Sarah Rutledge gave, in addition to her receipt for "Okra Soup," one for "New Orleans Gumbo," and the juxtaposition allows us to examine the essential differences between the two versions. While her receipt for "Okra Soup" does not call for cymlings nor further liaison than that of okra, it more nearly corresponds to the Virginia versions than to New Orleans gumbos. Her receipt for "New Orleans Gumbo" lacks a basic characterizing element, that of the brown roux; however, the telltale New Orleans use of "pulverized sassafras-leaves" is present, which are to be stirred in at the very end "until it become mucilaginous," this in lieu of okra. In that respect, Mrs. G. W. Randolph's receipt is in fact more traditionally New Orleans than that of Miss Rutledge in that it calls for flouring the meat and frying it in lard "till it is well browned"—that is, the sanctified dark brown roux of the New Orleans gumbo, giving an altogether different aspect and character than that of the okra stews of either Virginia or South Carolina.

Nineteenth-century Southern cookbooks almost invariably included receipts for okra, including okra soups, ranging from *The Kentucky Housewife* by Mrs. Lettice Bryan (1839) to *Mrs. Hill's New Cook Book* by Mrs. A[nnabella] P. Hill (1872), widow of Hon. Edward Y. Hill of Georgia. After a quick rundown, they seem not to have published receipts for any okra dish that could be called New Orleans gumbo, although occasionally the name was used; that is, except for that in *The Carolina Housewife*, and that receipt was not altogether typical, nor did it call for okra. But in 1881, an emancipated slave, Mrs. Abby Fisher, late of Mobile, Alabama, gave three proper receipts in *What Mrs. Fisher Knows about Old Southern Cooking*, two of which call for *ocra*, the other for *gumbo*, meaning pulverized sassafras leaves, an alternate New Orleans word for filé. In all three, she calls for brown roux, always adding, "Don't let it burn," a cautionary note that I wish cooks in New Orleans would take to heart. I realize that Creoles have acquired a taste for much darker roux than is countenanced in French cuisine, where brown roux may fairly be described as golden brown. But don't scorch it! It ends: "To be sent to table with dry boiled rice. Never stir rice while boiling." Naturally. She was an African American who originally hailed from South Carolina, where they know how to cook rice, their grandmothers having taught them how. No soggy rice for Abby Fisher.

New Orleans itself was inexplicably late on the scene with publication of receipts for its very own gumbo, something that did not occur until 1885, at least insofar as I can ascertain, when Lafcadio Hearn, a foreigner in the midst of Creoles, made up for lost time in *La Cuisine Creole*. He gave nine extraordinary receipts for *gombo*, two of which called for filé rather than okra. Among his directions, he counseled the reader to "keep one vessel sacred to soup." In making the brown roux, he warned: "Let it brown slowly so as not to scorch." And he added a reminder: "Serve with rice as usual." His flair and astuteness with *gombo* may have had something to do with the fact that he is said to have kept company—as we used to say so chastely—with an African American woman. He wrote marvelously about the Creole patois, recording *gumbo* proverbs, proverbs that would otherwise not have been known to us, many of them concerned with food, indeed, many with gumbo. That work is entitled *Gombo Zhèbes*, meaning gumbo of greens (also 1885). One from Martinique goes: "Jadin loin, gombo gat [When the garden is far, the gumbo is spoiled]." Remember that *gumbo* or *gomba* also refers to the patois of Francophone African Americans. Lafcadio Hearn was born Greek; educated in Ireland, England, and France; lived and traveled in the Francophone African diaspora; died in Japan as Yakumo Koizumi; wrote constantly in several languages, including Japanese; constantly drew cartoons, rather bitter comments on life. Nevertheless, it was his work that captured the spirit of New Orleans and of gumbo better than another work that came out the same year, *Creole Cookery*, issued by the Christian Woman's Exchange of New Orleans. The good ladies who published that work were somewhat apart from the true Creoles of New Orleans, not quite understanding some of the Creole expressions—rendering *calas* as *callers*, for example, possibly reflecting pronunciation—and there is massive "borrowing" from earlier Southern cookbooks. It was not until the turn of that century that *The Picayune's Creole Cook Book* appeared, that is, 1900. And we had to wait until 1904 for the charming work of Célestine Eustis, *Cooking in Old Créole Days* or *La cuisine créole à l'usage des petits ménages*. Well, actually two works; the French work is not a simple translation but effectively a separate work. In issuing his so-called facsimile edition of it, Louis Szathmáry completely excised the French work without so much as mentioning it.

There are a number of interesting receipts for okra in the *Carolina Rice Cookbook* (1901), compiled by Mrs. Samuel G. Stoney of Charleston, some from published sources, some from ladies of Charleston; two are attributed to Maum Sarah, an African American as indicated by her sobriquet but otherwise unidentified. To be sure, most of the receipts came from the good ladies' black cooks, so attributed or not. This work is featured in facsimile in *The Carolina Rice Kitchen*, a culinary study of the role of African slaves in providing the requisite expertise in the cultivation and cooking of rice, rice being exceedingly persnickety in both respects.

The Mason-Dixon Line can almost be said to be the Okra Line, that is, historically: As a rule, Southern writers gave receipts for okra, even when their works were published in the North. Northern writers did not, with the exception of those of Philadelphia, an anomaly explained by the early presence of West Indians who came to very nearly dominate the catering business in that city. This also explains the identification of "Pepper Pot" with Philadelphia, albeit a very pale version. To be sure, climate also played a role in this demarcation, but the critical factor was demographics.

If you were expecting a scientific treatise, complete with cultivars, etc., you will have been disappointed. I am a *culinary* historian, and historical receipts my primary documentation. Finally, that is what gets the food on the table.

As for the published historical receipts for okra, many of the works I cited have been issued over the years in facsimile editions; some are still in print and may be bought from our own Hoppin' John Taylor. The receipts for okra from the Jefferson family papers, however, are more difficult to come by. In the not-too-distant future, I hope, you can read them in *Mr. Jefferson's Table: The Culinary Legacy of Monticello*.

CONTRIBUTORS

Brett Anderson is the restaurant reviewer for the *New Orleans Times-Picayune*.

Colman Andrews is the editor-in-chief of *Saveur* and author or coauthor of six food books.

Jim Auchmutey is a reporter for the *Atlanta Journal-Constitution* and author of two books on Southern food.

Roy Blount Jr.'s books include *Be Sweet, Roy Blount's Book of Southern Humor*, and *Crackers*. He is a columnist for the *Oxford American* and a contributing editor for the *Atlantic Monthly*.

Gene Bourg is a freelance food and travel writer based in New Orleans.

Janet L. Boyd grew up in eastern Kentucky, where she was satisfyingly fed on her grandmother's Southern cooking.

Rick Bragg is a writer for the *New York Times* and the author of two personal histories, the latest of which is *Ava's Man*. His food writing has appeared in *Food & Wine*.

Carrie Brown, along with photographer Elizabeth DeRamus, is at work on *Faces of the South*.

Brian Carpenter is a Ph.D. candidate in American and Southern literature at the University of North Carolina at Chapel Hill. He is at work on a book about architecture in Southern literature.

Fred Chappell teaches in the English Department of the University of North Carolina, Greensboro. He has published twenty-five or so books of poetry, fiction, and critical commentary.

John T. Edge is director of the Southern Foodways Alliance. He has two books to his credit, and his magazine work has been published widely.

John Egerton of Nashville, Tennessee, is a writer of nonfiction. He wrote *Southern Food: At Home, on the Road, in History*.

Lolis Eric Elie is a columnist for the *New Orleans Times-Picayune* and author of *Smokestack Lightning: Adventures in the Heart of Barbecue Country*.

Marcie Cohen Ferris is a Ph.D. candidate in American studies at George Washington University, where she is writing a dissertation on Southern Jewish foodways. She has worked at the Museum of the Southern Jewish Experience.

Damon Lee Fowler is a culinary historian, journalist, culinary educator, and author of four cookbooks, including *Classical Southern Cooking* and *New Southern Kitchen*.

Sarah Fritschner is the food editor at the *Louisville Courier-Journal* and the author of three books, including *Express Lane Cookbook*.

Denise Gee of Birmingham, Alabama, directs food and entertaining coverage at *Coastal Living* magazine, where she is managing editor.

Nikki Giovanni is a poet who teaches at Virginia Tech University. She is the author of numerous books, including *Love Poems.*

Jessica B. Harris is a consultant, food historian, and cookbook author. Her latest book, *Beyond Gumbo: Creole Fusion Food from the Atlantic Rim,* will be published in 2003.

Jim Henderson is a freelance writer who contributes to *Bon Appetit.*

Karen Hess is the editor of *The Virginia Housewife, The Carolina Rice Kitchen: The African Connection,* and *What Mrs. Fisher Knows about Old Southern Cooking.*

Amanda Hesser is a writer for the *New York Times* and author of *The Cook and the Gardener: A Year of Recipes and Writings for the French Countryside.*

Jack Hitt is a contributing writer for the *New York Times Magazine, Harper's,* and the National Public Radio program *This American Life.*

Tara Hulen and Thomas Spencer are former senior reporters and editors at *Birmingham Weekly.* Hulen is now a freelance writer, and Spencer is a staff writer at the *Birmingham News.*

Dan Huntley has written for the *Charlotte Observer* since 1982. He has cooked paschal lamb in the Greek Peloponnese, but he prefers whole-hog barbecue from the Carolina Piedmont.

Honorée Fanonne Jeffers's first book, *The Gospel of Barbecue,* won the Wick Prize for poetry.

Lu Ann Jones, who teaches history at East Carolina University, is the author of *Mama Learned Us to Work: Farm Women in the New South.*

Craig LaBan is the restaurant critic for the *Philadelphia Inquirer.* He learned to love Southern food (and whiskey) during his tenure at the *New Orleans Times-Picayune.*

Christiane Lauterbach, French by birth, Atlantan by choice, is the longtime dining critic for *Atlanta* magazine. She publishes and edits *Knife and Fork,* a newsletter about restaurants.

Matt and Ted Lee grew up in Charleston, South Carolina. They are contributing editors for *Travel and Leisure* and write frequently for *Food & Wine,* the *New York Times,* and *Martha Stewart Living.*

Ronni Lundy is the author of *Shuck Beans, Stack Cakes, and Honest Fried Chicken, The Festival Table,* and *Butter Beans to Blackberries.*

Jann Malone, columnist for the *Richmond Times-Dispatch,* learned to love good food in her native New Orleans.

Larry T. McGehee is vice president and professor of religion at Wofford College, Spartanburg, South Carolina. His weekly column, "Southern Seen," appears in many small Southern newspapers.

Peter McKee is a banjo-playing Yankee lawyer from Seattle, Washington, who has been a willing hostage of Southern 'cue since 1974.

Mary E. Miller is a features columnist for the *Raleigh News and Observer.*

Debbie Moose, a native North Carolinian and former newspaper food editor, writes freelance food columns and radio essays.

Robert Morgan, a native of Henderson County, North Carolina, is the author of the novel *Gap Creek*, along with ten books of poetry.

MM (Mary Margaret) Pack writes about food and culture in Austin, Texas, for, among other publications, the *Austin Chronicle*.

Mary Jane Park is a writer and editor at the *St. Petersburg Times*.

Donna Pierce is an adjunct assistant professor at the University of Missouri School of Journalism, where she is developing a food-reporting class. She is a contributing editor at *Upscale* magazine.

Lynn Powell, a poet and native of Tennessee, has published widely. Among her books is *Old & New Testaments*.

Kathleen Purvis has been the food editor at the *Charlotte Observer* since 1989.

Julia Reed was born in Greenville, Mississippi. She is senior writer at *Vogue* and writes about food for the *New York Times* magazine.

Amy Rogers of Charlotte, North Carolina, is an author and editor. Among her works are *Red Pepper Fudge and Blue Ribbon*.

Elizabeth Schatz writes for *Vogue* and *In Style*. She lives in New York City, where she cooks in a very small kitchen.

Kathy Starr, granddaughter of Frances Fleming Hunte, is the author of *The Soul of Southern Cooking*.

Courtney Taylor is the food columnist for the *Jackson (Miss.) Clarion Ledger*. Her latest book is *The Southern Cook's Handbook*. A collection of her columns will be published later this year.

James Villas was born and raised in Charlotte, North Carolina. He has been food and wine editor at *Town and Country* for twenty-seven years and is the author of twelve books on food.

Reagan Walker grew up in Kentucky and has worked at newspapers in the South for fifteen years. She has been a food writer for the *Atlanta Journal-Constitution* for the past four years.

Robb Walsh is the restaurant critic of the *Houston Press* and author of *Legends of Texas Barbecue Cookbook: Recipes and Recollections from the Pit Bosses*.

ACKNOWLEDGMENTS

The Southern Foodways Alliance is grateful to the writers and photographers whose works appear herein. Many contributors waived their reprint fees, and we are doubly grateful for that. We have made every effort to trace and contact copyright holders. If an error or omission is brought to our attention, we will make corrections in future editions.

If you wish to submit an essay to be considered for inclusion in *Cornbread Nation 2*, please write to John T. Edge in care of the Southern Foodways Alliance, Center for the Study of Southern Culture, P.O. Box 1848, University, MS 38677, or send an e-mail message to johnt@olemiss.edu.

Transcriptions, permissions, and the like were handled, in part, by students at the Center for the Study of Southern Culture. We thank Warren Ables, Lauchlin Fields, and Mary Beth Lasseter for their good work.

Last, thanks to the team at the University of North Carolina Press—David Perry and Mark Simpson-Vos, to name just a few—who were a marvel of efficiency and intellect.

The following is a list of permissions to reprint the essays that appear in this book.

"Leah Chase" by Lolis Eric Elie. Originally published in *Gourmet*, February 2000. Reprinted by permission of the author.

"Marie Rudisill" by Damon Lee Fowler. Originally published in the *Savannah Morning News*, November 29, 2000. Reprinted by permission of the author.

"Eugene Walter" by John T. Edge. Originally published in the *Oxford American*, May/June 2001. Reprinted by permission of the author.

"Edna Lewis and Scott Peacock" by Christiane Lauterbach. Originally published in *Atlanta* magazine, November 2001. Copyright 2001 by Christiane Lauterbach. Reprinted by permission of the author.

"To Edna Lewis" by Nikki Giovanni. Originally published in Nikki Giovanni, *Love Poems*. Copyright 1997 by Nikki Giovanni. Reprinted by permission of the author.

"The Legendary Coe Dupuis, Moonshiner" by Craig LaBan. Originally published in the *Philadelphia Enquirer*, July 9, 2000. Reprinted by permission of the author.

"Dori Sanders, Peach Farmer" by Amy Rogers. Originally published in *Gaston Seasons*, Summer 1999. Copyright 1999 by Amy Rogers. Reprinted by permission of the author.

"From the Recipe File of Luba Cohen" by Marcie Cohen Ferris. Longer version originally published in *Southern Jewish History*. Copyright 1999 by Marcie Ferris. Reprinted by permission of the author.

"A Confederacy of Sauces" by Jack Hitt. Originally published in the *New York Times Magazine*, August 26, 2001. Reprinted by permission of the author.

"Interview with Kim Wong, Clarksdale, Mississippi" by Carrie Brown. From the forthcoming book by Carrie Brown and Elizabeth DeRamus, *Faces of the South*. Used by permission of the author.

"Craig Claiborne Remembered" by James Villas. Originally published in *Gourmet*, April 2000. Copyright 2000 by James Villas. Reprinted by permission of the author.

"Dinner Rites" by Rick Bragg. Originally published in *Food & Wine*, November, 1999. Copyright 1999 by American Express Publishing Corporation. All rights reserved. Reprinted by permission.

"Potluck Traditions" by Jim Auchmutey. Originally published in the *Atlanta Journal-Constitution*, August 2, 1998. Reprinted by permission of the author.

"The Peach Continuum" by MM Pack. Originally published in the *Austin Chronicle*, July 14, 2000. Reprinted by permission of the author.

"Canning Time" by Robert Morgan. Originally published in his book *Groundwork*. Reprinted by permission of Gnomon Press.

"Dead Men Don't Eat Brownies" by Janet L. Boyd. Originally published in the *Louisville Eccentric Observer*. Reprinted by permission of the author.

"Passing and Repasting" by Elizabeth Schatz. Originally published in *Newsday*, September 12, 2000. Copyright 2000 by Elizabeth Schatz. Reprinted by permission of the author.

"Reunion Time" by Reagan Walker. Originally published in the *Atlanta Journal-Constitution*, June 29, 2000. Reprinted by permission of the author.

"Ode to Joy" by Sarah Fritschner. Originally published in the *Louisville Courier-Journal*, January 25, 2002. Reprinted by permission of the author.

"Vacant Kitchens for Sale" by Larry T. McGehee. Originally syndicated in "Southern Seen" in various newspapers, June 4, 2001. Reprinted by permission of the author.

"In Praise of Dinnertime" by Mary Jane Park. Originally published in the *St. Petersburg Times*, November 24, 1999. Reprinted by permission of the author.

"Iced Tea: A Contrarian's View" by Fred Chappell. Originally published in *Gastronomica*, Fall 2001. Copyright 2001 by Fred Chappell. Reprinted by permission of the author.

"You Can't Eat 'Em Blues: Cooking Up a Food Song Movie" by Roy Blount Jr. Originally published in the *Oxford American*, July 1997. Reprinted by permission of the author.

"Summer Feeding Frenzy" by Debbie Moose. Originally published in the *Raleigh News and Observer*, September 24, 2000. Reprinted by permission of the author.

"The Gospel of Barbecue" by Honorée Fanonne Jeffers. Originally published in her book *The Gospel of Barbecue*. Reprinted by permission of the author.

"Welcome to Livermush Land" by Kathleen Purvis. Originally published in the *Charlotte Observer*, October 18, 2000. Copyright 2000 *Charlotte Observer*. Reprinted by permission.

"Aspiration" by Lynn Powell. Originally published in *Now and Then*, Summer 2000. Reprinted by permission of the Center for Appalachian Studies and Services.

"Here's One for the Birds" by Donna Pierce. Originally published in the *Columbia Daily Tribune*, June 21, 2000. Reprinted by permission of the author.

"My Blue Heaven" by Julia Reed. Originally published in the *New York Times Magazine*, August 19, 2001. Copyright 2001 by The New York Times Agency. Reprinted by permission.

"The Green Bean Conundrum" by Jann Malone. Originally published in the *Richmond Times-Dispatch*, June 6, 1991. Copyright 1991 *Richmond Times-Dispatch*. Reprinted by permission.

"A Butter Lover Spreads the Word" by Mary E. Miller. Originally published in the *Raleigh News and Observer*, February 11, 1998. Reprinted by permission of the author.

"What the Angels Eat" by Jim Henderson. Originally published in *Bon Appétit*, August 1998. Copyright 1998 Conde-Nast Publications. All rights reserved. Reprinted by permission.

"Dueling Steaks" by Denise Gee. Originally published in *Southern Living*, March 1998. Reprinted by permission of *Southern Living*.

"The South's Thirsty Muse" by Brian Carpenter. Originally published in *Southern Cultures*, Spring 2000. Reprinted by permission of *Southern Cultures*.

"Dinner at Darrington" by Robb Walsh. Originally published in the *Austin Chronicle*, December 3, 1993. Reprinted by permission of the author.

"Dirt Rich" by Ronni Lundy. Shorter version originally published in *Gourmet*, June 2001. Reprinted by permission of the author.

"In the 'Ham, the Hot Dog Rules" by Tara Hulen and Thomas Spencer. Originally published in *Birmingham Weekly*, June 11, 1998. Copyright 1998 by Tara Hulen and Thomas Spencer. Reprinted by permission of the authors.

"Stalking the Wild Hog" by Dan Huntley. Originally published in the *Charlotte Observer*, March 1, 1998. Copyright 1998 the *Charlotte Observer*. Reprinted by permission.

"The Watermelon Market" by Amanda Hesser. Originally published in the *New York Times*, April 15, 2001. Copyright 2001 by The New York Times Agency. Reprinted by permission.

"East of Houston, West of Baton Rouge" by Colman Andrews. Originally published in *Saveur*, May/June 2000. Reprinted by permission of the author.

"Isleño Pride" by Gene Bourg. Originally published in *Saveur*, March 2001. Reprinted by permission of the author.

"A Sweet and Soulful South Carolina Tour" by Matt Lee and Ted Lee. Originally published in *Travel + Leisure*, January 1999. Reprinted by permission of the authors.

"Dinner with Moth" by Brett Anderson. Originally published in the *New Orleans*

Times-Picayune, September 25, 2001. Copyright 2001 by The Times-Picayune Publishing Corporation. All rights reserved. Reprinted by permission.

"Your Greens Ain't Like Mine—Or Are They?" by Jessica B. Harris. Originally presented at the 1998 Southern Foodways Symposium. Used by permission of the author.

"The Soul of Southern Cooking" by Kathy Starr. Slightly different version originally published in her book *The Soul of Southern Cooking*. Reprinted by permission of the author.

"It's the Cue: The Life-Altering Impact of Southern Food on One Unsuspecting Yankee" by Peter McKee. Originally presented at the 2000 Southern Foodways Symposium. Used by permission of the author.

"Taking What She Had and Turning It into Money: The Female Farm Economy" by Lu Ann Jones. Originally presented at the 2001 Southern Foodways Symposium. Used by permission of the author.

"My Love Affair with the Sweet Potato" by Courtney Taylor. Originally presented at the 2001 Southern Foodways Symposium. Copyright 2001 by Courtney Taylor. Used by permission of the author.

"Okra in the African Diaspora of Our South" by Karen Hess. Originally presented at the 2001 Southern Foodways Symposium. Copyright 2001 by Karen Hess. Used by permission of the author.

The Southern Foodways Alliance (SFA), an affiliated institute of the Center for the Study of Southern Culture at the University of Mississippi, celebrates, teaches, preserves, and promotes the diverse food cultures of the American South. Along with sponsoring the Southern Foodways Symposium and Southern Foodways Field Trips, we document Southern foodways through oral history collection and archival research.

Established in 1977 at the University of Mississippi, the Center for the Study of Southern Culture has become a focal point for innovative education and research by promoting scholarship on every aspect of Southern culture. The center offers both B.A. and M.A. degrees in Southern studies and is well known for its public programs, including the annual Faulkner and Yoknapatawpha conference and the Conference for the Book.

The fifty founding members of the SFA are a diverse bunch: they are cookbook authors and anthropologists, culinary historians and home cooks, chefs, organic gardeners and barbecue pitmasters, food journalists and inquisitive eaters, native-born Southerners and outlanders too. For more information, point your browser to www.southernfoodways.com or call 662-915-5993.

SFA Founding Members

Ann Abadie, Oxford, Miss.
Kaye Adams, Birmingham, Ala.
Jim Auchmutey, Atlanta, Ga.
Marilou Awiakta, Memphis, Tenn.
Ben Barker, Durham, N.C.
Ella Brennan, New Orleans, La.
Ann Brewer, Covington, Ga.
Karen Cathey, Arlington, Va.
Leah Chase, New Orleans, La.
Al Clayton, Jasper, Ga.
Mary Ann Clayton, Jasper, Ga.
Shirley Corriher, Atlanta, Ga.
Norma Jean Darden, New York, N.Y.
Crescent Dragonwagon, Eureka Springs, Ark.
Nathalie Dupree, Social Circle, Ga.

John T. Edge, Oxford, Miss.
John Egerton, Nashville, Tenn.
Lolis Eric Elie, New Orleans, La.
John Folse, Donaldsonville, La.
Terry Ford, Ripley, Tenn.
Psyche Williams Forson, Beltsville, Md.
Damon Lee Fowler, Savannah, Ga.
Vertamae Grosvenor, Washington, D.C.
Jessica B. Harris, Brooklyn, N.Y.
Cynthia Hizer, Covington, Ga.
Portia James, Washington, D.C.
Martha Johnston, Birmingham, Ala.
Sally Belk King, Richmond, Va.
Sarah Labensky, Columbus, Miss.
Edna Lewis, Atlanta, Ga.
Rudy Lombard, Chicago, Ill.

Ronni Lundy, Louisville, Ky.
Louis Osteen, Charleston, S.C.
Marlene Osteen, Charleston, S.C.
Timothy W. Patridge, Atlanta, Ga.
Paul Prudhomme, New Orleans, La.
Joe Randall, Savannah, Ga.
Marie Rudisill, Hudson, Fla.
Dori Sanders, Clover, S.C.
Richard Schweid, Barcelona, Spain
Ned Shank, Eureka Springs, Ark.

Kathy Starr, Greenville, Miss.
Frank Stitt, Birmingham, Ala.
Pardis Stitt, Birmingham, Ala.
Marion Sullivan, Mt. Pleasant, S.C.
Van Sykes, Bessemer, Ala.
John Martin Taylor, Charleston, S.C.
Toni Tipton-Martin, Austin, Tex.
Jeanne Voltz, Pittsboro, N.C.
Charles Reagan Wilson, Oxford, Miss.